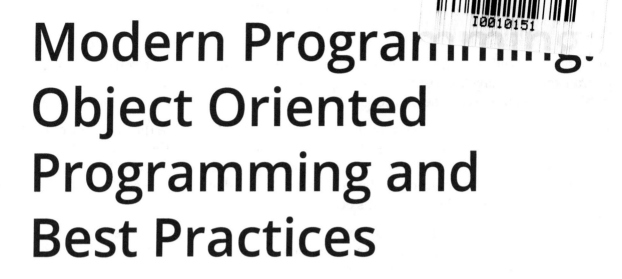

Modern Programming: Object Oriented Programming and Best Practices

Deconstruct object-oriented programming and use it with other programming paradigms to build applications

Graham Lee

Modern Programming: Object Oriented Programming and Best Practices

Author: Graham Lee

Managing Editor: Aditya Shah

Acquisitions Editor: Bridget Neale

Production Editor: Samita Warang

Editorial Board: David Barnes, Mayank Bhardwaj, Ewan Buckingham, Simon Cox, Mahesh Dhyani, Taabish Khan, Manasa Kumar, Alex Mazonowicz, Douglas Paterson, Dominic Pereira, Shiny Poojary, Erol Staveley, Ankita Thakur, and Jonathan Wray

First Published: June 2019

Production Reference: 1270619

ISBN: 978-1-83898-618-6

Published by Packt Publishing Ltd.

Livery Place, 35 Livery Street

Birmingham B3 2PB, UK

Table of Contents

Coding Practices   79

Testing   101

Architecture   113

Documentation   125

Requirements Engineering   139

Learning   155

Critical Analysis   167

Business   179

Philosophy 227

Index 247

Preface

About

This section briefly introduces the author and coverage of the book.

About the Book

Your experience and knowledge always influence the approach you take and the tools you use to write your programs. With a sound understanding of how to approach your goal and what software paradigms to use, you can create high-performing applications quickly and efficiently.

In this two-part book, you'll discover the untapped features of object-oriented programming and use it with other software tools to code fast and efficient applications. The first part of the book begins with a discussion on how OOP is used today and moves on to analyze the ideas and problems that OOP doesn't address. It continues by deconstructing the complexity of OOP, showing you its fundamentally simple core. You'll see that, by using the distinctive elements of OOP, you can learn to build your applications more easily.

The next part of this book talks about acquiring the skills to become a better programmer. You'll get an overview of how various tools, such as version control and build management, help make your life easier. This book also discusses the pros and cons of other programming paradigms, such as aspect-oriented programming and functional programming, and helps to select the correct approach for your projects. It ends by talking about the philosophy behind designing software and what it means to be a "good" developer.

By the end of this two-part book, you will have learned that OOP is not always complex, and you will know how you can evolve into a better programmer by learning about ethics, teamwork, and documentation.

About the Author

Graham Lee is an experienced programmer and writer. He has written books including *Professional Cocoa Application Security, Test-Driven iOS Development, APPropriate Behaviour,* and *APPosite Concerns.* He is a developer who's been doing this stuff for long enough to want to start telling other people about the mistakes he's made, in the hope that they'll avoid repeating them. In his case, this means having worked for about 12 years as a professional. His first programming experience can hardly be called professional at all: that was done in BASIC on a Dragon 32 microcomputer. He's been paid for software written in Perl, Python, Bash, LISP, Pascal, C, Objective-C, Java, Applescript, Ruby, C++, JavaScript, and probably some other things.

Please find me on *Twitter* (https://twitter.com/iwasleeg), *quitter* (https://quitter.se/leeg), or *my blog* (https://sicpers.info) to comment or query anything here.

Learning Objectives

- Untangle the complexity of OOP by breaking it down to its essential building blocks.

- Realize the full potential of OOP to design efficient, maintainable programs.

- Utilize coding best practices, including **Test-Driven Development (TDD)**, pair programming, and code reviews, to improve your work.

- Use tools, such as source control and IDEs, to work more efficiently.

- Learn how to most productively work with other developers.

- Build your own software development philosophy.

Audience

This book is ideal for programmers who want to understand the philosophy behind creating software and what it means to be "good" at designing software. Programmers who want to deconstruct the OOP paradigm and see how it can be reconstructed in a clear, straightforward way will also find this book useful. To understand the ideas expressed in this book, you must be an experienced programmer who wants to evolve their practice.

Approach

This book takes an autobiographical approach to explain the various concepts. The information in this book is based on the author's opinions and desired future directions. The author introduces key ideas and concepts, before going on to explain them in detail, outline their pros and cons, and guide you in how to most effectively use them in your own development.

Acknowledgements

This book is the result of a long-running research activity, and I hope that any work I have built upon is appropriately cited. Nonetheless, the ideas here are not mine alone (that distinction is reserved for the mistakes), and many conversations online, at conferences, and with colleagues have shaped the way I think about objects. A complete list would be impossible to construct, and an incomplete list would be unfair. So, I'll just say thank you.

Part One – OOP The Easy Way

What is object-oriented programming? My guess is that object-oriented programming will be in the 1980's what structured programming was in the 1970's. Everyone will be in favor of it. Every manufacturer will promote his products as supporting it. Every manager will pay lip service to it. Every programmer will practice it (differently). And no one will know just what it is.

Tim Rentsch, **Object oriented programming**–https://dl.acm.org/citation.cfm?id=947961

Object-Oriented Programming (**OOP**) has its beginnings in the simulation-focused features of the Simula programming language but was famously developed and evangelized by the Smalltalk team at Xerox's Palo Alto Research Center. They designed a computing system intended to be personal, with a programming environment accessible to children who could learn about the world and about the computer simultaneously by modeling real-world problems on their computer.

I recently researched the propagation and extension of OOP from PARC to the wider software engineering community, which formed the background to my dissertation *We Need to (Small)Talk: object-oriented programming with graphical code browsers*– https://www.academia.edu/34882629/We_need_to_Small_talk_object-oriented_ programming_with_graphical_code_browsers. What I found confused me: how had this simple design language for children to construct computer programs become so complicated and troublesome that professional software engineers struggled to understand it before declaring it a failure and reaching for other paradigms?

A textbook on my shelf, "A Touch of Class," by Bertrand Meyer, claims to be "a revolutionary introductory programming textbook that makes learning programming fun and rewarding." At 876 pages, it makes it a good workout, too: not for the schoolchild, but for the "entering-computer-science student" at degree level.

Digging further showed that the field of object thinking, object technology, OOP, or whatever you would like to call it had been subject to two forces:

- **Additive complexity**. Consultants, academics, and architects keen to make their mark on the world had extended basic underlying ideas to provide their own, unique, marketable contributions. While potentially valuable in isolation, the aggregation of these additions (and they were, as we shall see, deliberately aggregated in some cases) yields a rat's nest of complexity.

- **Structured on-ramps**. To make OOP appear easier and more accessible, people developed "object-oriented" extensions to existing programming tools and processes. While this made it easy to access the *observable features* of OOP, it made it ironically more difficult to access the *mental shift* needed to take full advantage of what is fundamentally a thought process and problem-solving technique. By fitting the object model into existing systems, technologists doomed it to stay within existing mindsets.

About the Example Code

In this part of the book, I have consciously chosen to use "mainstream," popular programming languages wherever possible. I have not stuck to any one language, but have used things that most experienced programmers should be able to understand at a glance: Ruby, Python, and JavaScript will be common. Where I've used other languages, I've done so to express a particular historical context (Smalltalk, Erlang, and Eiffel will be prevalent here) or to show ideas from certain communities (Haskell or Lisp).

One of the points of this part of the book is that as a cognitive tool, OOP is not specific to any programming language, and indeed many of the languages that are billed as object-oriented languages make what (or at least large parts of what) harder. Picking any one language for the sample code would then mean only presenting a subset of OOP.

1

Antithesis

Telling an Object What to Do

The big idea is "messaging" – that is, what the kernal [sic] of Smalltalk/Squeak is all about (and it's something that was never quite completed in our Xerox PARC phase). The Japanese have a small word – ma – for "that which is in between" – perhaps the nearest English equivalent is "interstitial." The key in making great and growable systems is much more to design how its modules communicate rather than what their internal properties and behaviors should be.

Alan Kay, (squeak-dev mailing list – http://lists.squeakfoundation.org/pipermail/ squeak-dev/1998-October/017019.html)

A huge amount of complexity is wrapped up in that most common of operations: invoking an object's method. In many programming languages – C++, Java, Python, and others – this takes the form **anObject.methodName()**, which means "there will be a method on the class that **anObject** is an instance of, or some antecedent class, where the method is called **methodName**, please find it and run it, with the **self** or **this** value aliased to **anObject**." So, for example, in Java we would expect to find a (non-abstract) **public void methodName() { /* ... */ }** somewhere in **anObject**'s class or parent.

This guarantee introduces a lot of coupling between the caller and the object that holds the method:

1.   The caller knows that the object is an instance of some class (there are so many issues bound up with inheritance that it gets its own chapter, later).

2.   The caller knows that the object's class, or some ancestor of it, provides a method with the given name.

3.   The method will run to completion in this context, then give control back to the caller (this is not particularly evident from the syntax in isolation, but nonetheless is assumed).

What would it mean to lift those assumptions? It would make the object a truly independent computer program, communicating from a distance over an agreed protocol based on message passing. What that object does, how it does it, even what programming language it's implemented in, are all private to the object. Does it collaborate with a class to find out how to respond to the message? Does that class have one parent or multiple parents?

The *idea* behind message-passing is exactly that arms-length separation of concerns, but even programming languages that are based on the message-passing scheme usually treat it as a special case of "look up a method," to be followed only if the usual method-resolution fails. These languages typically have a particular named method that will be run when the requested method isn't found. In Smalltalk, it's called **doesNotUnderstand:**, while in Ruby it's called **method_missing()**. Each one receives the *selector* (that is, the unique name of the method the caller was hoping to invoke) to decide what to do with it. This gets us a higher level of decoupling: objects can send messages to one another without having to peek at the others' implementations to discover whether they implement a method matching the message.

Why is that decoupling valuable? It lets us build our objects as truly standalone programs, considering only what their contract is with the outside world and how their implementation supports that contract. By requiring, for example, that an object will only receive a message if it is an instance of a class that contains a Java function of the same name that can be pushed onto the call stack, even if via a Java interface (a list of methods that a Java class can provide), we adopt a lot of assumptions about the implementation of the message receiver, turning them into constraints that the programmer must deal with when building the sender. We do not have independent, decoupled programs collaborating over a message interface, but a rigid system with a limited amount of modularity. Understanding one object means pulling in information about other parts of the system.

This is not merely an academic distinction, as it constrains the design of real systems. Consider an application to visualize some information about a company's staff, which is located in a key-value store. If I need every object between the view and the store to know about all of the available methods, then I either duplicate my data schema everywhere in the app by defining methods like `salary()` *or* `payrollNumber()`*, or I provide meaningless generic interfaces like* `getValue(String key)` *that remove the useful information that I'm working with representations of people in the company.*

Conversely, I could say to my `Employee` object "if you get a message you do not recognize, but it looks like a key in the key-value store, reply with the value you find for that key." I could say to my view object "if you get a message you do not recognize, but the `Employee` gives you a value in response to it, prepare that value for display and use the selector name as the label for that value." The behavior – looking up arbitrary values in the key-value store – remains the same but the message network tells us more about *why* the application is doing what it does.

By providing lazy resolution paths like `method_missing`, systems like Ruby partially lift these assumptions and provide tools to enable greater decoupling and independence of objects in the network. To fully take advantage of this, we must change the language used and the way we think about these features.

A guide to OOP in Ruby will probably tell you that methods are looked up by name, but if that fails, the class can optionally implement `method_missing` to supply custom behavior. This is exactly backwards: saying that objects are bags of named methods until that stops working, when they gain some autonomy.

Flip this language: an object is responsible for deciding how it handles messages, and one particular convenience is that they automatically run methods that match a received selector without any extra processing. Now your object truly is an autonomous actor responding to messages, rather than a place to store particular named routines in a procedural program.

There are object systems that expose this way of thinking about objects, a good example being the CMU Mach system. Mach is an operating system kernel that supplies communication between threads (in the same or different tasks) using message passing. A sender need know nothing about the receiver other than its port (the place to put outgoing messages) and how to arrange a message to be put in the port. The receiver knows nothing about the sender; just that a message has appeared on its port and can be acted on. The two could be in the same task, or not even on the same computer. They do not even need to be written in the same language, they just need to know what the messages are and how to put them on a port.

In the world of service-oriented architecture, a microservice is an independent program that collaborates with peers over a loosely coupled interface comprised of messages sent over some implementation-independent transport mechanism – often HTTPS or protocol buffers. This sounds a lot like OOP.

Microservice adopters are able to implement different services in different technologies, to think about changes to a given service only in terms of how they satisfy the message contract, and to independently replace individual services without disrupting the whole system. This, too, sounds a lot like OOP.

Designing an Object

The object-oriented approach attempts to manage the complexity inherent in real-world problems by abstracting out knowledge and encapsulating it within objects. Finding or creating these objects is a problem of structuring knowledge and activities.

Rebecca Wirfs-Brock, Brian Wilkerson, and Lauren Wiener, Designing Object-Oriented Software

An early goal of OOP was to simplify the work of software system design by reducing the big problem "design this large system to solve these problems" into the small problems "design these small systems" and "combine these small systems such that they solve these problems in concert". Brad Cox, an object technologist who built the Objective-C language and cofounded a company to exploit it, wrote an article "*What if there's a Silver Bullet...And the Competition Gets It First?*" in which he asserted that OOP represented a significant reduction in software complexity.

In the broadest sense, "object-oriented" refers to the war and not the weapons, the ends and not the means, an objective rather than technologies for achieving it. It means orienting on objects rather than on processes for building them; wielding all the tools programmers can muster, from well-proven antiques like Cobol to as-yet missing ones like specification/testing languages, to enable software consumers, letting them reason about software products with the common-sense skills we all use to understand the tangible objects of everyday experience.

It means relinquishing the traditional process-centered paradigm with the programmer-machine relationship at the center of the software universe in favor of a product-centered paradigm with the producer-consumer relationship at the center.

Nonetheless, many "object-oriented" design techniques still rely on considering the system as a whole, building artisanal, bespoke objects from scratch that will comprise the system that satisfies the customer's needs. In this sense, Cox's vision has not come to pass: he hoped for the "software industrial revolution" in which standardized components (software-ICs, analogous with integrated circuits in electronics design) could be specified based on their externally visible behavior and composed into a system relevant to the task at hand. Rather, we still have a craft industry, but now the application-specific components we build every time are called "objects."

This approach – designing a whole system as a single software product but calling the bits "objects" – goes under the name of **Object-Oriented Analysis and Design**. Typically, it is expressed as a way to decompose big problems according to the *data* used to solve the problem, so that OOP becomes an "alternative" to functional programming, in which the big problem is decomposed according to the *operations* used in its solution. An uncaptioned table in "Using Functions for Easier Programming" by Neil Savage – https://dl.acm.org/citation.cfm?id=3193776 from 2018 describes the term Object-Oriented:

The central mode for abstraction is the data itself, thus the value of a term isn't always predetermined by the input (stateful approach).

The term Functional programming is described as:

The central mode for abstraction is the function, not the data structure, thus the value of a term is always predetermined by the input (stateless approach).

Never mind that "functional" languages like Haskell have mechanisms designed for handling state, or that plenty of problems we might want to solve in the world have both stateful and stateless aspects!

This idea of objects-as-data does have its roots in the OOP movement. In his textbook "*A Touch of Class*" from 2009, in Section 2.3 "*What is an object?*", Bertrand Meyer uses the following definition:

An object is a software machine allowing programs to access and modify a collection of data.

This is in exact opposition to the usual goals of "encapsulation" or "data hiding" that we have heard about, in which we try to *forbid* programs from accessing and modifying our data! In this view, we have the object as a "software machine," which is good as it suggests some kind of independent, autonomous function, but unfortunately, we get the idea that the purpose of this machine is to look after some slice of our data from the overall collection used throughout the program.

It is this mindset that leads to objects as "active structures," like this typical example in C#:

```
class SomeClass

  {

    private int field;

    public int Field => field;

  }
```

This satisfies our requirement for encapsulation (the field is private), and our requirement that an object allows programs to access and modify a collection of data. What we have ended up with is no different from a plain old data structure:

```
struct SomeClass

  {

    int Field;

  }
```

The exception is that the C# example requires a function call on each access of the field. There is no *real* encapsulation; objects with their own fields can make no guesses about the status of those fields, and a system including such objects can only be understood by considering the whole system. The hoped-for advantage that we could turn our big problem into a composition of small problems has been lost.

A contributor to this objects-as-data approach seems to have been the attempt to square object-oriented programming with **Software Engineering**, a field of interest launched in 1968 that aimed to bring product design and construction skills to computer scientists by having very clever computer scientists think about what product design and construction might be like and not ask anybody. Process-heavy and design-artefact-heavy systems, approaches, and "methodologies" (a word that used to mean "the study of method" until highfalutin software engineers took it to mean "method, but a longer word") recommended deciding on the objects, their methods, and properties; the data involved; and the presentation and storage of that data in excruciating detail, all in the name of satisfying a **Use Case**, which is Software Engineering speak for "a thing somebody might want to do."

The inside cover of "*Applying UML and Patterns*" by Craig Larman (1997) has 22 detailed steps to follow before **Construction** when constructing a product.

Objects can be thought of as *simulations* of some part of the problem we're trying to solve, and a great way to learn from a simulation is to *interact* with it. If our objects are just active structures that hold some data on behalf of a program, then we don't get that benefit: we can't interact with the simulation without building out all of the rest of the program. And indeed that is the goal behind a lot of the "engineering" processes that use objects: while they may pay lip service to iterative and incremental development, they still talk about building a system at once, with each object being a jigsaw puzzle piece that satisfactorily fits its given gap in the puzzle.

So, let's go back to Bertrand Meyer's definition, and remove the problematic bit about letting a program access an object's data:

An object is a software machine

A machine is a useful analogy. It's a device (so something that was built by people) that uses energy to produce some effect. Notice the absence of any statement about *how* the machine produces that effect, *how* the machine consumes its materials, or *how* the machine's output is supplied. We've got a thing that does a thing, but if we're going to compose these things together to do other things, we're going to need to know how to do that composition. Adding a constraint takes us from "it's a machine" to "it's a machine that we can use like this".

An object is a software machine that can collaborate with other software machines by sending and receiving messages.

Now we've got things that do things and can be used together. We don't restrict the level of complexity of the things that are done by each machine (so booking a flight and representing a number are both things that we could build machines to do); just how we would combine them. This has parallels with Brad Cox's software ICs analogy, too. An "integrated circuit" could be anything from a **NAND** gate to an **UltraSPARC T2**. We can use any of the IC's together, of any size, if we just know how to deal with their inputs and outputs: what voltage should appear on each pin and what that represents.

This analogy tells us that our software system is like a big machine that does something useful by composing, powering, and employing smaller component machines. It tells us to worry about whether the things coming out of one machine are useful as inputs to another machine, but not to worry about what's going on inside each machine except in the restricted context of the maintenance of those machines. It tells us to consider at each point whether the machine we have is more useful than not having that machine, rather than tracking the progress toward the construction of some all-powerful supermachine.

It even tells us that building an **assembly line** in which input of a certain type is transformed into output of a certain type is a thing we might want to do; something that, otherwise, we might believe is solely the domain of the functional programmer.

Drawing an Object

I see a red door and I want to paint it black. No colors any more I want them to turn black.

Rolling Stones, Paint it Black

If object-oriented programming is the activity of modelling a problem in software, then the kinds of diagrams (and verbal descriptions) that software teams use to convey the features and behavior of those objects are metamodeling – the modeling of models. The rules, for example, the constraints implied when using **CRC cards**–https://dl.acm.org/citation.cfm?id=74879, are then `metametamodels`: the models that describe how the models of the models of the problems will work.

Unified Modeling Language

Plenty of such systems (I will avoid the word `metametamodels` from now on) have been used over time to describe object systems. The **UML** (**Unified Modeling Language**) is the result of combining three prior techniques: the three Elven Kings, Grady Booch, Ivar Jacobson, and James Rumbaugh bent their rings of power (respectively, the **Booch Method**, **Object-Oriented Software Engineering**, and the **Object Modelling Technique** – the latter mostly recognized today because the majority of diagrams in the famous *Design Patterns* book are drawn to its rules) to the *One Rational Ring*, wielded by Mike Devlin.

As an aside, Rational started as a company making better Ada applications and tools for other Ada programmers to make better Ada applications, including the R1000 workstation, optimized for running Ada programs and featuring an integrated development environment. The R1000 did not take off but the idea of an IDE did, and through a couple of iterations of their Rose product (as well as the UML and Rational Unified Process), made significant inroads into changing the way organizations planned, designed, and built software.

The UML and, to differing extents, its precursor modelling techniques, represent a completist approach to object modelling in which all aspects of the implementation can be represented diagrammatically. Indeed, tools exist to "round-trip" convert UML into compatible languages like Java and back again into the UML representation.

The model you create that both encapsulates enough of the "business" aspects of the system to demonstrate that you have solved a problem and enough of the implementation aspects to generate the executable program is not really a model, it *is* the program source. In shooting for completeness, the UML family of modelling tools have missed "modelling" completely and simply introduced another implementation language.

If the goal of message-passing is to solve our big problem through the concerted operation of lots of small, independent computer programs loosely coupled by the communications protocol, then we should be able to look at each object through one of two lenses: internal or external. In fact, the boundary itself deserves special consideration, so there are three views:

1. The "external" lens: What messages can I send to this object? What do I need to arrange in order to send them? What can I expect as a result?

2. The "internal" lens: What does this object do in response to its messages?

3. The "boundary" lens: Does the behavior of this object satisfy the external expectations?

The final two of these things are closely intertwingled. Indeed some popular implementation disciplines, such as **Test-Driven Development** lead you to implement the object internals only through the boundary lens, by saying "I need this to happen when this message is received," then arranging the object's internals so that it does, indeed, happen.

The first is separated from the others, though. From the outside of an object I *only* need to know what I can ask it to do; if I also need to know how it does it or what goes on inside, then I have not decomposed my big problem into independent, small problems.

UML class diagrams include all class features at all levels of visibility: public, package, protected, and private; simultaneously. Either they show a lot of redundant information (which is not to a diagram's benefit) or they expect the modeler to take the completist approach and solve the whole big problem at once, using the word "objects" to give some of that 1980s high-technology feel to their solution. This is a downhill development from Booch's earlier method, in which objects and classes were represented as fluffy cloud-shaped things, supporting the idea that there's probably some dynamism and complexity inside there but that it's not relevant right now.

Interestingly, as with Bertrand Meyer's statement that "an object is a software machine allowing programs to access and modify a collection of data," explored in the section on *analysis and design*, we can find the point at which Grady Booch overshot the world of modelling tools in a single sentence in *Chapter One of his 1991 book Object-Oriented Design with Applications.*

> ### Note
>
> Perhaps there is a general principle in which the left half of a sentence about making software is always more valuable than the right half. If so, then the (**Agile Manifesto** — http://agilemanifesto.org/) is the most insightfully-designed document in our history.

The sentence runs thus:

Object-oriented design's underlying concept is that one should model software systems as collections of cooperating objects...

So far, so good.

... treating individual objects as instances of a class ...

I would suggest that this is not necessary, and that classes, and particularly inheritance, deserve their own section in this part of the book (see *Finding a Method to Run* section).

... within a hierarchy of classes.

And here we just diverge completely. By situating his objects within "a hierarchy of classes," Booch *is* encouraging us to think about the whole system, relating objects taxonomically and defining shared features. This comes from a good intention – inheritance was long seen as the object-oriented way to achieve reuse – but promotes thinking about reuse over thinking about *use*.

Class-Responsibility-Collaborator

Just as the UML represents a snapshot in the development of a way of describing objects, so do CRC cards, introduced by Kent Beck and Ward Cunningham in 1989, and propagated by Rebecca Wirfs-Brock, Brian Wilkerson, and Lauren Wiener in their textbook *Designing Object-Oriented Software.*

The CRC card describes three aspects of an object, none of which is a cyclic redundancy check:

- The *Class* names
- The *Responsibilities* of the object
- The *Collaborators* that the object will need to work with

Not only does this school of design focus on the messaging aspect of objects (the responsibilities will be things I can ask it to do and the collaborators will be other objects it asks to do things), but it introduces a fun bit of *anthropomorphism*. You and I can each pick up a card and "play object," having a conversation to solve a problem, and letting that drive our understanding of what messages will be exchanged.

David West, in his 2004 book, *Object Thinking*, presents the object cube, which extends the CRC card into three dimensions by adding five more faces:

- A textual description of instances of the class
- A list of named contracts (these are supposed to indicate "the intent of the class creator as to who should be able to send particular messages," and in his examples are all either "public" or "private")
- The "knowledge required" by an object and an indication of where it will get that knowledge
- The message protocol is a list of messages the object will respond to
- Events generated by the objects

Some bad news: you can't make a cube out of 3x5 index cards; and you can't buy 5x5 index cards. But that's just an aside. Again, as with using the UML, we've got to record the internals and externals of our object in the same place, and now we need to use large shelves rather than index boxes to store them.

With both of these techniques, the evolution seems to have been one of additive complexity. Yes, you can draw out the network of objects and messages, oh and while you're here you can also...

And rationally, each part of each of these metamodels seems to make sense. Of course, at some point, I need to think about the internals of this object; at some point, I need to consider its instance variables; and at some point, I need to plan the events emitted by the object. Yes, but not at the *same* point, so they don't need to be visible at the same time on the same model.

Jelly Donuts and Soccer Balls

Ironically, there *is* a form of object diagram that makes this separation between the externals and internals clear, though I have only seen it in one place: The NeXT (and subsequently Apple) **jelly-donut model** – http://www.cilinder.be/docs/next/ NeXTStep/3.3/nd/Concepts/ObjectiveC/1_OOP/OOP.htmld/index.html This isn't a tool that programmers use for designing objects, though: it's an analogy used in some documentation.

It's an analogy that some authors disagree with. In *Object Thinking*, David West says that the jelly donut model (which he calls the **soccer-ball model**, after Ken Auer) is the model of choice of the "traditional developer," while "an object thinker" would represent an object anthropomorphically, using a person.

West may well argue that the jelly donut/soccer ball model represents traditional thinking because it reflects the Meyer-ish view that your system is designed by working out what data it needs and then carving that up between different objects. Ironically, Bertrand Meyer would probably also reject the soccer ball model, for an unrelated reason: Eiffel follows the **Principle of Uniform Reference**, in which an object field or a member function (method) is accessed using the same notation. To an Eiffel programmer, the idea that the data is "surrounded" by the methods is superfluous; the jelly donut indicates the use of a broken language that allows the sweet jelly to escape and make everything else sticky.

Opposing Functional Programming

[An] important aspect of functional programming is that functions do not change the data with which they work [...] Object-oriented imperative languages such as C, Java, or Python change their state as they run.

Neil Savage, (Using Functions for Easier Programming – https://dl.acm.org/citation. cfm?id=3193776)

Many programmers define themselves through their tools, and therefore define themselves as *against* certain other tools. If you are a .NET programmer, then you do not use Java. If you are a native mobile programmer, then you do not use JavaScript. If you are a React programmer, then you do not use Angular. An affiliation with one tool automatically means a disaffiliation with others.

Such partisanship is a confirming example of Sayre's law: the arguments are so fierce because the stakes are so low. For people who supposedly work in a field of rationality and science, we're really good at getting emotionally brittle when somebody wants to use a different library, language, text editor, or whitespace symbol than the one we have chosen.

This fierce disagreement over strongly defended similarities extends to the programming paradigm, too. If you are an object-oriented programmer, then your mortal enemy is the functional programmer—http://www.sicpers.info/2015/03/inspired-by-swift/, and vice versa.

Messages Are Just Requests

Not so fast! Recall the working definition of objects I have used throughout the antithesis: an object is an isolated, independent computer program that communicates with other programs by passing messages. This tells us nothing about *how* to build those isolated, independent computer programs. Particularly, there is no *mandate* to have mutable state anywhere. The following interface works as a messaging interface for a time-varying list:

```
public interface MutableList<T> {

    void setElements(T[] elements);

    void appendObject(T element);

    void removeObject(int index) throws OutOfBoundsException;

    void replaceObject(int index, T element) throws OutOfBoundsException;

    int count();

    T at(int index);

};
```

And so, does this one:

```
public interface TemporalList<T> {

    void setInitialState(T[] elements);

    void appendObject(T element, Time when);

    void removeObject(int index, Time when) throws
    InconsistentHistoryException;

    void replaceObject(int index, T element, Time when) throws
    InconsistentHistoryException;

    void revertMostRecentChange(Time beforeNow);

    int count(Time when);

    T at(int index, Time when);

};
```

In the first, time in the list's lifespan is modeled using successive states of the computer memory. In the second, time in the list's lifespan is modeled explicitly, and the history of the list is preserved. Another option is to model evolution using *different objects*, turning time into space:

```
public interface ImmutableList<T> {

  ImmutableList<T> addObject(T element);

  ImmutableList<T> removeObject(int index) throws OutOfBoundsException;

  ImmutableList<T> replaceObject(int index, T element) throws
OutOfBoundsException;

  int count();

  T at(int index);

}
```

Now the list looks a lot like a sort of a functional programming list. But it's still an object. In each case, we have defined what *messages* the object responds to but, remembering the section on *Telling an Object What to Do*, we have not said *anything* about what methods exist on that object, and certainly not how they are implemented. The `MutableList` and `TemporalList` interfaces use Bertrand Meyer's principle of **Command-Query Separation**, in which a message either instructs an object to do something (like add an element to a list) or asks the object for information (like the number of elements in a list), but never does both. This does not automatically imply that the commands act on local mutable state though. They could execute `Datalog` programs, or SQL programs, or be stored as a chain of events that is replayed when a query message is received.

In the `ImmutableList` interface, commands are replaced by transforms, which ask for a new list that reflects the result of applying a change to the existing list. Again, no restriction on *how* you implement those transforms is stated (I could imagine building `addObject()` by having a new list that delegates every call to the original list, adding 1 to the result of `count()` and supplying its own value for `at(originalCount)`; or I could just build a new list with all of the existing elements and the new element), but in this case, it's clear to see that every method can be a pure function based on the content of the object and the message parameters.

We can see that "pure function based on the content of the object and the message parameters" is the same as "pure function" more clearly by rewriting the interface in Python syntax (skipping the implementations):

```python
class ImmutableList:

    def addObject(this, element):

        pass

    def removeObject(this, index):

        pass

    def replaceObject(this, index, element):

        pass

    def count(this):

        pass

    def at(this, index):

        pass
```

It's now easier to see that each of these methods is a pure function in its parameters, where **this/self** is a parameter that's automatically prepared in other languages (or a part of the method's environment that's automatically closed over in others).

Nothing about message-passing says, "please do not use functional programming techniques."

An Object's Boundary is Just a Function

The following subsections were deeply informed by the article Objects as Closures: abstract semantics of object-oriented languages – https://dl.acm.org/citation.cfm?id=62721, which builds this view of objects much more rigorously.

The interface to an object is the collection of messages it responds to. In many cases, this is backed by a collection of methods, each with the same name as the message selector that will invoke it. Not only is this the easiest thing to do, it's also an implementation constraint in many programming languages. The preceding Python implementation of **ImmutableList** can be visualized in this table:

Message Selector	Method to Invoke
addObject	ImmutableList.addObject
removeObject	ImmutableList.removeObject
replaceObject	ImmutableList.replaceObject
count	ImmutableList.count
at	ImmutableList.at

Figure 3.1: Visualization of ImmutableList after implementation

This table can equivalently be replaced by a pure function of type **Message Selector->Method to Invoke**. A trivial implementation of the function would look up its input in the left-hand column of the table and return the value it finds in the same row in the right-hand column. An implementation of **ImmutableList** doesn't need to have any methods at all, choosing functions based on the message selector:

```
class ImmutableList:
    def __init__(this, elements):
        this.elements = elements
    def __getattr__(this, name):
        if name == "count":
            return lambda: len(this.elements)
        elif name == "at":
            return lambda index: this.elements[index]
        # ...
```

Using this object works the same way as using an object where the methods were defined in the usual way:

```
>>> il = ImmutableList([1,2,3])
>>> il.count()
3
>>> il.at(0)
1
>>>
```

So, whichever way you write out an object, its methods are functions that have access to (close over) the object's internals, and its message interface is one such function that uses the message selector to choose which method to invoke.

Freed from the fetters of the language's idea of where methods live, we see that the function to look up implementations from selectors can use *any* information available to it. If the object knows about another object, it can send the message on to the other object, send a different method in its place, or it could compile a new function and use that. The important idea is that *an object is a function for finding other functions.*

That Function-Like Boundary? Actually, a Closure Over the Constructor Arguments

Our **ImmutableList** has a constructor method called **__init__**, which sets up the initial state of the object using its arguments, and then the message-finding **__getattr__** function, which chooses functions to respond to the messages that are sent to the object.

An equivalent way to arrange this is to have the constructor function return the message-finding function as a closure over the constructor's arguments (and any transformation implied in "setting up the initial state of the object" can be arranged using local variables that are captured in the closure, too). So, all in all, an object is a single higher-order function: a function that captures its arguments and returns a closure over those arguments that accept messages and then chooses a method to execute the code:

```
(constructor arguments) -> message -> (method arguments) -> method
return type
```

Sticking with Python, and using this insight, **ImmutableList** is reduced to a single expression:

```
def ImmutableList(elements):

        return type('ImmutableList',

                      (object,),

                      {'__getattr__':

                       (lambda this, name:

                       (lambda: len(elements)) if name=="count"

                       else (lambda index: elements[index]) if
  name=="at"

                       else False)

                      })()
```

By the way, this demonstrates why so many object-oriented languages don't seem to have a type system. If "*everything is an object*," then even in the most stringent of type systems, everything is a **message->method** function, so everything has the same type, and everything type checks.

The preceding definition of **ImmutableList** does escape the "everything is an object" type scheme by ending with the phrase **else False**, meaning "if I didn't find a method, return something that isn't callable, so the user gets a **TypeError**." A more complete object system would have the object send itself a **doesNotRespond** message here, and no breaking out into Python's usual world of computation would occur.

Capturing Elements of Reusable Design

A *pattern for increased monitoring for intellectual property theft by departing insiders*

Title of (an article in the Proceedings of the 18th Conference of Pattern Languages of Programs – https://dl.acm.org/citation.cfm?id=2579157*), PLoP'11*

Christopher Alexander, while evidently seminal in the field of built architecture, seems pretty lazy as architects go. Why? Because rather than designing a building or even a town *himself*, he expects the people who will live, work, shop, and play there to do that for him, and even to build its prototype.

In fact, this has little to do with laziness; it's because he believes that they are the best people to do the designing as they are the people who best know the uses to which the structure will be put and the problems it will solve. What does he know about that? Not much; what he knows is the expertise architects have gained in solving problems that crop up when designing and constructing towns and buildings.

In A *Pattern Language: Towns, Buildings and Construction*, Alexander and his coauthors and reviewers sought to encapsulate that professional knowledge in a grammar that would allow a user to solve their own construction problems by taking advantage of the solutions known to work by the expert architects. Each pattern describes the problem it solves, the context in which it solves it, and the advantages and limitations of the solution. Some represent instant decisions to be made – the placement of columns in a building construction; others represent experiences to be nurtured gradually – the opening of street cafes to facilitate relaxed interaction between people and their environment. The grammar developed in A *Pattern Language* is additive, so each pattern develops ideas that have been introduced previously without depending on patterns that will be seen later, and there are no cyclic references. Each pattern is hyperlinked (old-school and using page numbers) to the preceding patterns it builds upon.

We could expect that, in taking inspiration from A *Pattern Language*, software designers and builders would create a pattern language that allowed users of computers to design and build their own software, by elucidating the problems the users are facing and expressing known approaches to solving those problems. And indeed, that is exactly what happened when Kent Beck and Ward Cunningham published *Using Pattern Languages for Object-Oriented Programs* – http://c2.com/doc/oopsla87.html. The five Smalltalk UI patterns listed in that report are like a microcosm of a **Human Interface Guidelines** document, written for the *people who will use the interface*.

However, what most of us will find when looking for examples of a pattern language for software construction are the 23 patterns in the 1994 "Gang of Four" book *Design Patterns: Elements of Reusable Design* by Gamma, Helm, Johnson, and Vlissides. Compared with the 253 architectural design patterns documented by Alexander et al., the software pattern language seems positively anemic. Compared with practice, the situation looks even worse. Here are the three patterns that see regular use in modern development:

- **Iterator**: You won't have implemented the `Iterator` pattern yourself; it's the one that programming language designers have worked out how to supply for you, via the `for (element in collection)` construct.

- **Singleton**: You'll have only built *Singleton* so that you could write that blog post about why *Singleton* is "Considered Harmful."

- **Abstract Factory**: The butt of all jokes about Java frameworks by people who haven't used Java frameworks.

Here's the thing: the *Gang of Four* book is actually very good, and the patterns are genuinely repeatable patterns that can be identified in software design and that solve common problems. But as Brian Marick argued in Patterns Failed. Why? Should we care?—https://www.deconstructconf.com/2017/brian-marick-patterns-failed-why-should-we-care, the 23 patterns discussed therein are *implementation* patterns, and software implementors (that's us) don't want repeatable patterns; we want *abstraction*. Don't tell me "Oh, I've seen that before, what you do is..."; tell me "Oh, I've seen that before, here's the `npm` module I wrote."

The big winner for software reuse was not information that could be passed from one programmer to another, but information that could be passed from one *lawyer* to another, which allowed other information to be passed from one programmer to *another's program*. The free software license (particularly, due to the conservative nature of technologists in business, the non-copyleft free software licenses like the MIT or BSD) permitted some programmers to publish libraries to CTAN and its spiritual successors, and permitted a whole lot of other programmers to incorporate those libraries into their works.

In that sense, the end situation for software reuse has been incredibly similar to the "software ICs" that Brad Cox described, for example, in *Object-Oriented Programming: An Evolutionary Approach*. He proposed that we would browse the catalogue (the `npm` repository) for software ICs that look like they do what we want, compare their data sheets (the `README.md` or Swagger docs), then pick one and download it for integration into our applications (`npm install`).

Anyway, back to design patterns. Marick suggested that the way we work means that we can't benefit from implementation patterns because we don't rely on repeated practice in implementation. Some programmers do participate in **Code Kata** – http://codekata.com/, a technique for instilling repeated practice in programming, but by and large we try to either incorporate an existing solution or try something new, not find existing solutions and solve problems in similar ways.

Indeed, we could vastly shrink the Gang of Four book by introducing **Strategy (315)** and describing all of the other problems in its terms. Abstract Factory? A **Strategy (315)** for creating objects. Factory Method? The same. Adapter? A **Strategy (315)** for choosing integration technologies. State? A **Strategy (315)** for dealing with time. But we don't do that, because we think of these as different problems, so describe them in different terms and look for different solutions.

So, abstraction has to stop somewhere. Particularly, it has to stop by the time we're talking to the product owners or sponsors, as we're typically building specific software tools to support specific tasks. Built architecture has techniques for designing residences, offices, shops, and hotels, rather than "buildings," A house for a young single worker is different from a house for a retired widow, although both are residences with one occupant. So, this points us, as Brian Marick concludes, to having design patterns in our software's problem domain, telling us how domain experts address the problems they encounter. We might have good abstractions for stateful software, or desktop application widgets, or microservice-based service architecture, but we have to put them to specific ends, and the people who know the field know the problems they're trying to solve.

And indeed, that is one of the modern goals of the Pattern Language of Programming conference series and the software patterns community. I expected that, on first reading, the pull quote chosen for this section ("A pattern for increased monitoring for intellectual property theft by departing insiders") would raise a few cynical laughs: "Wow, the patterns folks are so far down the rabbit hole that they're writing patterns for *that*?" Well, yes, they are, because it's a problem that is encountered multiple times by multiple people and where knowledge of the common aspects of the solution can help designers. Any enterprise IT architect, CISO, or small company HR person is going to know that leavers, particularly those who left due to disagreements with management or being poached by competitors, represent an increased risk of IP theft and will want a way to solve that problem. Here, the pattern language shows the important dimensions of the problem, the facets of the solution, and the benefits and drawbacks of the solution.

A quote from the pattern description is revealing:

The authors are unaware of any implementation of the pattern in a production environment.

This means that, while the solution does (presumably and hopefully) capture expert knowledge about the problem and how to solve it, it is not tested. The design patterns from the Beck and Cunningham paper (and Beck's later *Smalltalk Best Practice Patterns*), and indeed the Gang of Four book, were all based on *observation* of how problems had commonly been solved. There were not lots of C++ or Smalltalk programs that all had classes called `AbstractFactory`, but there *were* lots of C++ or Smalltalk programs that solved the "We need to create families of related or dependent objects without specifying their concrete classes" problem.

On the other hand, there is nobody outside of an SEI lab who has used "Increased Monitoring for Intellectual Property Theft by Departing Insiders" as their solution to, well, that. So, perhaps patterns have gotten out of hand.

Finding a Method to Run

Don't go out of your way to justify stuff that's obviously cool. Don't ridicule ideas merely because they're not the latest and greatest. Pick your own fashions. Don't let someone else tell you what you should like.

*Larry Wall, (Perl, the first postmodern computer language–*https://www.perl.com/pub/1999/03/pm.html/*)*

The Perl community has a mantra: TIMTOWTDI (pronounced "Tim Toady"). It stands for "There Is More Than One Way to Do It" and reflects the design principle that the language should enable its users to write programs in the way in which they are thinking and not in the way that the language designer thought about it. Of course, TIMTOWTDI is not the only way to do it, and the **Zen of Python**–http://wiki.c2.com/?PythonPhilosophy takes a different (though not incompatible) tack:

There should be one-- and preferably only one --obvious way to do it.

So, how is a method found? There is more than one way to do it. The first, and easiest to understand, is that an object has a method with the same name as the message selector, and the language assumes that when you send that message, it's because you want to invoke that method. That's how this looks in Javascript:

```
const foo = {
    doAThing: () => { console.log("I'm doing a thing!"); }
}


    foo.doAThing();
```

The next way is the most general, and doesn't exist in all languages and is made difficult to use in some. The idea is to have the object *itself* decide what to do in response to a message. In Javascript that looks like this:

```
const foo = new Proxy({}, {
    get: (target, prop, receiver) => (() => {
      console.log("I'm doing my own thing!");
    }),
});


    foo.doAThing();
```

While there are many languages that don't have *syntax* for finding methods in this way, it's actually very easy to write yourself. We saw in the section on functional programming that an object is just a function that turns a message into a method, and so any language that lets you write functions returning functions will let you write objects that work the way you want them to. This argument is also pursued in the talk Object-Oriented Programming in Functional Programming in Swift–https://www.dotconferences.com/2018/01/graham-lee-object-oriented-programming-in-functional-programming-in-swift.

Almost all programming languages that have objects have a fall-through mechanism, in which an object that does not have a method matching the message selector will look by default at *another* object to find the method. In Javascript, fully bought into the worldview of Tim Toady, there are two ways to do this (remember that this is already the *third* way to find methods in Javascript). The first, classic, original recipe Javascript way, is to look at the object's prototype:

```
function Foo() {};

    Foo.prototype.doAThing = () => { console.log("Doing my prototype's
thing!"); };


    new Foo().doAThing();
```

And the second way, which in some other languages is the *only* way to define a method, is to have the object look at its class:

```
class Foo {
    doAThing() { console.log("Doing my class's thing!"); }
}


    new Foo().doAThing();
```

A little bit of honesty at the expense of clarity here: these last two are actually just different syntax for the same thing; the method ends up being defined on the object's prototype and is found there. The mental model is different, and that's what is important.

But we can't stop there. What if *that* object can't find the method? In the prototype case, the answer is clear: it could look at its prototype, and so on, until the method is found, or we run out of prototypes. To an external user of an object, it looks like the object has all of the behavior of its prototype *and* the things it defines (which may be other, distinct features, or they may be replacements for things that the prototype already did). We could say that the object *inherits* the behavior of its prototype.

The situation with inheritance when it comes to classes is muddier. If my object's class doesn't implement a method to respond to a message, where do we look next? A common approach, used in early object environments such as Simula and Smalltalk, and in Objective-C, Java, C#, and others, is to say that a class is a refinement of a *single* other class, often called the superclass, and to have instances of a class inherit the behavior defined for instances of the superclass, and its superclass, until we run out of `superclasses`.

But that's quite limiting. What if there are two different classes of object that one object can be seen as a refinement of? Or two different classes that describe distinct behaviors it would make sense for this object to inherit? Python, C++, and others allow a class to inherit from *multiple* other classes. When a message is sent to an object, it will look for a method implementation in its class, then in...

...and now we get confused. It could look breadth-first up the tree, considering each of its parents, then each of *their* parents, and so on. Or it could look depth-first, considering its first superclass, and *its* first superclass, and so on. If there are multiple methods that match a single selector, then which is found will depend on the search strategy. And of course, if there are two matching methods but with different behavior, then the presence of one may break features that depend on the behavior of the other.

Attempts have been made to get the benefits of multiple inheritance without the confusion. **Mixins**–https://dl.acm.org/citation.cfm?id=97982 represent "abstract subclasses," which can be attached to any superclass. This turns a single-superclass inheritance system into one that's capable of supporting a limited form of multiple inheritance, by delegating messages to the superclass *and any mixins*.

However, this does not address the problem that conflicts will arise if multiple mixins, or a superclass and a mixin, supply the same method. A refinement to the idea of mixins, called **traits**, introduces additional rules that avoid the conflicts. Each trait exposes the features it provides, and the features it requires, on the class into which it is mixed. If the same feature is provided by two traits, it must either be renamed in one or be removed from both and turned into a requirement. In other words, the programmer can choose to resolve the conflict themselves by building a method that does what both of the traits need to do.

So, inheritance is a great tool for code reuse, allowing one object to borrow features from another to complete its task. In "*Smalltalk-80: The Language and its Implementation*," that is the justification for inheritance:

Lack of intersection in class membership is a limitation on design in an object-oriented system since it does not allow any sharing between class descriptions. We might want two objects to be substantially similar, but to differ in some particular way.

Over time, inheritance came to have stronger implications for the intention of the designer. While there was always an "is-a" relationship between an instance and its class (as in, an instance of the `OrderedCollection` class *is* an `OrderedCollection`), there came to be a subset relationship between a class and its subclasses (as in, `SmallInteger` is a subclass of `Number`, so any instance of `SmallInteger` is also an instance of `Number`). This then evolved into a subtype relationship (as in, you have only used inheritance correctly if any program that expects an instance of a class also works correctly when given an instance of any subclass of that class), which led to the restrictions that tied object-oriented developers in knots and led to "favor composition over inheritance": you can only get reuse through inheritance if you also conform to these other, unrelated requirements. The rules around subtypes are perfectly clear, and mathematically sound, but the premise that a subclass *must* be a subtype does not need to be upheld.

Indeed, there's another assumption commonly made that implies a lot of design intent: the existence of classes. We have seen that Javascript gets on fine without classes, and when classes were added to the language, they were implemented in such a way that there is really no "class-ness" at all, with classes being turned into prototypes behind the scenes. But the *presence* of classes in the design of a system implies, well, the presence of classes: that there is some set of objects that share common features and are defined in a particular way.

But what if your object truly is a hand-crafted, artisanal one-off? Well, the class design community has a solution for that: Singleton – the design pattern that says, "class of one." But why have a *class* at all? At this point, it's just additional work, when all you want is an *object*. Your class is now responsible for three aspects of the system's behavior: the object's work, the work of making the object, and the work of making sure that there is only one of those objects. This is a less cohesive design than if you just made one object that did the work.

If it were possible (as it is in Javascript) to first make an object, then make another, similar object, then more, then notice the similarities and differences and encapsulate that knowledge in the design of a class that encompasses all of those objects, then that one-off object would not need to be anything more than an object that was designed once and used multiple times. There would be no need to make a class of all objects that are similar to that one, only to constrain class membership again to ensure that the singleton instance cannot be joined by any compatriots.

But as you've probably experienced, most programming languages only give you one kind of inheritance, and *that* is often the "single inheritance, which we also assume to mean subtyping" variety. It's easy to construct situations where multiple inheritance makes sense (a book is both a *publication* that can be catalogued and shelved and it is a *product* that can be priced and sold); situations where single inheritance makes sense (a *bag* has all the operations of a *set*, but adding the same object twice means it's in the *bag* twice); and situations where customizing a prototype makes sense (our hypothesis is that simplifying the **Checkout** interaction by applying a fixed shipping cost instead of letting the customer choose from a range of options will increase completion among customers attempting to check out). It's easy to consider situations in which all three of those cases would simultaneously apply (an online bookstore could easily represent books, bags, and checkouts in a single system), so why is it difficult to model all of those in the same object system?

When it comes down to it, inheritance is just a particular way to introduce delegation – one object finding another to forward a message on to. The fact that inheritance is constrained to specific forms doesn't stop us from delegating messages to whatever objects we like, but it does stop us from making the *reasons* for doing so obvious in our designs.

Building Objects

What then is a personal computer? One would hope that it would be both a medium for containing and expressing arbitrary symbolic notions, and also a collection of useful tools for manipulating these structures, with ways to add new tools to the repertoire.

Alan C. Kay, "A Personal Computer for Children of All Ages"

Smalltalk is both a very personal and a very live system. This affected the experience of using, building, and sharing objects built in the system, which were all done in a way very different from the edit-compile-assemble-link-run workflow associated with COBOL and later languages.

As an aside, I'm mostly using "Smalltalk" here to mean "Smalltalk-80 and later things that derived from it without changing the experience much." Anything that looks and feels "quite a lot like" a Smalltalk environment, such as Pharo or Squeak, is included. Things that involve a clearly more traditional workflow, like Java or Objective-C, are excluded. Where to draw the line is left intentionally ambiguous: try out **GNU Smalltalk**–http:// smalltalk.gnu.org/) *and decide whether you think it is "a Smalltalk" or not.*

A Smalltalk environment is composed of two parts: the virtual machine can execute Smalltalk bytecode, and the image contains Smalltalk sources, bytecode, and the definitions of classes and objects.

So, the image is both personal and universal. Personal in the sense that it is unique to me, containing the objects that I have created or acquired from others; universal in the sense that it contains the whole system: there are no private frameworks, no executables that contain the Directory Services objects but not the GUI objects, and no libraries to link before I can use networking.

This makes it very easy to build things: I make the objects I need, and I find and use the objects that I can already take advantage of. On the other hand, it makes sharing quite fraught: if I need to make a change to a system object for some reason, you cannot take in my change without considering the impact that change will have on everything else in your image. If you want to add my class to your image, you have to make sure that you don't already have a class with that name. We cannot both use the same key on the `Smalltalk` dictionary for different purposes.

It's also live, in that the way you modify the image is by interacting with it. Methods are implemented as Smalltalk bytecode (though that bytecode may simply be a request to execute a "primitive method" stored on the virtual machine) by writing the method into a text field and sending a message to the compiler object asking it to compile the method. Classes are added by sending a message to an existing class, asking it to create a subclass. Objects are created by sending a **new** message to a class.

While there is editing, compilation and debugging, this all takes place within the image. This makes for a very rapid prototype and feedback experience (unsurprising, as one vision behind Smalltalk was to let children explore the world and computers in tandem – https://mprove.de/diplom/gui/kay72.html. Any change you make affects the system you are using, and its effects can be seen without rebuilding or quitting an application to launch it again. Similarly, the system you are using affects the changes you are making: if an object encounters a message to which it does not respond or an assertion is not satisfied, then the debugger is brought up, so you can correct your code and carry on.

The fast feedback afforded by building UIs out of the objects that represent UI widgets was used by lots of **Rapid Application Development** tools, such as NeXT's Interface Builder, Borland's Delphi and Microsoft's Visual Basic. These tools otherwise took a very different position to the trade-offs described previously.

While an IDE like Eclipse might be made out of Java, a Java developer using Eclipse is not writing Java that modifies the Eclipse environment, even where the Java package they are writing is an Eclipse plugin. Instead, they use the IDE to host tools that produce *another* program containing their code, along with references to other packages and libraries needed for the code to work.

This approach is generic rather than personal (anyone with the same collection of packages and libraries can make the standalone code work without any step integrating things into their image) and specific rather than universal (the resulting program – mistakes aside – contains only the things needed by that program).

This one key difference – that there is a "build phase" separating the thing you're making from the thing you're making it in – is the big distinction between the two ways of building objects, and one of the ways in which the transfer of ideas in either direction remains imperfect.

Those Rapid Application Development tools with their GUI builders let you set up the UI widgets from the vendor framework and configure their properties, by working with live objects rather than writing static code to construct a UI. In practice, the limitations on being able to do so are:

- To understand the quality of a UI, you need to work with the real information and workflows the interface exposes, and that is all in the program source that's sat around in the editor panes and code browsers, waiting to be compiled and integrated with the UI layout into the (currently dormant) application.

- Changes outside the capability of the UI editor tool cannot be reflected within it. Changing the font on a label is easily tested; writing a new text transform to be applied to the label's contents is not.

- The bits of a UI that you can test within a UI builder are usually well-defined by the platform's interface guidelines anyway, so you never *want* to change the font on a label.

In practice, even with a UI builder you still have an edit-build-debug workflow.

A similar partial transfer of ideas can be seen in test-driven development. A quick summary (obviously, if you want the long version, you could always *buy my book*– https://qualitycoding.org/test-driven-ios-development-book/) is that you create an object incrementally by thinking of the messages you want to send it, then what it should do in response, then you send those messages and record whether you get the expected responses. You probably do not get the expected response, as you have not told the object how to behave yet, so you add the bit of behavior that yields the correct response and move on to the next message, after doing a bit of tidying up.

In the world of Smalltalk, we have already seen that something unexpected happening leaves you in the debugger, where you can patch up the thing that's broken. So, the whole of the preceding process can be resummarised as "think of a message, type it in, hit *do it*, edit the source until the debugger stops showing up," and now you have an increment of working software in your image.

In the world of Java, even though the same person wrote both the SUnit and JUnit testing tools, the process is (assuming you already have a test project with the relevant artefacts):

1. Write the code to send the message

2. Appease the compiler

3. Build and run the test target

4. Use the output to guide changes, back in the editor

5. Repeat 3 and 4 until the test passes

So, there's a much longer feedback loop. That applies to any kind of feedback, from acceptance testing to correctness testing. You can't build the thing you're building from within itself, so there's always a pause as you and your computer switch context.

The reason for this context switch is only partly due to technology: in 2003, when Apple introduced Xcode, they made a big deal of "fix and continue," a facility also available in Java environments, amongst others: when the source code is changed, within certain limits, the associated object file can be rebuilt and injected into the running application without having to terminate and re-link it. However, that is typically not how programmers *think* about their activities. The worldview that lends us words like "toolchain" and "pipeline" is one of sequential activities, where a program may *end up* "in production" but certainly doesn't *start* there. People using the programs happens at the end, when the fun is over.

Conclusion to Part One

We have seen that Object-Oriented Programming is indeed, as many detractors suggest, a complex paradigm with many moving parts. We have also seen that this complexity is not essential: at its core is a single idea that a problem can be modeled as lots of distinct, interacting agents, and that each of those agents can be modeled as a small, isolated computer program. The solution to the original problem is found in the interaction between those agents, which is mediated by message passing.

Some of the incidental complexity seems to have been added by people wanting to make their mark: the proliferation in design patterns appears to have occurred because it is always easier to add a new pattern than to consolidate existing ones; however much some people might like to erase Singleton from history. Objects are not "just" decomposition and message-passing, they are that *and* providing access to a program's data, or that *and* a hierarchy of classes.

Much of the complexity associated with objects comes from another source: trying to treat object-oriented programming as much like the structured, procedural, imperative processes that came before, and map its terminology onto the thought structures and workflows of the established ways of writing software. This is the "structured on-ramp" of this section's introduction, in which OOP is seen as an extension to existing ideas, and programs are made "better" by adding objects in the same way that food is made "better" by sprinkling paprika on top. Thus, it is that Ann Weintz could say that "A NeXT Object is simply a piece of C code" in *Writing NeXT Applications*. Thus, object-oriented software engineering is about building complex software systems by careful, top-down analysis of the procedures (or bottom-up analysis of the data and its manipulations), while also as a side activity creating a hierarchy of classes with particular relationships.

If objects are something you do *as well as* writing software, then no wonder it is harder than not using the objects! OOP seems to have failed, but it may not even have been attempted.

2

Thesis

Objects Are Independent Programs

The thread running through a lot of different presentations is that objects are isolated computer programs that communicate by sending and receiving messages. Often, there is an *and*, but the second clause differs greatly. Let's ignore it and focus on that first clause.

For example, in Smalltalk-80 and (most of) its descendants, objects could be described as isolated computer programs that communicate by sending and receiving messages *and* are instances of classes that are organized in a tree structure. The second part here, the part about classes, weakens the first part by reducing the scope of isolation. Why is it required that both the sender and recipient of a message are instances of a class, and that both classes are members of the same tree structure? It is not, so let's strengthen the idea of isolated programs by removing the constraint on inheritance.

An existing example of an OOP environment with this form of isolation is COM (yes, the Microsoft **Component Object Model**, that **COM**). When you receive an object, you know nothing about it but that it responds to the messages defined in the **IUnknown**–https://docs.microsoft.com/en-us/windows/desktop/api/unknwn/nn-unknwn-iunknown interface, which let you keep a reference to the object, relinquish that reference, or find out what other interfaces it supports. It tells you nothing about where that object came from, whether it inherited from another object, or whether it has fresh, hand-crafted, artisanal implementations of each of its methods.

An inference you can make about both `COM` objects and `Smalltalk` objects is that they exist in the same process, that is, the same blob of memory and execution context, as the thing sending them the message. Maybe they internally forward their messages over some **IPC (inter-process communication)** or **RPC (remote procedure call)** mechanism, but there is at least part of the object that needs to be in your part of the computer. If it crashes that process, or accesses memory beyond its own instance variables, that impacts the other objects around it. If a `Smalltalk` object hogs the CPU, other objects do not get to run.

So, while `Smalltalk` objects *approximate* the **isolated computer programs** concept, the approximation is inexact. Meanwhile, on Mach, the only thing a sender knows about an object is a "port," a number that the kernel can use to work out what object is being messaged. An object could be on a different thread, on the same thread, in a different process, or (at least in theory) on a different computer, and sending it a message works in the same way. The receiver and the sender could share all of their code, inherit from a common ancestor, or be written in different programming languages and running on CPUs that store numbers in a different way, but they can still send each other a message.

Between the extreme of `Smalltalk` (all objects are the same sort of objects and are related to each other) and Mach there is the concept of the `MetaObject`–http://wiki.c2.com/?MetaObjectProtocol. As the objects in a software system define how the system models some problem, the metaobjects define how the software system expresses the behavior of its objects. The `MetaObject` protocol exposes messages that change the meaning of the *object model* inside the system.

A `MetaObject` protocol, in other words, lets a programmer choose different rules for their programming environment for different sections of their program. Consider method lookup, for example: in Part One, we saw how any of prototypical inheritance, single inheritance and multiple inheritance, have benefits and drawbacks, and each impose different constraints on the design of an object system. Why not have all of these inheritance tools – and indeed any others, and other forms of delegation – to hand at the same time? With a `MetaObject` protocol, that's possible.

The Open-Closed Nature of Independent Objects

In his book *Object-Oriented Software Construction*, Bertrand Meyer introduced the Open-Closed Principle. This principle may be one of the most confusingly stated ideas in all of computing and has led to a whole sub-industry of articles and podcasts explaining how a **ShapeRenderer** can draw **Squares** and **Circles** (of course, I have also partaken of such, and will continue here).

The Open-Closed Principle says that a module (an object, in our case) should be open to extension – it should be possible to extend its behavior for new purposes – and yet closed to modification – you should not need to change it. This design principle comes with a cost, as you need to design your objects to support extensibility along lines that are not yet known (or at least, to make it clear which lines are or are not going to be fruitful) in return for the benefit that maintainers and users of the objects know that they are going to be stable and will not introduce breakages into a system through unexpected changes.

The nature of objects explored above, their treatment as completely independent programs, supports the Open-Closed Principle by keeping each object at arm's length from the others. Their only point of contact is their messaging interface, even to their parent classes (remembering, of course, that they may not have any).

Therefore, to be open and closed, an object also needs to be ignorant: it should know as little as possible about its context. It knows what to do when it receives messages, and it knows when to send messages, but should otherwise remain uninformed as to what is happening around it. An ignorant object can be used in multiple contexts – open to extensions of its use – due to the fact that it cannot distinguish these contexts. It requires no contextual changes, and thus is closed to modification.

The Correctness of Independent Objects

When each object is its own separate program, then we turn the problem of "does this big system work" into two separate problems:

- Do these independent objects work?
- Are these independent objects communicating correctly?

Each of these problems has been solved repeatedly in software engineering, and particularly in OOP. An object's message interface makes a natural boundary between "this unit" and "everything else", for the purposes of defining unit tests. Kent Beck's Test-Driven Development approach sees developers designing objects from the message boundary inwards, by asking themselves what messages they would like to send to the object and what outcomes they would expect. This answers the question "do these independent objects work?" by considering each of the objects as a separate system under test.

The London School of TDD, exemplified by the book *Growing Object-Oriented Software, Guided by Tests*, takes an extreme interpretation of the message-boundary-as-system-boundary rule, by using **mock objects**–http://xunitpatterns.com/Mock%20Object. html as stand-ins for all collaborators of the object under test. *This* object (the one being tested) needs to send a message to *that* object (some collaborator), but there's no reason to know anything about that object other than that it will respond to the message. In this way, the London School promotes the ignorance described above as supporting the **Open-Closed Principle**.

With the Eiffel programming language, Bertrand Meyer also addressed the question of whether each object works by allowing developers to associate a *contract* with each class. The contract is based on work Edsger Dijkstra and others had done on using mathematical induction to prove statements about programs, using the object's message interface as the natural outer edge of the program. The contract explains what an object requires to be true before handling a given message (the preconditions), what an object will arrange to be true after executing its method (the postconditions), and the things that will always be true when the object is not executing a method (the invariants). These contracts are then run as checks whenever the objects are used, unlike unit tests which are only executed with the inputs and outputs that the test author originally thought of.

Contracts have turned up in a limited way in the traditional software development approach in the form of **property-based testing**–http://blog.jessitron.com/2013/04/ property-based-testing-what-is-it.html, embodied in Haskell's **QuickCheck**, Scala's **ScalaCheck**, and other tools. In Eiffel, the contract is part of the system being constructed and describes how an object is to be used when combined with other objects. Property-based tests encapsulate the contract as an external verifier of the object under test by using the contract as a test oracle from which any number of automated tests can be constructed. A contract might say "if you supply a list of e-mail messages, each of which has a unique identifier, this method will return a list containing the same messages, sorted by sent date and then by identifier if the dates are equal". A property-based test might say "for all lists of e-mail messages with unique identifiers, the result of calling this method is...". A developer may generate a hundred or a thousand tests of that form, checking for no counter-examples as part of their release pipeline.

The second part of the problem – are these independent objects communicating correctly? – can also be approached in multiple ways. It is addressed in a contract world such as Eiffel by ensuring that at each point where an object sends a message to a collaborator, the preconditions for that collaborator are satisfied. For everybody else, there are integration tests.

If a unit test reports the behavior of a single object, then an integration test is trivially any test of an assembly containing more than one object. Borrowing Brad Cox's Software ICs metaphor, a unit test tells you that a chip works, an integration test tells you that a circuit works. A special case of the integration test is the system test, which integrates all of the objects needed to solve some particular problem: it tells you that the whole board does what it ought to.

The Design of Independent Objects

It is appropriate to digress into a discussion of design here, because the activities of testing and design are closely related. Eric Evans's book **Domain-Driven Design** discusses a form of what was previously called object-oriented analysis: finding the objects needed to solve a problem by interpreting a description of the problem. The process is straightforward. Take a description of the problem, and the *things* that do things are objects, the things they *do* are methods, and the things they *tell* or *ask* other things are messages. Evans proposes having a single "ubiquitous" language across the whole development team, so that the words used by the person who has the problem – the **Goal Donor**–http://wiki.c2.com/?GoalDonor are the same words as those used by the people building the solution. Borrowing an idea from Christopher Alexander, it is the ubiquitous language of the problem and solution domain in which one would expect to find a pattern language, as common aspects of problems become addressed in similar ways.

Behavior-Driven Development marries the technical process of **Test-Driven Development** with the design concept of the ubiquitous language by encouraging developers to collaborate with the rest of their team on defining statements of desired behavior in the ubiquitous language and using those to drive the design and implementation of the objects in the solution domain. In that way, the statement of what the Goal Donor needs is also the statement of sufficiency and correctness – that is, the description of the problem that needs solving is also the description of a working solution. This ends up looking tautological enough not to be surprising.

Constructing Independent Objects

The theme running through this is that sufficiency is sufficient. When an object has been identified as part of the solution to a problem and contributes to that solution to the extent needed (even if for now that extent is "demonstrate that a solution is viable"), then it is ready to use. There is no *need* to situate the object in a taxonomy of inherited classes, but if that helps to solve the problem, then by all means do it. There is no *need* to show that various objects demonstrate a strict subtype relationship and can be used interchangeably, unless solving your problem requires that they be used interchangeably. There is no *need* for an object to make its data available to the rest of the program, unless the problem can be better solved (or cheaper solved, or some other desirable property) by doing so.

I made quite a big deal earlier of the **Open-Closed Principle**, and its suggestion that the objects we build be "open to modification." Doesn't that mean that anticipating the ways in which a system will change and making it possible for the objects to flex in those ways?

To some extent, yes, and indeed that consideration can be valuable. If your problem is working out how much to bill snooker players for their time on the tables in your local snooker hall, then it is indeed possible that your solution will be used in the same hall on the pool tables, or in a different snooker hall. But which of those will happen first? Will either happen soon? Those are questions to work with the Goal Donor and the **Gold Owner**—http://wiki.c2.com/?GoldOwner, the person paying for the solution) on answering. Is it worth paying to solve this related problem *now*, or not?

Regardless of the answer, the fact is that the objects are still ready to go to work as soon as they address *the problem you have now*. And there are other ways to address related problems anyway, which don't require "future-proofing" the object designs to anticipate the uses to which they may be put. Perhaps your `SnookerTable` isn't open to the extension of representing a pool table too, but the rest of the objects in your solution can send messages to a `PoolPlayer` in its stead. As the variant on the Open-Closed Principle showed, these other objects could be ignorant of the game played on the table.

Some amount of planning is always helpful, whether or not the plan turns out to be. The goal at every turn should be to understand how we get to *what we now want* from *what we have now*, not to *already have* that which *we will probably want sometime*. Maybe the easiest thing to do is to start afresh: so, do that.

Working with Independent Objects

The traditional way of writing and changing software has led to Continuous Deployment, a principle of automating the pipeline between writing source code and deploying the production artifact in a live environment, with a goal of reducing the time taken for changes to flow through the pipeline while maintaining a high level of quality.

Environments such as **Pharo**–https://pharo.org/, **SqueakJS** (https://squeak. js.org/run/#url=https://freudenbergs.de/bert/squeakjs&zip=[Squeak5.0-15113. zip,SqueakV50.sources.zip], or even in their limited ways **Swift Playgrounds**–https:// www.apple.com/swift/playgrounds/ and **Project Jupyter**–https://jupyter.org/ show that this pipeline *can* be zero length, and that software can be written directly in the environment it is intended for. The result of a test failure does not need to be a log file served by Jenkins that must be pored over so a fix can be hypothesized in "local dev", it can be an opportunity to correct the program running in the live environment and continue (or, at worst, restart) the operation that failed.

This liveness property is not restricted to Smalltalk-like environments or REPLs. Consider the Mach microkernel operating system; any server that is registered to the name server (or, in the case of the HURD, as a translator on the filesystem) is a "live object" that can receive messages from the rest of the system and participate in its behavior. They are also tasks that can be inspected, debugged, changed, restarted, or replaced.

A server application composed of microservices presents similar properties. The "objects" (the running instances of the services) find each other by URL: whatever service is configured to receive HTTP requests at a given route "responds" to the "messages". Each of these services can be independently inspected, debugged, edited, or replaced.

Conclusion to Part Two

When the additional complexity, and the attempts to appeal to traditional software delivery techniques, are removed, Object-Oriented Programming is an attempt to represent complicated problems through a network of small, independent programs that each model one (simpler) aspect of the problem. These programs can be independently written, verified, deployed, changed, and used. They should ideally be ignorant of each other as much as possible, relying only on the knowledge that they should respond to certain messages and can send other messages to other objects.

3

Synthesis

In *Chapter 2, Thesis*, we saw that the core benefits of OOP can be achieved with a small number of considerations:

- Objects are *independent programs*, ignorant of context to the largest possible extent

- Objects communicate by *sending messages*

- Objects behave in ways described in *contracts* expressing their responses to messages

- Objects can be written, changed, inspected, and adapted *in context*

There is no system currently available that supports all of these requirements simultaneously. Ironically, while OOP has become *overcomplicated*, as demonstrated in *Chapter 1, Antithesis*, it has also remained *incomplete*. In the final part of this book, let's consider what such a system would look like.

Objects Are Independent Programs

The easiest problem to solve is allowing developers to independently design objects without expressing constraints that inhibit the developers' design freedoms. One way is to provide a `MetaObject` protocol that allows developers to adapt the rules of a language to fit a particular context. An even easier way (both to create and to use) is to make the *primitive parts of the message system* available to developers, to combine as needed to fulfill their design goals.

This is easier to create because any more complex system would need these primitives anyway. It is easier to use because it allows the developers to construct solutions to problems as they encounter them, rather than trying to work out how to adapt existing rules onto the models they have for their solutions. That adaptation was one of the difficulties with using OOP we explored in *Chapter 1, Antithesis*: if what you've got is Java inheritance, you need to solve your problem using Java inheritance, even if your problem doesn't seem like it fits with Java inheritance.

The primitives needed are small in number. Here is a worked example in Python that is based on the functional programming view of objects explored in *Chapter 1, Antithesis*.

A selector type. This is a type that can be used to name messages, and thus it must be comparable: the receiver needs to know which selector was named in a message so it can decide what to do. Python's string type is sufficient as a selector type, though many OO languages use an interned string type (Ruby's symbols, for example) to make comparison cheaper.

A lookup function. This is a way, given a message, to decide what code to run. Python already uses a `__getattr__()` function to do this, both for its `object.attribute` syntax and to implement the `getattr(object, attribute)` function, and conveniently, it expects the attribute's name to be a string, so this works with the message selectors.

A way to send a message. This will let the object find the appropriate method implementation using its own lookup function, then execute that method with the arguments supplied in the message. It looks like this:

```
def msg_send(obj, name, *args):
        message_arguments = [obj]
        message_arguments.extend(args)
        return getattr(obj,name)(*message_arguments)
```

Notice the convention that the first argument to any message is the receiving object. This allows the object to recursively message itself, even if the method being invoked was not found on the receiver but on a delegated object that would otherwise be ignorant of the receiver.

A recursive case for message lookup. If an object does not know how to implement a given message, it can ask a different object. This is *delegation*. It looks like this:

```
def delegate(other, name):

    return getattr(other, name)
```

A base case for message lookup. Eventually, an object will need a way to say "sorry, I was sent a message that I do not understand". The **doesNotUnderstand** function provides that behavior (in our case, raising an error), and we'll also supply a **Base** type that uses **doesNotUnderstand** and can terminate any delegation chain:

```
def doesNotUnderstand(obj, name):

    raise ValueError("object {} does not respond to selector {}".
format(obj, name))

  Base = type('Base', (), {

    '__getattr__': (lambda this, name:

        (lambda myself: myself) if name=="this"

        else (lambda myself: doesNotUnderstand(myself, name)))

  })
```

Due to the message-sending convention, **myself** is the object that received the message, while **this** is the object that is handling the message on its behalf: these could be, but do not have to be, the same.

Now these 13 lines of Python (found in **objective-py** at https://gitlab.labrary.online/leeg/objective-py) are sufficient to build any form of object-oriented delegation, including the common forms of inheritance.

An **object** can inherit from a prototype by delegating all unknown messages to it.

A **class** is an object that implements methods on behalf of its instances. A created instance of a class contains all of its own data, but delegates all messages to the class object.

The class can have no parents (it does not delegate unknown messages), one parent (it delegates all unknown messages to a single parent class object) or multiple parents (it delegates unknown messages to any of a list of parent class objects). It can also support traits or mixins, again by adding them to the list of objects to search for method implementations in.

A class could even have a **metaclass**: a class object to which it delegates messages that it has received itself. That **metaclass** could have a **metametaclass**, if desired.

Any, or multiple, of these schemes can be used within the same system, because the objects are ignorant of each other and how they are constructed. They simply know that they can use **msg_send()** to send each other messages, and that they can use **delegate** to have another object respond to messages on their behalf.

But, Python being Python, these objects all run synchronously on the same thread, in the same process. They are not truly independent programs yet.

Sticking with Python, it is easy to separate our objects out into separate processes by using a different Python interpreter for each object via the **execnet**—https://codespeak. net/execnet/index.html module.

> **A quick, but important, aside**
>
> The example here (and available at https://gitlab.labrary.online/leeg/objactive-py) focuses on demonstrating the possibility of running isolated objects, and is not really appropriate for using in a real application or system. The lack of production systems based around the simple object-oriented principles described in this book is the motivation for writing the book in the first place!

Each object can live in its own module. Creating an object involves creating a new Python interpreter and telling it to run this module:

```python
def create_object():
    my_module = inspect.getmodule(create_object)
    gw = execnet.makegateway()
    channel = gw.remote_exec(my_module)
    return channel
```

When **execnet** runs a module, it has a special name that we can use to store the receiving channel and install the message handler. In this code, the receiver is stored in a global variable; as this is running in its own Python interpreter in a separate process from the rest of our system, that *global* is in fact unique to the receiving object:

```python
if __name__ == '__channelexec__':
    global receiver
    receiver = channel
    channel.setcallback(handler)
    channel.waitclose()
```

The **handler** function is our object's message dispatch function: it inspects the message selector and decides what code to run. This can work in exactly the same way as in previous examples—in other words, it can work however we want. Once an object receives a message, it should be up to *that object* to decide what to do with it, and how to act in response.

An Object's Behavior Can Be Described in A Contract

While it is up to any one object to decide how it responds to messages, we need to know whether that object represents a useful addition to our system. In other words, we want to know *what* the object will do in response to *what* messages.

As seen in *Chapter 2, Thesis*, the Eiffel language encapsulates this knowledge about an object in the form of a *contract*, describing the preconditions and postconditions for each method along with the invariants that hold when the object has been created and whenever it is not executing a method.

This contract is, as the language in *Object-Oriented Software Construction* implies, a useful *design* tool: describe your object in terms of the messages it receives, what it expects when it receives those messages, and what the sender can expect in return.

Eiffel also demonstrates that the contract is an effective *correctness testing* tool, because the assertions contained in an object's contract can be checked whenever appropriate, whether the object is being used in a test or a production system. In principle, the contract could even be used to *generate* tests in the style of property-based testing; what is "for all (expected input structure) -> (assertions that some properties hold of results)" other than a statement of preconditions and postconditions? In practice, this integration does not yet exist.

As the contract describes what an object can do, what must be true for the object to do it, and what will be true after the object has done it, it's also a great candidate for the position of *standard documentation structure* for each object. We already see in the world of HTTP APIs that the **Open API Specification** (formerly Swagger, https:// swagger.io/specification) is a machine and human-readable description of what operations an API supports, its parameters and responses. An approach like this could easily be adopted for individual objects; after all, an object represents a model of a small, isolated computer program and so its message boundary is an API supporting particular operations.

Objects Can Be Written, Inspected, And Changed in Context

David West describes objects as *actors* on the computer stage, and even the meta-acting of programmers picking up the CRC card representing an object and role-playing its part in the system, explaining what data they're using and what messages they're sending to the other objects. Objects are fundamentally a live, interactive way of *thinking about software*, so they would be best supported by a live, interactive way of *turning thought into software*.

The Smalltalk environments, including modern ones such as **Pharo** and **Amber**—https://www.amber-lang.net/, demonstrate that such tools are possible. Pharo in particular features novel additions to the developer experience, one of the bullet points on the project's About page (https://pharo.org/about) tells us that "yes, we code in the debugger."

Distributing the software that is made with such an environment, currently, can be suboptimal. With Pharo, you either export specific classes into a package that somebody else who already has Pharo set up can use, or you write the state of your whole Pharo environment to an *image file*, and give the Pharo VM and the image file to the person who will use your software. Amber works like this too, but in the background is using the popular Bower package manager for JavaScript and its *image* contains just a few classes that implement JavaScript functions. Additionally, many JavaScript developers do not *distribute* their software in the conventional sense, as it is either served as needed to the browser or run by the developers themselves in a Node.js service.

Such live interaction is not confined to the Smalltalk world. I am writing this section of the book using the **GNU Emacs**—https://www.gnu.org/software/emacs/ text editor, which is really an Emacs Lisp interpreter with a dynamic text-centric user interface. At any time, I can type some Emacs Lisp in and evaluate it, including defining new functions or redefining existing functions. For example, given a paragraph containing the following:

```
(defun words () (interactive) (shell-command (concat "wc -w " buffer-
file-name)))
```

I can move my cursor to the end of the paragraph, run the Emacs Lisp **eval-last-sexp** function, and then have a new **words** function that returns 1909, the number of words (at the time of writing) in this part of the manuscript. If it didn't do that, if I had accidentally counted characters instead of words, I could edit the function, re-evaluate it, and carry on using the fixed version. There's no need to quit Emacs while I re-build it, because I'm editing the code in the same environment that it runs in.

Put That All Together

All of the parts explored here exist, but not in the same place. Putting these together is a significant undertaking; building message passing and delegation between objects in separate processes may only take a few source lines, design-by-contract is a judicious application of the `assert()` statement, but a whole interactive environment to allow live development and debugging of such a system is a much bigger undertaking. So why consider it?

Speed

When the development environment and the deployment environment are the same, developers get a higher fidelity experience that makes turnaround time on development lower by reducing the likelihood that a change will "break in CI" (or even in production) due to differences in the environments.

The people using the software can have higher confidence too, because they know that the developer has built the thing in the same environment it will be used in. Additionally, the use of contracts in this proposed development system increases confidence, because the software is stated (and demonstrated) to work for *all* satisfactory inputs rather than merely a few test cases thought of by the developer.

Such fidelity is typically provided to developers at the *expense* of speed. Programmers connect over the network to a production-like server or wait for virtual machine or container images to be constructed on their local system. This time gets added to the typical steps, such as compiling or linking that come from separating development and deployment, giving us time to get distracted and lose our thread of concentration while getting validation of our work so far.

Ultimately, though, the speed comes from *experimentation*. When development is close to deployment, it's easier to ask questions such as "what if I change this to be like that?" and to answer them. When systems are decomposed into small, isolated, independent objects, it's easier to change or even discard and replace objects that need improvement or adaptation.

While there is value in *designing* by contract, there is also value in *progressively* adding details to an object's contract as more properties of the system being simulated become known, and confidence in the shape of the objects increases. Contracts are great for documentation and for confidence in the behavior of an object, but those benefits need not come at the expense of forcing a developer's train of thought to call at particular stations in a prescribed order. As we saw in Chapter 1, *Antithesis*, a lot of complexity in object-oriented programming to date came from requiring that software teams consider their use cases, or their class hierarchies, or their data sharing, or other properties of the system at particular points in an object-oriented software engineering process.

It's far better to say, "here are the tools, use them when it makes sense," so that the developer experience is not on rails. If that means taking time designing the developer system so that use, construction, documentation, testing, and configuration of the thing being developed can happen in any order, then so be it.

Tailoring

Such experimentation also lends itself to *adaptation*. A frequent call for the industrialization of software involves the standardization of components and the ability for end users to plug those components together as required. Brad Cox's Software ICs, Sal Soghoian's AppleScript dictionaries, and even the NPM repository represent approaches to designing reuse by defining the boundary between "things that are reused" and "contexts in which they are reused."

In all of these situations, though, the distinction is arbitrary: a Software IC could implement a whole application, or the innards of a Mac app could be written in AppleScript. In a live development environment, the distinction is erased, and any part is available for extension, modification, or replacement. There is a famous story about Dan Ingalls adding smooth scrolling to a running Smalltalk system (http://www.righto.com/2017/10/the-xerox-alto-smalltalk-and-rewriting.html) during a demo for a team from Apple Computer that included Steve Jobs. At that moment, Dan Ingalls' Alto computer had smooth scrolling, and nobody else's did. He didn't need to recompile his Smalltalk machine and take the computer down to redeploy it, it just started working that way.

My assertion is that the addition of contracts to a live programming environment *enables* experimentation, customization, and adaptation by increasing confidence in the replacement parts. Many object-oriented programmers already design their objects to adhere to the Liskov Substitution Principle, which says (roughly) that one object can act as a replacement for another if its preconditions are at most as strict as the other object's, and its postconditions are at least as strict.

In current environments, however, this idea of substitutability is unnecessarily coupled to the type system and to inheritance. In the proposed system, an object's inheritance or lack thereof is its own business, so we ask a simpler question: is this object's contract compatible with that use of an object? If it is, then they can be swapped and we know that things will work (at least to the extent that the contract is sufficient, anyway). If it is not, then we know *what* will not work, and what adaptation is required to hook things up.

Propriety

"But how will we make money?" has been a rallying cry for developers who don't want to use a new tool or technique for decades. We said we couldn't make money when free and open source software made our source code available to our users, then started running GNU/Linux servers that our users connect to so they can download our JavaScript source code.

The system described here involves combining the development and deployment environments, so how could we possibly make money? Couldn't users extract our code and run it themselves for free, or give it to their friends, or sell it to their friends?

Each object on the system is an *independent program* running in its own process, and its interface is the loosely coupled abstraction of message-sending. Any particular object could be a compiled executable based on a proprietary algorithm, distributed without its source code. Or it could be running on the developer's own server, handling messages remotely, or it could be deployed as a **dApp** to **Ethereum** or **NEO**. In each case, the developer avoids having to deploy their source code to the end user, and while that means that the user can't inspect or adapt the object, it does not stop them from *replacing* it.

It is interesting to consider how the economics of software delivery might change under such a system. At the moment, paid-outright applications, regular subscription fees, and free applications with paid-for content or components are all common, as are free (zero cost) applications and components. Other models do exist: some API providers charge per use, and blockchain dApps also cost *money* (albeit indirectly via tokens) to execute the distributed functions. An app or a web service has a clear brand, visible via the defined entry point for the user (their web address, or home screen icon). How might software businesses charge for the fulfilment of a programmatic contract, or for parts of an application that are augmented by other objects, or even replaced after deployment?

Security

It was mentioned when discussing the propriety of objects that each object is hidden behind the loosely coupled message-sending abstraction. Implications on the security of such a system are as follows:

- For an object to trust the content of a message, it must have sufficient information to make a trust decision and the confidence that the message it has received is as intended with no modifications. Using operating system IPC, the messages sent between objects are mediated by the kernel, which can enforce any access restrictions.

- "Sufficient information" may include metadata that would be supplied by the messaging broker, for example, information about the context of the sender or the chain of events that led to this message being sent.

- The form in which the object receives the message does not have to be the form in which it was transmitted; for example, the messaging layer could encrypt the message and add an authentication code on sending that is checked on receipt before allowing the object to handle the message. Developers who work on web applications will be familiar with this anyway, as their requests involve HTTP verbs such as GET or POST and readable data such as JSON, but are then sent in a compressed format over encrypted, authenticated TLS channels. There is no reason such measures need to be limited to the network edges of an application nor (as evinced with a microservices architecture) for the network edge and the physical edge of the system to be in the same place.

Multiprocessing

Computers have not been getting faster, in terms of single-task instructions per second, for a very long time. Nonetheless, they still *are* significantly faster than the memory from which they are loading their code and data.

This hypothesis needs verifying, but my prediction is that small, independent objects communicating via message passing are a better fit for today's multi-core hardware architectures, as each object is a small self-contained program that should do a better job of fitting within the cache near to a CPU core than a monolithic application process.

Modern high-performance computing architectures are already massively parallel systems that run separate instances of the workload that synchronize, share data, and communicate results via message sending, typically based on the MPI standard. Many of the processor designs used in HPC are even *slower* in terms of instruction frequency than those used in desktop or server applications, but have many more cores in a single package and higher memory bandwidth.

The idea of breaking down an application to separate, independent objects is compatible with the observation that we don't need *a fast program*, but *a fast system* comprising multiple programs. As with cloud computing architectures, such systems can get faster by scaling. We don't necessarily need to make a faster widget if we can run tens of copies of the same widget and share the work out between them.

Usability

All of this discussion focuses on the benefits (observed or hypothesized) of the approach to writing software that has been developed in this book. We need to be realistic, though, and admit that working in the way described here is untested and is a significant departure from the way programmers currently work.

Smalltalk programmers already love their Smalltalk, but then C++ programmers love their C++ too, so there isn't a one-size-fits-all solution to the happiness of programmers, even if it could be shown that for some supposed objective property of the software construction process or the resulting software, one tool or technique had an advantage over others.

Some people may take a "better the devil you know" outlook, while others may try this way (assuming such a system even gets built!) and decide that it isn't for them. Still others may even fall in love with the *idea* of working in this way, though we could find that it slows them down or makes lower quality output than their current way of working! Experimentation and study will be needed to find out what's working, for whom, and how it could be improved.

This could turn out to be the biggest area of innovation in the whole system. Developer experiences are typically extremely conservative. "Modern" projects use the edit-compile-link-run-debug workflow that arose to satisfy technical, not experiential, constraints decades ago. They are driven from a **DEC VT-100** emulator. Weirdly, that is never the interface of choice for consumer products delivered by teams staffed with designers and user experience experts.

Conclusion to Part Three

The story of this book has been one of deconstruction and reconstruction. The enormous complexity of three decades of OOP was deconstructed, to find a simple core, and an object-oriented programming experience was reconstructed around that core. The reconstruction contains all of the distinctive and important elements of the paradigm, while shedding the complexity borne of additive consultancy and capitulation to existing processes.

Importantly, this new reconstruction still takes lessons from the two schools of thought in computing, which I call the *laboratory school* and the *library school*.

The Laboratory School

The Laboratory School is the experimental approach. Go out, make a thing, and adapt, refine, or reject it based on your observations of how it performs. Don't worry about making the right thing, or making the thing right, just ensure it is made. You can adapt it later.

Extreme Programming (**XP**) and the Lean Startup movement both exhibit influences of the laboratory school. Both schemes advocate experimentation and fast feedback. Both recommend starting small and simple – XP with its *Ya Ain't Gonna Need It* principle and the Lean Startup with its *minimum viable product* – and then rapidly iterating based on feedback.

The Smalltalk style of object-oriented programming also evinces the laboratory way of thinking. Loose coupling via message-sending lets programmers replace the collaborating objects in a system with other objects easily and quickly. Integrated development and deployment environments enable a style called **Debugger-Driven Design**–https://medium.com/concerning-pharo/pharo-50c66685913c: find the thing that breaks the system because you haven't built it yet, build it, then let the system carry on with its new behavior.

The Library School

The library school is the research-driven approach. Understand your problem, discover the properties of a solution that appropriately addresses the problem, implement the solution with those properties.

The disciplines related to *object-oriented software engineering* show associations with the library school. While the Rational Unified Process, as one example, does promote *iterative and incremental* development, the increments tend to be additive rather than exploratory: build the walking skeleton, then design, implement, and test this use case, then that use case. Add more use cases until the funding runs out. Make sure that at each step you retain your carefully-considered hierarchy of class relationships.

The *if it type checks, it works* principle in programming appears to come from the library school. A type system is a machine for constructing proofs about the software that uses types from that system. Design your software with consistent application of those types and you get theorems for free (https://ecee.colorado.edu/ecen5533/fall11/reading/free.pdf) about the behavior of the software.

Design by contract demonstrates library-school thinking applied to OOP. The principle characteristic of an object is not its named type, but its *shape*: the messages it responds to and the things it does in response to those messages. Taking the mathematical proof tools from formal methods and applying them to the shape of objects, you end up with the *contract*: a mathematical statement about the messages an object responds to and the behavior resulting from receiving those messages.

The Labrary

There are lessons to be learned from each of these schools of thought, and rather than siding with either one, the system described here adopts details from both. Not in an additive *let's do all the things these people do, and add all the things these people do* way, but in a synthetic *let's see what ideas these people promote and how they can be combined* way. We have contracts from the library, but don't require *design by contract*: they are part of a live, experimental system from the laboratory that can be added and removed at any time.

There is of course, one big problem with this environment, produced by the synthetic "Labrary" school of thought. That problem is that the environment doesn't exist. Yet. To the Labrary!

Part Two –
APPropriate Behavior

One of the key things that motivated me to write this part was picking up my copy of *Code Complete, 2nd Edition*–http://www.cc2e.com. I've had a copy of either this or the first edition of the book for most of my developer career. I hadn't read it in a while, though, so I flicked through the table of contents looking for an interesting section to re-read.

The only parts that caught my eye were the sections at the back on the personality of a developer and on self-improvement. I find this odd; *Code Complete* is widely recommended as a comprehensive book on the craft of writing software. Rightly so; it's helped lots of programmers (myself included) to introspect the way they practice their work, to understand and improve it.

Code Complete is certainly thick enough to be considered comprehensive. Why, then, when it has so much content on *how code should be written*, has it so little to say on *the people doing the writing*?

I'm now in a position to answer the question that titles this section; this part is about the things that go into being a programmer that aren't specifically the programming. *Coder Complete*, if you will. It starts fairly close to home, with chapters on working with other coders, on supporting your own programming needs, and on other "software engineering" practices (I'm currently not sure whether I think software *is* an engineering discipline, nor, for people interested in that movement, a craftsmanship–the term is commonly encountered so I'll use it anyway) that programmers should understand and make use of. But as we go through this part of the book, we'll be talking about psychology and metacognition–about understanding how you, the programmer, *function* and how to improve that functioning. My hope is that thinking about these things will help to formulate a *philosophy* of making software; a coherent argument that describes what's good and worthwhile and desirable about making software, what isn't, and how the things discussed throughout this part, fit into that philosophy.

A very small amount of this part of the book has appeared before *on my blog*–https://sicpers.info. More was destined for my blog but was incorporated here instead. Still more would never have been written if I hadn't planned out the table of contents of the empty sections of my head.

Tools That Support Software Development

Introduction

Yes, there are loads of different tools. Yes, everybody has their favorite. No, there's no reason to look down on people who use different tools than yours. Yes, people who like **vi** are weird. In this chapter, I'm not going to recommend specific tools, but maybe certain classes of tools and ways I've found of working with them that help me.

If you're new to programming – perhaps you've just taken a few classes or worked through some books – this chapter should tell you something about what programmers do beyond typing **public static void** into text editors. If you're more experienced, you may still find the odd useful nugget here.

Version Control/Source Code Management

I imagine many readers are currently thinking that the battle over version control must surely be over by now, and that all developers are using some system. This is, unfortunately, demonstrably untrue. Let me start with an anecdote. It's 2004, and I've just started working as a systems manager in a university computing lab. My job is partly to maintain the computers in the lab, partly to teach programming and numerical computing to physics undergraduates, and partly to write software that will assist in said teaching. As part of this work, I started using version control, both for my source code and for some of the configuration files in **/etc** on the servers. A more experienced colleague saw me doing this and told me that I was just generating work for myself; that this wasn't necessary for the small things I was maintaining.

Move on now to 2010, and I'm working in a big scientific facility in the UK. Using software and a *lot* of computers, we've got something that used to take an entire PhD to finish down to somewhere between 1 and 8 hours. I'm on the software team and, yes, we're using version control to track changes to the software and to understand what version is released. Well, kind of, anyway. The "core" of the files/source code is in version control, but one of its main features is to provide a scripting environment and DSL in which scientists at the "lab benches," if you will, can write up scripts that automate their experiments. These scripts are not (necessarily) version controlled. Worse, the source code is deployed to experimental stations so someone who discovers a bug *in the core* can fix it locally without the change being tracked in version control.

So, a group does an experiment at this facility, and produces some interesting results. You try to replicate this later, and you get different results. It could be software-related, right? All you need to do is to use the same software as the original group used... Unfortunately, you can't. It's vanished.

That's an example of how scientists failing to use the tools from software development could be compromising their science. There's a lot of snake oil in the software field, both from people wanting you to use their tools/methodologies because you'll pay them for it, and from people who have decided that "their" way of working is correct and that any other way is incorrect. You need to be able to cut through all of that nonsense to find out how particular tools and techniques impact the actual work you're trying to do. Philosophy of science currently places a high value on reproducibility and auditing. Version control supports that, so it would be beneficial for programmers working in science to use version control. But they aren't; not consistently, anyway.

In its simplest guise - the one that I was using in 2004 - version control is a big undo stack. Only, unlike a series of undo and redo commands, you can leave messages explaining who made each change and why. Even if you're working on your own, this is a great facility to have – if you try something that gets confusing or doesn't work out, you can easily roll back to a working version and take things from there.

Once you're more familiar with the capabilities of a version control system, it can become a powerful tool for configuration management. Work on different features and bugfixes for the same product can proceed in parallel, with work being integrated when it's ready into one or more releases of the product. Discussing this workflow in detail is more than I'm willing to cover here: I recommend the **Pragmatic Programmer** books on version control such as **Pragmatic Version Control Using Git**–http://pragprog.com/book/tsgit/pragmatic-version-control-using-git by Travis Swicegood.

On Version Control and Collaboration

Version control is *no* more of a collaboration tool than other document management systems, such as SharePoint. Integrating (or merging) related work by different people is hard and requires knowledge of the meaning of the code and how changes interact. Version control systems don't have that knowledge, and as a result cannot simplify this merging process in any but the most trivial cases. It *does* let you defer the problem until you want to face it, but that's about it.

Some tools - for example, **GitHub** – http://www.github.com – provide social features around a core version control system. However, the problems of knowing what to integrate from whom, and when, and resolving conflicts all still exist. The social features give you somewhere to talk about those problems.

Distributed Version Control

I've used a good few version control systems over the years, from simple tools that work with the local filesystem to hugely expensive commercial products. My favored way of working now is with a **DVCS (Distributed Version Control System)** (though, as promised earlier, I'm not going to suggest that you choose a particular one; with the exception of `darcs`, they all work in much the same way).

With a DVCS, it's very easy to get a local project into version control, so even toy projects and prototypes can be versioned. A feature that makes them great for this, over earlier systems that version local files, such as **RCS (Reaction Control System)** and **SCCS (Source Code Control System)**, is that the whole repository (that is, all of the files that comprise the versioned project) is treated atomically. In other words, the repository can be at one version or another, but never in an in-between state where some files are at an earlier revision than others.

Earlier systems, like RCS, do not impose this restriction. With RCS, every file is versioned independently so each can be checked out on a different version. While this is more flexible, it does introduce certain problems. For example, consider the files in the following figure. One of the files contains a function that's used in code in the other file. You need to make a change to the function's signature, to add a new parameter. This means changing all three files.

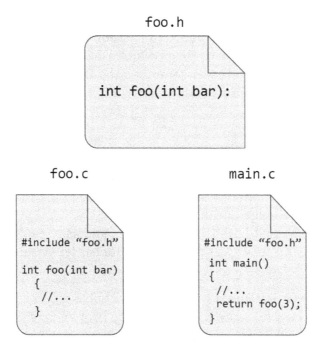

Figure 4.1: A dependency that crosses multiple files

In an atomic version control system, the files can either both be checked out at the revision with one parameter or both be checked out at the revision with two parameters. A per-file versioning system will allow any combination of versions to be checked out, despite the fact that half of the possible combinations do not make sense.

Once you've got a project that's locally versioned in a DVCS repository, sharing it with others is simple and can be done in numerous ways. If you want to back up or share the repository on a hosted service like **BitBucket**−http://www.bitbucket.org, you set that up as a remote repository and push your content. A collaborator can then clone the repository from the remote version and start working on the code. If they're on the same network as you, then you can just share the folder containing the repository without setting up a remote service.

Personal Experience

In some situations, a combination of these approaches is required. The DVCS tools that I've used all support that. On one recent project, everything was hosted on a remote service but there were hundreds of megabytes of assets stored in the repository. It made sense for the computers in the office to not only clone the remote repository, but also to peer with each other to reduce the time and bandwidth used when the assets changed. The situation looked like the following figure.

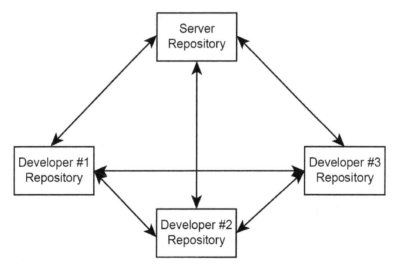

Figure 4.2: A DVCS configuration can break out of the "star" topology required by centralized systems

Doing this with a centralized version control system would've been possible, but ugly. One of the developers would've needed to fully synchronize their working copy with the server, then fully copy the repository and its metadata to all of the other developer systems. This is less efficient than just copying the differences between the repositories. Some centralized version control systems wouldn't even support that way of working, because they track which files they think you have checked out on the server.

Another benefit brought by DVCS – as much due to improved algorithms as their distributed nature – is the ease with which you can create and destroy branches. When I mainly worked with centralized version control (primarily Subversion and Perforce), branches were created for particular tasks, such as new releases, and the teams I worked on invented workflows for deciding when code migrated from one branch to another.

With DVCSes, I often create a branch every hour or so. If I want to start some new work, I create a branch in my local version of the repository. After a while, I'm either done, and the branch gets merged and deleted; convinced that the idea was wrong – in which case, it's just deleted; or I want someone else to have a look, and I push that branch without merging it. All of this was possible with centralized VCS, though much slower – and you needed network access to even create the branch.

Continuous Integration and Deployment

Having just discussed version control, it's time to announce which VCS mistake I see more often than any other – the mistake that's made by everyone (myself included), regardless of their experience or expertise. And the winner is...

Adding new files to a project but forgetting to add them to the repository.

I don't do this *very* often - maybe less than once per month. But whenever I do, when the other developers on the team synchronize their repositories, we're left in a situation where everything works for me, but they can't build.

If we're lucky, the error will report that the file wasn't found, and we can quickly resolve the problem. If not, there'll be some other error about a missing symbol or something that will take time to track down before discovering the root cause.

If only we had some form of robot that would see every check-in, grab the source code, and try to build the product. If it couldn't do that, it'd be great if it came over and complained to the person who made the change that broke the build.

It turns out that we've been living in the future for quite a while now, and that robot already exists. It goes by the name of **Continuous Integration**, or CI.

Why Use CI?

Finding those missing files isn't the only thing CI is good for. If you have automated tests (see the *Chapter 5, Coding Practices*), a CI system can run the tests on every change and report any problems. My team's CI server is configured to run the analysis tool (discussed in this chapter) and consider a build failed if that tool discovers any problems. Some projects automatically generate API documentation and publish it to a web server.

It can even make the build available for people to install once it's passed all of the tests. This is related to the idea of **Continuous Deployment**: if a version of the software seems good enough to use (that is, it doesn't fail any test you put it through), then start using it. You may still find problems that weren't exposed by the automated tests, but you'll do so earlier than if you didn't deploy right away.

A final benefit to CI - one that's quite subtle but very useful – is that it forces you to set your project up so that it can be checked out of version control and built automatically. This means that even when a human programmer is working with the project, it's easy for them to get set up with the source and start being productive. That person could be you, when you get a new laptop. It could be a contractor or a new employee joining the team. Either way, if there's a single step to fetch the project and build it, then they'll be up to speed quickly, rather than asking you how to fetch some library or configure some plugin.

CI On Real Teams

Some teams I've worked on have been so heavily invested in using CI that they've employed someone to maintain the CI infrastructure (it's not a full-time occupation, so they usually look after other supporting tools and consult on their use). In other teams, it's been up to the developers to keep it running.

The difficulty in that second case is in knowing when to look after the CI versus doing project work. As an example, in the month before this section was written, I had to migrate my team's CI system onto different hardware. Despite trying to ensure that the configuration of the system didn't change between the two environments, the tests in one of the projects would no longer run.

The thing is, the tests worked fine in the IDEs on all of the developer machines. Is it really important to take more time away from adding value to the products our clients are paying for to handhold some confused robot?

I consider running without CI to be proceeding at risk these days. Yes, I *could* avoid all problems without it. Yes, it's *possible* that nothing will go wrong. But why take the chance? Why not spend that little extra to ensure I discover problems as early as possible? It's spending a little now to potentially save a lot in the future. I therefore try to find the time to maintain the CI service when it's necessary.

Build Management

I wrote in the previous section that a benefit of adopting CI is that it forces you to simplify the building of your project (by which I mean compiling sources, translating assets, creating packages, and anything else that takes the inputs created by the project team and converts them into a product that will be used by customers). Indeed, to use CI you will have to condense the build down until an automated process can complete it given any revision of your source code.

There's no need to write a script or an other program to do this work, because plenty of build management tools already exist. At a high level, they all do the same thing: they take a collection of input files, a collection of output files, and some information about the transformations needed to get from one to the other. How they do that, of course, varies from product to product.

Convention or Configuration

Some build systems, like `make` and `ant`, need the developer to tell them nearly everything about a project before they can do anything. As an example, while `make` has an implicit rule for converting C source files into object files, it won't actually execute that rule until you tell it that you need the object file for something.

Conversely, other tools (including Maven) make certain assumptions about a project. Maven assumes that every `.java` file in a folder called `src/main/java` must be compiled into a class that will be part of the product.

The configuration approach has the advantage that it's discoverable even to someone who knows little about the system. Someone armed with a collection of source files, `grep`, and a little patience could work out from a `Makefile` or `Xcode` project which files were built as which targets, and how. Because there's a full (or near full) specification of how everything's built, you can find what you need to change to make it act differently, too.

The downside to that discoverability is that you *have* to specify all that stuff. You can't just tell Xcode that any `.m` file in a folder called `Classes` should be passed to the Objective-C compiler; you have to give it a big list of all of them. Add a new file, and you must change the list.

With a convention-based build system, this situation is exactly reversed. If you follow the conventions, everything's automatic. However, if you don't *know* the conventions, they can be hard to discover. I once had a situation on a *Rails* project where the folder that static resources (such as images) were saved in changed between two releases. On launching the app, none of my images were being used and it wasn't clear why. Of course, for someone who *does* know the conventions, there's no learning curve associated with transferring between different projects.

On balance, I'd prefer a convention-led approach, provided the conventions are well-documented somewhere so it's easy to find out what's going on and how to override it if you need to. The benefit of reduced effort and increased consistency, for me, outweighs the occasional surprise that's encountered.

Build Systems That Generate Other Build Systems

Some build procedures get so complicated that they spawn another build system that configures the build environment for the target system before building. An archetypal example is GNU Autotools, – which actually has a three-level build system. Typically, developers will run **autoconf**, a tool that examines a project to find out what questions the subsequent step should ask and generates a script called **configure**. The user downloads the source package and runs **configure**, which inspects the compilation environment and uses a collection of macros to create a Makefile. The Makefile can then compile the source code to (finally!) create the product.

As argued by *Poul-Henning Kamp*–http://queue.acm.org/detail.cfm?id=2349257), this is a bad architecture that adds layers of cruft to work around code that has not been written to be portable to the environments it will be used in. Software written to be built with tools like these is hard to read, because you must read multiple languages just to understand how one line of code works.

Consider a bug reported in a particular C function in your project. You open that function to find two different implementations, chosen by a **#ifdef/#else/#endif** preprocessor block. You search for the macro used by that block and find it in **config.h**, so you must read the **configure** script to find out how it's set. To discover whether *that* test is doing the right thing, you need to look at the **configure.ac** file to find out how the test is generated.

About the only justification for using such a convoluted process is that it's thought of as conventional and expected by your target users, but even then, I'd question whether that expectation is driven by a technical need or by **Stockholm syndrome** – http://en.wikipedia.org/wiki/Stockholm_syndrome. If your product doesn't need to be portable, then there's no need to add all that complexity – and even if it does, there may be better ways to solve the problem that'll work for your product. One obvious approach is to target a portable platform such as Mono or Python.

Bug and work tracking

For most of their history, computers have excelled at doing things one at a time. Even a single client or customer can parallelize much better than that and will think of (and make) multiple requests while you're still working on one thing.

It's really useful to write all of these requests down, and keep track of where you and your colleagues are on each of them so that you don't all try to solve the same problem, and can let the client know which of them you've fixed. Bug trackers (sometimes more generally called issue trackers or work trackers) are designed to solve that problem.

What Goes in And When?

I've worked on projects where the bug tracker gets populated with all of the project's feature requests at the beginning (this discussion overlaps slightly with the treatment of software project management patterns, in *Chapter 13, Teamwork*). This introduces a couple of problems. One is that the **Big List** needs a lot of grooming and editing to stay relevant as features are added and removed, split between multiple developers, or found to be dependent on other work. The second is psychological: for a long time, members of the project team will be looking at a soul-destroying list of things that still haven't been done, like Sisyphus standing with his rock looking up from the base of the hill. The project will seem like a death march from the beginning.

My preference is to attack the work tracker with an iterative approach. When it's decided what will go into the next build, add those tasks to the work tracker. As they're done, mark them as closed. The only things that stay in the tracker from one iteration to the next are those things that don't get completed in the build when they were scheduled to. Now, the big list of items in the tracker is always the big list of what we've already completed, not the big list of things still remaining. This is something akin to the Kanban system, where a team will have a fixed "capacity" of pending work. As they pull work from the pending bucket to start working on it, they can request that the bucket get topped up–but never past its capacity.

My approach to reporting bugs is different. Unless it's something trivial in the code I'm working on now, so that I can fix the problem in under a couple of minutes and move on, I'll always report it straight away. This means I won't forget about the problem; the fix is implicitly planned for the next iteration, following the **Joel Test** rule of fixing bugs before adding new code, and we can see how many bugs are being discovered in each build of the product. (Now that I reflect on the Joel Test, I realize that this chapter covers a lot of points that are included in the test. Perhaps you should just measure your team's performance with respect to the Joel test's 12 points and fix any that you answer "no" to–http://www.joelonsoftware.com/articles/fog0000000043.html.).

How Precisely to Track?

So, you managed to fix that bug in 2 hours. But, was it *actually* 2 hours, or was it 125 minutes? Did you spend those 2 hours solely fixing the bug, or did you answer that email about the engineers-versus-sales whist drive during that time?

Being able to compare estimated time versus actual time can be useful. I'm not sure that "velocity" – the ratio between the estimated time and the actual time spent on tasks – is particularly helpful, because in my experience estimates are not consistently wrong by a constant factor. It's knowing *what* work you're bad at estimating that's helpful. Do you fail to appreciate the risks involved in adding new features, or do you tend to assume all bug fixes are trivially simple?

So, precise measurements are not particularly helpful, which is useful to know, because the accuracy probably doesn't exist to back up that precision. I usually just look at my watch when I start work and when I end work, and round to the nearest quarter or half hour. That means my time records include all those interruptions and little tasks I did while fixing the bug – which is fine because they slowed me down and that needs recording.

Estimates aren't even that accurate. The game I play with my team goes like this: every developer on the team (and no one else) independently writes down an estimate of how long the tasks we're planning will take. They're allowed to pick one of these: 1 hour, 2 hours, 4 hours, 8 hours, or don't know. If we think a task will take longer than 8 hours, we break it down and estimate smaller chunks of the task.

For each task, everyone presents their estimates. If they're roughly the same, then we just pick the highest number and go with that. If there's a spread of opinion – maybe one developer thinks something will take an hour when someone else thinks it'll take a day – we'll discuss that. Probably, one (or more) of the team is relying on tacit knowledge that needs to be brought into the open. It's usually possible to resolve such differences quickly and move on to the next thing.

Integrated Development Environment

Well, really, I suppose your environment doesn't need to be fully integrated. For a long time, my toolset was a combination of Project Builder, Interface Builder, WebObjects Builder, EOModeler, and Edit. It *does* need to make you more efficient than the simple "text editor and `make`" combo of yore.

What's the big problem? Why so harsh on the text editor? Any time you have to stop making software to deal with your tools, there's a chance you'll lose concentration, forget what you were doing, and have to spend a few minutes reacquainting yourself with the problem. Losing a couple of minutes doesn't sound like too big a deal, but if you're doing it a couple of times an hour every working day, it quickly adds up to a frustrating drop in productivity.

You're going to be using your IDE for most of your working day, *every* working day, for the next few years. You should invest heavily in it. That means spending a bit of money on a good one that's better than the free alternatives. It means training yourself in the tricks and shortcuts so you can do them without thinking, saving the occasional second and (more importantly) keeping you focused on the work. It can even mean writing plugins, if your environment supports them, so you can do more without context-switching.

In some plugin-rich environments, you could go a whole day without ever leaving the IDE. For example, Eclipse now includes the **Mylyn** (http://eclipse.org/mylyn/start/) task-focused plugin, so you can interact with your bug tracker inside the IDE. It'll also let you focus your views on only those files related to the task you're currently working on.

Not only do you need to go deep on your chosen IDE, you need to go broad on alternatives. A future version of your favorite tool might change things so much that you'd be more efficient switching to a different app. Or you might start working on a project where your preferred IDE isn't available; for example, you can't (easily) write a Mono app in Xcode, or an Eclipse RCP application in Visual Studio.

This restriction of development environments to particular platforms, whether done for technological or business reasons, is unfortunate. This is where the "just use a text editor" crowd has a point: you can learn `emacs` just once and whatever language you end up programming in, you don't need to learn how to use the editor again just to write code. As you're going to spend your whole working life in one of these environments, every change to features you already know how to use represents horrendous inefficiency.

Notice that all of the aforementioned IDEs follow the same common pattern. When people have the "which IDE is best?" argument, what they're actually discussing is "which slightly souped-up monospace text editor with a **build** button do you like using?" Eclipse, Xcode, IntelliJ, Visual Studio... All of these tools riff on the same design—letting you see the source code and change the source code. As secondary effects, you can also do things like build the source code, run the built product, and debug it.

The most successful IDE in the world, I would contend (and then wave my hands unconvincingly when anyone asks for data), is one that's not designed like that at all. It's the one that is used by more non-software specialists than any of those already mentioned. The one that doesn't require you to practice being an IDE user for years before you get any good. The one that business analysts, office assistants, accountants, and project managers alike all turn to when they need their computer to run through some custom algorithm. The most successful IDE in the world is Excel.

In a spreadsheet, it's the inputs and results that are front-and-center in the presentation, not the intermediate stuff that gets you from one to the other. You can test your "code" by typing in a different input and watching the results change in front of you. You can see intermediate results, not by breaking and stepping through, or putting in a log statement then switching to the log view, but by breaking the algorithm up into smaller steps (or functions or procedures, if you want to call them that). You can then visualize how these intermediate results change right alongside the inputs and outputs. That's quicker feedback than even REPLs can offer.

Many spreadsheet users naturally adopt a "test-first" approach; they create inputs for which they know what the results should be and make successively better attempts to build a formula that achieves those results. And, of course, interesting visualizations such as graphs are available (though the quality does vary between products). Drawing a graph in Xcode is... challenging. Indeed, you can't do it at all, but you can get Xcode to create an application that can itself generate a graph. The results are a significant distance away from the tools.

Static Analysis

In the *Chapter 5, Coding Practices*, there's a section on *Code Reviews*. Knowing that reviewers will find and fixate upon the simplest problems they can find, wouldn't it be great to remove all the trivial problems so that they're forced to look for something more substantial?

This is what static analysis does. It finds problems in code that can be automatically discovered without running the product, but that are either off-topic for compiler warnings or take too long to discover for the compiler to be an appropriate tool to search for them.

What are off-topic problems? Typically, those that require knowledge of the semantics of the functions or methods you're using – knowledge that's beyond the scope of the compiler. For example, consider a C++ **destroyObject<T>(T t)** function that *deletes* its parameter. Calling that function twice with the same argument would be an error – but the compiler doesn't know that if it's just inspecting the function signature. Others are a matter of style. For example, Apple's C APIs have a naming convention related to their memory management rules: a function name contains **Create** when the caller owns the returned object or **Get** when the **callee** does. It's not a mistake to use C language to mix those up, so the compiler won't tell you about it, but an analyzer can.

There is basically no reason to avoid using a static analyzer (if your reason is that there isn't one for your language/framework/whatever yet, you might have chosen a language/framework/whatever that isn't ready yet. There's a section about that in *Chapter 12, Business*). It'll discover easily fixable bugs for you and quickly train you into not making those mistakes in the first place.

Code Generation

There are, in many applications, plenty of features that are trivial to implement but must be done over and over. Perhaps it's taking an array of model objects and preparing a list view, creating classes from database schemata, or creating a list of compile-time constants from a text file.

These situations can usually be automated by generating code. The idea is to express the problem in a succinct representation, then translate that into something that can be incorporated into your program. This is pretty much what a compiler does; though many programming languages are far from succinct, they're still much less unwieldy than the machine's native instruction code.

Writing Your Own Generator Shouldn't Be A First Resort

Just as a code generator makes it easier to create a product, it makes it harder to debug. For a concrete example, consider the **autotools** build system discussed earlier in this chapter. Imagine that a developer is looking into a reported problem in which one of the tests fails (a problem that I had to deal with today). The log file tells them what the C program was that encapsulated the test, but the developer cannot just modify that program. They must discover where the **configure** script is generating that program, and what it's trying to achieve by doing so. They must then find out where in **configure. ac** that section of the shell script is generated and work out a change to the **m4** macros that will result in the desired change to the C program, two steps later.

In short, if your target environment offers facilities to solve your problem natively, such a solution will require less reverse engineering when diagnosing later problems. It's only if such a solution is overly expensive or error-prone that code generation is a reasonable alternative.

Many of the cases given at the beginning of this section were data-driven, like the situation deriving class descriptions from a database schema for some **Object-Relational Mapping (ORM)** system. This is a case where some programming languages give you the ability to solve this problem without generating code in their language. If you can resolve messages sent to an object at runtime, then you can tell that object which table its object is in and it can decide whether any message corresponds to a column in that table. If you can add classes and methods at runtime, then you can generate all of the ORM classes when the app connects to the database.

The existence and applicability of such features depends very much on the environment you're targeting but look for and consider them before diving into writing a generator.

When the Generator Won't Be Used by A Programmer

If the target "customer" for this facility isn't going to be another developer, then a generator can often be a better choice than a full-featured programming language, despite the increase in implementation complexity.

A solution that's often explored in this context is a **Domain-Specific Language (DSL)**, a very limited programming language that exposes grammar and features much closer to the problem that the customer understands than to computer science concepts. Many projects that I've been involved with have used DSLs, because they offer a nice trade-off between letting the customer modify the system as they see fit and avoiding complex configuration mechanisms.

Case study

The "customer" using the application doesn't need to be the end user of the finished product. On one project I worked on, I created a DSL to give to the client so that they could define achievements used in the project's gamification feature. A parser app told them about any inconsistencies in their definitions, such as missing or duplicate properties, and also generated a collection of objects that would implement the rules for those achievements in the app. It could also generate a script that connected to the app store to tell it what the achievements were.

5
Coding Practices

Introduction

If you learned programming by studying a book or an online course, you probably sat at your computer with a text editor or IDE, solving each problem completely as it came. Most software teams have two additional problems to contend with—the applications they're writing are much larger, and there's more than one of them working on the product at once. In this chapter, I'll look at some common ways to set about the task of programming on a larger project (though, teamwork plays such a big part in this that it has its own chapter later in the book).

Most of this chapter will act as a quick reference, with an inline reading list and a few opinions thrown in for good measure. The reason is that the concepts are too large to cover in detail in a single section of a novel-length book like this.

Test-Driven Development

TDD (**Test-Driven Development**) is such a big topic, plenty of books have been written about it. Indeed, one of those books was written by me: **Test-Driven iOS Development** (http://www.pearsoned.co.uk/bookshop/detail.asp?item=100000000444373). So, I won't go into too much detail here. If you've never come across test-driven development before, or the phrase "red-green-refactor," I recommend **Growing Object-Oriented Software, Guided By Tests** (http://www.growing-object-oriented-software.com/) (unless you're focusing on iOS, of course).

The point of TDD

People talk about test-driven development as a way to ensure high test coverage. It does that, for sure. But its main utility is as a *design tool*. You can construct an executable specification of a module or class, based on how you need to use that class in your product. Often, I'll create some tests while I'm designing a class, but remove them as the code changes and they become obsolete.

I've delegated classes to other developers before by writing a suite of tests and asking them to fill in the implementation. I've left myself a failing test on a Friday evening, so I know what I'm supposed to be doing on Monday morning (the `#error` C preprocessor command, which inserts a compiler error with a custom message, is also useful for this). TDD has plenty of utilities beyond generating automated regression tests.

Notice that TDD only helps you with your design when you limit yourself to designs that can be (easily) achieved by doing TDD. That's no bad thing, as it means that everything will be designed in similar, understandable ways. It's like a magazine having a tone and style guide, so readers have a base level of expectations of any article.

Particular constraints, or at least *suggestions*, derived from allowing TDD to elicit design choices include that your design will probably be loosely coupled (that is, each module will not depend greatly on other modules in the system) with interchangeable dependencies injected from the outside. If your response to that is "great - that's what I'd want," then you'll have no problem.

The Software I'm Writing Can't Be Tested

Actually, it probably can. Apart from the sample code from the afore-mentioned book, there's code in every project I've written that hasn't been tested. In most cases, it probably *can* be tested. Let's look at some of the real reasons the tests haven't been written.

I've already written the code without tests, and can't work out how to retroactively test it

This is a common complaint. Don't let a TDD proponent smugly say "well, you should have written tests in the first place" – that's dogmatic and unhelpful. Besides, it's too late. Instead, you should decide whether you want to (and can) spend the time changing the code to make it amenable to testing.

It's not just time, of course; there's a risk associated with any change to software. – As mentioned elsewhere in this book, any code you write is a liability, not an asset. The decision regarding whether or not you adapt the code to support tests' adaptation should consider not only the cost of doing the work, but the potential risk of doing it. (I'm deliberately calling this work "adaptation" rather than "refactoring." Refactoring means to change the structure of a module without affecting its behavior. Until you have the tests in place, you cannot guarantee that the behavior is unchanged.) These need to be balanced against the potential benefits of having the code under test, and the opportunity cost of not getting the code into shape when you get the chance.

If you decide you *do* want to go ahead with the changes, you should plan your approach so that the work done to support the tests is not too invasive. You don't want to change the behavior of the software until you can see whether such changes reflect your expectations. A great resource for this is Michael Feathers' **Working Effectively With Legacy Code** (https://c2.com/cgi/wiki?WorkingEffectivelyWithLegacyCode).

I don't know how to test that API/design/whatever

Often, "this can't be tested" comes down to "I don't know how this could be tested." Sometimes, it's actually true that some particular API doesn't lend itself to being used in isolation. A good example is low-level graphics code, which often expects that some context exists into which you're drawing. It can be very hard (if indeed it's possible at all) to reproduce this context in a way that allows a test harness to capture and inspect the drawing commands.

You can provide such an inspection capability by wrapping the problematic API in an interface of your own design. Then, you can swap that out for a testable implementation – or for an alternative API, if that becomes desirable. OK, the adaptor class you wrote probably can't be tested still, but it should be thin enough for that to be a low risk.

In other cases, there is a way to test the code that can be brought out with a bit of thought. I'm often told that an app with a lot of GUI code can't be tested. Why not?

What's in a GUI app? For a start, there are a load of data models and "business" logic that would be the same in any other context and can easily be tested. Then, there's the interaction with the UI: the "controller" layer in the MVC world. That's code that reacts to events coming from the UI by triggering changes in the model and reacts to events coming from the model by updating the view. That's easy to test too, by simulating the events and ensuring that the controller responds to them correctly; mocking the "other end" of the interaction.

This just leaves any custom drawing code in the view layer. This can indeed be both difficult (see above) and irrelevant – sometimes, what's important about graphics isn't their "correctness" but their aesthetic qualities. You can't really derive an automated test for that.

If your app really is mainly custom drawing code, then: (i) I might be willing to concede that most of it can't be tested; (ii) you may need to rethink your architecture.

I don't have time right now

There! There's a real answer to "why aren't there tests for this?" It genuinely can be quicker and/or cheaper to write code without tests than to create both, particularly if working out how to test the feature needs to be factored in. As I said earlier though, a full cost analysis of the testing effort should include the potential costs of *not having the tests*. And, as we know, trying to predict how many bugs will be present in untested code is hard.

So Is Test-Driven Development A Silver Bullet?

As you will see later in this chapter, it is not believed that there *is* a silver bullet to making software. Plenty of people are happy with the results they get from TDD. Other people are happy with the results they get from other practices. My opinion is that if you are making something that solves problems and can demonstrate with high confidence that what you are doing is solving those problems, then you are making a valuable contribution. Personally, I am currently happy with TDD as a way to show which parts of a problem I have solved with software.

Domain-Driven Design

Domain-Driven Design (DDD) is a term introduced in the 2004 book *of the same name*– http://domaindrivendesign.org/books/evans_2003, though most of its principles have been around quite a bit longer among practitioners of object-oriented analysis and design. Indeed, the core of DDD can be thought of as deriving from the simulation techniques employed in Simula 67 – a language that influenced the design of C++.

Simply put, much software (particularly "enterprise" software) is created as a solution to a particular problem. Therefore, software should be designed by software experts in conjunction with domain experts. They should use a shared model of the problem domain, so that it's clear the whole team is trying to solve the same problem.

In an attempt to reduce communication problems, a "ubiquitous language" is defined – a common glossary of terms that's used throughout the documentation and the software. This includes the source code – classes and methods are named using the ubiquitous language to reflect the parts of the problem they address.

I think it was learning some of the principles of domain-driven design that finally made **Object-Oriented programming (OOP)** "click" with me (there's more on OOP later in this chapter). I'd been doing C and Pascal programming for a long time when I started to approach languages such as C++ and Java. While I could see that methods belonged to classes, in much the same way that modules work, deciding *what* should be an object, where its boundaries were, and how it interacted with other objects took me a long time to get to grips with.

At some point, I went on a training course that talked about domain modelling – and made it very simple. The core of it went something like this: listen to a domain expert describing a problem. Whenever they describe a concept in the problem domain with a noun, that's a candidate class, or maybe an attribute of a class. Whenever something's described as a verb, that's a candidate for a method.

That short description of how to translate a problem specification into objects and actions was a huge eye-opener for me; I can't think about OOP in any other way.

Behavior-Driven Development

I found it hard to decide whether to put BDD in this chapter or to discuss it with teamwork, because it's really an exercise in communication masquerading as a coding practice. But it's here, so there you go. Indeed, many of the sections in this chapter will skirt that boundary between coding and communication, because programming is a collaborative activity.

BDD is really an amalgamation of other techniques. It relies heavily on DDD ideas like the ubiquitous language and combines them with test-driven development. The main innovation is applying test-first principles at the feature level. Using the ubiquitous language as a **Domain-Specific Language** (http://martinfowler.com/books/dsl.html), the team works with the customer to express the specifications for features in an executable form, as an automated acceptance test. Then, the developers work to satisfy the conditions expressed in the acceptance tests.

My own experience has been that BDD tends to stay at the conversation level, not the implementation level. It's easy for an agile team (which includes its customers) to collaborate on the acceptance criteria for a story, and then for the technical members of the team to implement tests that evaluate the system according to those criteria. It's hard – – for the team – and I've never seen it happen – to collaborate on the authorship of automated tests whose outcomes convince the customer that the user story has been correctly built.

xDD

It seems like every time there's a developer conference, there's a new **(something)-Driven Development** buzzword introduced. TDD; BDD; **Acceptance Test-Driven Development**–(http://www.methodsandtools.com/archive/archive.php?id=72); **Model Driven Development** (https://social.msdn.microsoft.com/Forums/azure/en-US/d9fa0158-d9c7-4a88-8ba6-a36a242e2542/model-driven-development-net?forum=dslvsarchx). Some people think *it's too much*–http://scottberkun.com/2007/asshole-driven-development/.

Many of the new terms are introduced by people hoping to carve out their niche as a trainer or consultant in the field they just defined. Many are just catchy names that encompass existing practices. – Indeed, TDD is really a codification of the test-first practices popularized by **Extreme Programming**. This doesn't mean that they are devoid of value though; sometimes, the part that's truly original is indeed novel and worth knowing about. And often, the communities that congregate around these techniques have their own customs and ways of working that are worth exploring.

Design by Contract

A little confession about one of my most recent software projects: it has a lot of unit tests in it. But for every test assertion, there are more than three assertions *in the code itself*.

These have proven invaluable for documenting my assumptions about how the code is put together. While unit tests show that each method or class works as expected in isolation, these assertions are about ensuring that the boundaries respect the assumptions that are made within the methods – that is, they act as a form of integration test.

The assertions I've written mainly fall into three categories – testing that expectations are met when the method is entered, that its results are what I expected before it was returned, and that certain transformations done during the method yield results conforming to particular conditions. In developer builds, whenever one of these assumptions is not met, the app crashes at the failing assertion. I can then decide whether the method needs to be changed, or whether the way it's being used is wrong.

In designing the **Eiffel language** (http://docs.eiffel.com/book/method/object-oriented-software-construction-2nd-edition) in 1988, Bertrand Meyer formalized a "contract" comprising three distinct types of test that are similar to the assertions described above:

- *preconditions* should be true on function entry

- *postconditions* should be true on function exit

- *invariants* remain true at all "stable" times – immediately after the constructor exits, and at any time that one of the object's methods is not being executed.

Rather than codifying these conditions as assertions, in Eiffel they're actually part of a method definition. The contracts formalize the relationship between the caller of a method and its implementor: the caller is required to ensure that preconditions are met before calling the method. In return, the `callee` promises to satisfy the postconditions. These conditions can be inserted into the code by the compiler as assertions to verify that classes are behaving correctly at runtime. You could also imagine pointing an automated checker like **Klee** (http://klee.github.io/getting-started/), at a class; it could check all the code paths of a method and report on those that, even though they start with the preconditions and invariants satisfied, do not end up meeting the postconditions or invariants.

Meyer coined the term *Design by Contract* to refer to this practice of including preconditions, postconditions, and invariants in method definitions in Eiffel. The term is in fact a trademark that his company owns; implementations for other languages are called contract programming or contract coding (thankfully, not contract-driven development...).

As we've seen, I tend to use a poor replacement of contract programming even when I don't have language support for the capability. I see these contract-style assertions fail in development much more frequently than I see unit test failures; to me, contract programming is a better early warning system for bugs than TDD.

Development by Specification

This is, as far as I'm aware, not a common development practice currently. But as a natural progression from Test-Driven Development, I think it deserves a mention and consideration.

Unit tests, even when used as part of TDD, are employed in a craft way – as a bespoke specification for our one-of-a-kind classes. We could benefit from more use of these tests, substituting the static, error-prone type tests used in many APIs for dynamic specification tests.

A table view, for example, does not need something that merely responds to the data source selectors; it needs something that *behaves* like a data source. So, let's create some tests that any data source should satisfy, and bundle them up as a specification that can be tested at runtime. Notice that these aren't quite unit tests, in that we're not testing our data source – we're testing *any* data source.

A table view needs to know how many rows there are, and the content of each row. So, you can see that a dynamic test of a table view's data source would not simply test each of these methods in isolation; it would test that the data source could supply as many values as it said there were rows. You could imagine that, in languages that support design-by-contract, such as Eiffel, the specification of a collaborator could be part of the contract of a class.

These specifications would be tested by objects at the point their collaborators are supplied, rather than waiting for something to fail during execution. Yes, this is slower than doing the error-prone type hierarchy or conformance tests that usually occur in a method's precondition. No, that's not a problem: we want to make it right before making it fast.

Treating test fixtures as specifications for collaboration between objects, rather than (or in addition to) one-off tests for one-off classes, opens up new routes for collaboration between the developers of the objects. Framework vendors can supply specifications as enhanced documentation. Framework consumers can supply specifications of how they're using the frameworks as bug reports or support questions; vendors can add those specifications to a regression testing arsenal. Application authors can create specifications to send to contractors or vendors as acceptance tests. Vendors can demonstrate that their code is "a drop-in replacement" for some other code by demonstrating that both pass the same specification.

Pair programming

I've pair-programmed a lot during my career, though it has only accounted for the minority of my time. I've also watched other people pair programming; the interactions between partners can make for very interesting viewing.

Before diving into what I think makes *good* pair programming, I'm going to describe what makes *bad* pair programming.

Back-Seat Driving Is Not Pair Programming

Because I've been doing TDD for a while, I'm used to deliberately letting my code go through a little bit of a worthless phase before it gets good enough to integrate. Maybe I'll leave out handling a failure condition until I see it fail or add that in at the end. Perhaps I can't think of what to call a method so will name it `DoTheThing()` until I've got a clearer image.

What I have to remember is that *my partner might not work the same way*. Yes, it's annoying to see an unhandled condition, or a variable that isn't named according to my preferred convention, but is that the most urgent problem *right at this moment*? Probably not; the problem that the driver is currently working on has their attention and talking about something else is just a distraction. I should help them work on that and bring up other issues when it's appropriate.

A more extreme form of this problem: stealing the keyboard is not pair programming.

Being A Silent Partner Is Not Pair Programming

The situation in which I most frequently see this happen is when the navigator (for want of a better, more general word to describe the person who isn't driving – though not "passenger," for obvious reasons) feels either inferior to or intimidated by the driver. They feel afraid of contributing or unqualified to contribute, because they don't want to appear stupid or fear the response to their contribution.

This section is not for the driver in such circumstances – I'll come on to that; it's for the navigator. If you can't see how the code does what it ought, maybe it doesn't do it. If you ask about it to your partner, one of two things will happen:

- You'll find a bug, which will get fixed

- That bug won't exist, but you'll find out how the code addresses that issue

(Technically, there's a third option, which is that the driver will tell you to shut up. At that point, you want a book about human resources, not being a developer.)

If you don't ask, one of two things happen:

- The bug will exist, and won't get fixed

- The bug won't exist, and you won't find out how the code works

In short, there's a higher chance that the bug will remain in the code if you don't ask about it, so you should consider it your professional duty to ask.

So, Is Pair Programming Just The Balance Between Those Things?

That's an over-simplistic view of things, but yes. Pair programming works best when both people are involved; otherwise, one of them is redundant, even if they happen to be acting as a typist. How to do pair programming *well* depends on what you're trying to use it *for*.

Pair Programming As Programming

The few times I've used pair programming as a means to get code into an app, I've found that the simple rule to make sure both people are involved is nothing can happen until both people agree. This allows the driver to moderate back-seat driving: "That's a good point, but let's put it to one side until we've finished this bit." It also *requires* the driver to involve the silent partner.

Something I'm guilty of when navigating in pair programming is taking the helm: "Let me just show you what I mean." The **both people** rule is as much a rule for me as for other people, as it requires me to find better ways to describe what I'm thinking of than by destroying the partnership. Having a whiteboard available really helps.

If the goal is to write production code, pairing works best with two people of roughly the same skill level in the target environment, who can take turns at driving. When there's an imbalance between their abilities, it turns into...

Pairing As A Coaching Practice

Pairing is great as a teaching exercise. The same rule about not writing code until both people agree still applies, ensuring that the student discusses any issues with the tutor, who has the opportunity to guide the process.

I think pair coaching works best when the coach takes the navigator's seat. Their role is to encourage the student to ask questions, and then to be the petulant toddler who answers every question with another question.

Seriously. The best way I've found to help someone through a problem is to identify and raise the questions they should be asking themselves. It uncovers hidden assumptions, makes people come up with verbal arguments to support (or sometimes leads them to change) their position, and they end up trying to guess which questions will come next, meaning they have answers before they're asked. This technique is even useful when you have no knowledge of the subject you're coaching on – but for now, we'll assume that the coach programmer is the more accomplished programmer.

When the student is staring at a blank file in the IDE, questions can be very high-level. What does the code we're about to write interface with, and what constraints does that impose? Do we have a choice of the APIs we use, and if so, which shall we go with? The occasional "why?" helps to tease out the student's train of thought.

Action has a place in the learning process, and so sometimes the appropriate response is not a question but "well, let's try that." Even if your student hasn't hit upon what *you* think is the best solution, making a start is a quick way to find out which one of you is wrong about what's going to happen.

But Does It Work?

Is pair programming actually beneficial? It certainly appears to be *in the context of programming classes* (http://dl.acm.org/citation.cfm?id=563353), where pair programmers produce better software than sole programmers *and are more likely to get higher grades* (http://portal.acm.org/citation.cfm?doid=611892.612006). Whether these results can be generalized to all programmers is questionable; it'd be interesting to find out *why* these subjects do better when they're pairing and discover whether those conditions apply to more skilled programmers.

Code Reviews

Another thing it's safe to say that pair programming is *not* is a code review exercise; they have different goals. A code review should be conducted to discuss and improve existing code. Pair programming is about two people constructing some code *de novo*. If your pair programming is about one person writing code and one person saying they've done it wrong, you need to rethink your practices (or your partnership).

Mind you, that's true of code review when it's going badly, too. One problem with code reviews is that it's much easier to spot code that satisfies "I wouldn't have written it like that" than it is to spot code that satisfies "it should've been written to consider these things." This often gets in the way of getting useful information out of code reviews, because the reviewer gets frustrated with the tabs/spaces/variable names/other degenerate properties of the code.

It's problems like this that make me prefer asynchronous, distributed code reviews over face-to-face reviews. We frequently see that **people** (http://programmers. stackexchange.com/questions/80469/how-to-stand-ground-when-colleagues-are-neglecting-the-process) *don't understand* the **motivations** (http://thedailywtf.com) of their colleagues. Let the reviewer work out that initial frustration and anger on their own – preferably, *without the author present as a punching bag*. The reviewer gets a chance to calm down, to acquaint themselves with the requirements, and to study the code in detail... This is not true of in-person reviews, where there's someone else in the room, waiting for the first gem of wisdom to be granted.

On the subject of face-to-face reviews, be wary of people citing the "classics" in this field. People espousing the benefits of code reviews will often cite **Fagan's paper on code inspections** (http://ieeexplore.ieee.org/xpls/abs_all.jsp?arnumber=5388086), claiming that it shows a reduction in the cost of developing software after introducing code reviews. Well, it does. But not in any way you'd recognize from modern software development.

The code inspections performed in Fagan's group would, by and large, uncover problems that, today, would be reported by a modern IDE before you even compile the code. Indeed, Fagan specifically describes code being inspected *after* a product is written, but *before* it's submitted to the compiler. Think back to the last time you *completely* wrote an application before you tried building it. For most developers working today, that hasn't ever happened.

Fagan's reviews would've discovered things such as missing semicolons or spelling mistakes before a deck of punchcards was submitted to a batch compiler. That was, indeed, a valuable saving in terms of lost computer time and rework. For a modern code review, though, to be valuable, it has to save time elsewhere. The reviewer should be encouraged to focus on real issues at higher levels. Does the code represent a good abstraction? Is there an opportunity to reuse components of it elsewhere? Does it accurately solve the problem at hand?

The tool I've found most useful for achieving this is a checklist. A short collection of things the reviewer should focus on directs the review away from trivial questions about style and naming practice. Further, it also directs the *author* to think about these problems while writing code, which should make the actual review itself fairly short. After using the same checklist a few times, its effectiveness will be reduced, as everyone on the team will have a shared approach to dealing with the problems that appear on it. Therefore, the items on the checklist should be swapped in and out as old items become irrelevant and the importance of other problems increases.

Usually, the teams I'm working on do code reviews when integrating a piece of work into a release. This has worked better than scheduled reviews (the code is rarely baked, leading to the reviewer focusing on known rough edges) or reviews upon request (developers just don't ask). This is supported in tools like GitHub by "pull requests"– when the author wants to merge some code into an upstream branch or repository, they send a request, which is a chance to do the review. Other tools, such as **gerrit** (http://code.google.com/p/gerrit/), provide similar capabilities.

Code reviews should ideally be treated as learning activities. The author should learn *why* the reviewer is suggesting particular changes, what the problems are, and why the proposed changes address those problems in ways that the code, as submitted to the review, did not. The reviewer should be learning too: there are opportunities to learn from the submitted code and practice your rhetorical skills by coming up with convincing arguments for why your changes should be accepted arguments that aren't "because I know best." For this to work, the outcome of a code review must be a discussion, even if it's a comment thread in a review tool. Making some additional fixes and accepting the fixed changes without discussion loses a lot of the benefit of having the review.

Programming Paradigms And Their Applicability

On one (theoretically correct, though practically unpleasing) level, all software is just comprised of loads, stores, mathematics, and jumps, so any application can be written using any tool that permits the correct ordering of those basic operations. A key theme running through this book though, is the idea of software's interpersonal nature, and here, we have a concrete example of that: the application source code as a source of mutual understanding between the programmers who work on it.

Before exploring that though, a little diversion into history, to make an idea explicit so that we can leave it behind. This is the idea of successive layers of abstraction allowing people to build on what came before. Yes, all software is built out of the basic operations described above but thinking about your problem in terms of the computer's operations is hard. Within a few years of stored-program computers being invented, EDSAC programmers created an *assembler* that translated mnemonic operation names (such as A for add) into the operation **codes** used by the computer. Programmers could then worry just about the fact that they were adding things, not about which number the processor used to represent addition in this particular addressing mode (on computers that have more than one).

Other work, including that on macro assemblers and Grace Hopper's work on A-1 and other compilers, let programmers move a level away from computer operations (even with "friendly" names) and express *what they want to happen* in a way that can be translated into low-level instructions. For example, a loop over some code with an index variable taking even values from 2 to 20 can be expressed as `FOR I=2 TO 20 STEP 2:…:NEXT I` rather than the initialization, test, branch, and update steps the computer actually needs to execute.

So, when someone solves a problem in software once, others can (legality, compatibility, and availability permitting) build other software on top of that solution. This applies to the discussion that follows objects can be built out of other objects and functions can be built out of other functions. Functions can be built out of objects and objects out of functions, too. This is not that story. This is the story of *stories* being built out of functions and objects; of choosing programming paradigms as ways to *think* about software and to *describe* thoughts about software to other programmers.

Object-Oriented Programming

When it first became a popular technique in the middle of the 1980s, some people tried to position OOP as the solution to all of the software industry's ills (whether those ills existed in the forms described is probably a discussion for another time). Fred Brooks, a manager on IBM's infamous System/360 project, had told programmers that there is *no silver bullet*–http://www.cs.nott.ac.uk/~cah/G51ISS/Documents/NoSilverBullet.html; that the problems faced by the software industry are hard and no technology solution would make it any easier. Brad Cox asked rhetorically in response, *what if there is a silver bullet*–http://dl.acm.org/citation.cfm?id=132388 (that is, object technology), and your competitors are already using it?

As Cox saw it (or at least positioned it in marketing his company), object-oriented programming was the cultural shift that would move software construction from a cottage industry of separate one-off craft pieces to a true engineering discipline, by introducing the *object* as an interchangeable component with a standard interface, just like the pozidrive screw or the four-by-two plank. (Software-ICs: another metaphor Cox used, particularly in his book *Object-Oriented Programming: An Evolutionary Approach*–http://books.google.co.uk/books/about/Object_Oriented_Programming. html?id=deZQAAAAMAAJ&redir_esc=y, was that of the *Software Integrated Circuit*. Just as the development of computer hardware had accelerated by moving from assembling computers out of discrete components to connecting together standard ICs, he envisaged a sort of software Moore's Law arising from the successive development of applications assembled from standard objects or Software ICs.)

Software manufacturing companies could build these standard parts and make them available to an object marketplace. This would be the software equivalent of the trade store, where blue-collar tradesmen and do-it-yourself computer users could buy objects off the shelf and assemble them into the applications they needed.

As it happens, Brooks had already pointed out that there were two classes of problem associated with building software: the *essential* problems that arise from it being a complex activity and the *accidental* problems related to the current processes or technology and their flaws. Object-oriented programming did not solve the essential problems and replaced some accidental problems with others.

Anyway, all of this history may be of some interest but what *is* object-oriented programming? The problem we need to look at is not one of manipulating data or of instructing the computer, but one of *organizing* that data and those instructions to aid (human) comprehension.

The property of object-oriented software that distinguishes it from other techniques is the interrelated organization of code and the data that code acts on into autonomous units (the eponymous *objects*) that interact by sending each other messages. The argument in favor of this approach is that a programmer working on one such unit need only understand the *interface* of its collaborating units—the messages they understand along with the preconditions and results of those messages; not the *implementation*— how those units do what they do. A large program comprising many instructions is thus split into multiple independent entities that can be developed in isolation.

Plenty of programming languages that predate object-oriented programming already allow the organization of code into modules, each module having its own functions and data. Such modules can be restricted to communicating with each other only using particular interface functions. What OOP brings on top of this is the idea of the automaton, of the self-contained package of code and data that is independent both from unrelated parts of the software system and from other instances of things like itself. So, while a multiplayer game written in Modula-2 might have a module that controls the player characters and hides their details away from the rest of the game, were it written in an object-oriented language like Oberon-2, it might have an object representing each of the player characters that hides its internals from the rest of the game and from each other player object.

Given this desire to make a system of autonomous agents that communicate via messages (cpp-messages), some readers may take umbridge at the statement that OOP involves message sending, using languages such as C++ with its member functions as counter examples. Suffice it to say that the *mental model* of objects sending messages to each other is still useful, however the language actually implements it. Now, some other readers are going to dig up quotes by Alan Kay to assert that *only* languages with message-sending can be considered object-oriented. (If you dig hard enough, you'll find that, in Smalltalk, the phrase "object-oriented" was sometimes used to refer to the *memory management* paradigm; in other words, to the garbage collector. The programming model was called "message-passing." So, perhaps C++ with the Boehm-Demers-Weiser garbage collector truly *is* "object-oriented" as purists would understand it. Whatever. If you take issue with it, please find someone else to email.) The largest problem (if not *the* problem; the question being the only one introduced by adopting OOP) is choosing which objects are responsible for which actions. This is a difficult problem to solve; I remember getting it very wrong on the first object-oriented systems I created and still want to improve nearly a decade later. Programmers in all fields have written about heuristics for decomposing systems into component objects, and some people have developed tools to evaluate software in relation to those heuristics and to automatically change the composition.

Those heuristics range from woolly concepts (the open-closed principle, the single responsibility principle, and others) to precisely defined mathematical rules (the Liskov substitution principle, the Law of Demeter, and others). Most (or maybe all) of these have the high-level goal of increasing the *autonomy* of objects in the system, reducing the extent to which they depend on the rest of the system. The stated benefits of doing this are: the increased reusability of objects across different systems, and the reduced likelihood that a given object will need changing in reaction to a change elsewhere in the system.

Researchers have also found that **object-oriented software** is *harder to review*–http://dl.acm.org/citation.cfm?id=337343 than structured software. The desirable design properties that lead to a connected system of loosely coupled objects also produce a system where it's difficult to discover the flow of execution; you can't easily see where control goes as a result of any particular message. Tools do exist that aim to address this by providing multiple related views of an object-oriented system, such as Code Bubbles and Eclipse Mylyn. These are not (yet) mainstream. Then, of course, there are the documents that describe object-oriented software at a high level, often expressed diagrammatically using a notation such as UML. The value of these documents is described in the *Chapter 8, Documentation*.

I find that the most interesting reading on object-oriented programming is that written when it was new; new to the commercial programmer anyway. It's that material that attempts to persuade you of the benefits of OOP, and to explain the reasoning behind the paradigm. Specific practices have changed significantly in the intervening few decades, but modern books assume that you know *why* you want to do OOP, and often even that you know what it is.

I'd recommend that even readers who consider themselves experienced object-oriented programmers read *Object-Oriented Programming: An Evolutionary Approach*–http://books.google.co.uk/books/about/Object_oriented_programming.html?id=U8AgAQAAIAAJ&redir_esc=y) and **Object-Oriented Software Construction**–http://books.google.co.uk/books?id=v1YZAQAAIAAJ&source=gbs_similarbooks. These books not only tell you about particular languages (Objective-C and Eiffel, respectively) but also on the problems that those languages are supposed to solve.

What you may learn from these and other foundational texts in the field is that the reason OOP did not succeed is not because it failed, but because it was not attempted. Keen to make OOP accessible, the **Object Technology** companies made it clear that what you were already doing was already OOP. If you know how to write sequential statements in C, you'll *love* writing sequential statements in Java, and then you'll be doing OOP.

Aspect-Oriented Programming

An extension to object-oriented programming that so far has not reached the same level of application and currency, aspect-oriented programming sets out to solve a particular problem in the construction of object-oriented systems. More specifically, the problem exists in class-based object-oriented systems with single inheritance.

The previous section described the existence of many heuristics, created to guide the organization of code in object-based systems. One of these heuristics was the *Single Responsibility Principle*, which says that the code in one class should be responsible for just one thing. Imagine, then, a database application for a human resources department (almost the canonical OOP example, if recipe managers are ignored). One class might represent an employee, having a name, salary, manager, and so on. Not everyone should be able to change an employee's salary, so some access control will be needed. It could also be useful for auditing and debugging purposes to be able to log any change to an employee's salary.

There are then three responsibilities: updating the database, access control, and auditing. The Single Responsibility Principle means that we should avoid putting all the responsibilities in the `Employee` class. Indeed, that would lead to a lot of duplication because the access control and auditing facilities would be needed elsewhere in the application too. They are *cross-cutting concerns*, where the same facilities must be provided by many, otherwise different, classes.

While there are other ways to build these cross-cutting concerns into an application, aspect-oriented programming opens up configurable *join points* in an object-oriented system. These join points include method entry or exit, the transfer of execution to exception handlers, and fields being read or changed. An aspect defines the predicate a join point must satisfy for this aspect to be relevant (called a pointcut) and the code that is run at that join point (sometimes called advice).

AOP extensions are available for popular OOP environments (**AspectJ** (http://www.eclipse.org/aspectj/) for Java and **Aspect#** (http://sourceforge.net/projects/aspectsharp/) for .NET), but as previously mentioned, the style is not widely used. It adds further to the problem OOP already suffers from, in that it's hard to work out exactly what code is executed in response to a given event. Other systems, such as Ruby and Self (and C++), have "traits" or "mix-ins," which take the position of aspects but not the name.

Functional Programming

Something that's even less new—though needed a bit of rediscovery—than object-oriented programming is functional programming. As the name suggests, functional programming is all about functions; in this case, functions in the mathematical sense of operations that can be applied to some input domain and produce output in a corresponding range. Whereas object-oriented systems describe the imperative commands the computer must execute, a functional program describes the functions that are applied to given input.

This distinction leads to some interesting departures from imperative systems (though these departures can be modelled in OO code, they are prevalent in FP). Parts of functional systems can be *lazily evaluated*; in other words, the computer, seeing that an x^2 result is required, can defer the computation of that result until it's actually used, or the CPU is quiescent. That's not so interesting for calculating a square but can lead to tricks like working with a list of all integers. In imperative code, a list of all integers would need computing when it was created, which is impossible to do. Functional software can define something that evaluates to a list of all integers, then lazily evaluate only those entries that are actually accessed.

Similarly, results can be *memorized*: the result x times x for x==2 is always 4; we know it doesn't depend on anything else, such as the state of a database or what keys a user presses on the keyboard, so having calculated 2 times 2=4 once, we can always remember it and use the answer 4 again.

Recursion is a weapon frequently wielded in functional programs. How might we build a list of all integers? Let's restrict ourselves to a list of positive integers. Define the `f(x)` function such that:

- If x is at the head of a list `l`, `f(x)=1`

- Otherwise, `f(x)=1+f(previous entry)`

Then, for a list with one entry, the result of applying `f` is 1. With two entries, it becomes `1+f(single-entry)=2`, and so on.

Recursion and lazy evaluation are both useful properties, but neither is intrinsic to a functional style of programming; they are merely frequently found being employed in such fields. A more essential part of the program-as-function model is the absence of side effects.

Because mathematical functions have no side effects, the output of a function depends only on its input. Evangelists of functional programming say that this makes software easier to understand (nothing "magic" can happen), and that it makes for a good approach to building multi-threaded software as there can be no race conditions; if the input to a function can be prepared, the function can produce its output. If a function works well with a number as its input, it will work equally well with the (numeric) output of *another* function as its input; its execution depends only on what it receives.

Of course, many software systems have requirements to produce side effects such as drawing images on a display or modifying the saved state of a database. Different functional programming languages then provide different techniques for *encapsulating* – not completely removing – mutable state. For example, stateful components of a software system written in Haskell will be expressed as data types that are the results of functions and can themselves be executed to produce the required side effects; in this way, stateful parts can act as sinks or sources to the functional program.

Functional programming has gained a lot of popularity in the commercial sector in the last couple of years, primarily with the availability of functional languages that interface with existing (object-oriented) code; examples being **Clojure** (http://clojure.org) on the **Java Virtual Machine** (**JVM**) and **F#** (https://fsharp.org/learn.html) on the .Net VM. The principles though are a lot older—LISP was *first described in 1958*—http://www-formal.stanford.edu/jmc/recursive.html but based on mathematical concepts that *predate the programmable computer*—http://www.jstor.org/stable/1968337. A great reference on the how and why of functional programming is **Structure and Interpretation of Computer Programs** (https://web.mit.edu/alexmv/6.037/sicp.pdf), even though recent versions of this book use the not-at-first-glance functional language, Python.

6

Testing

Introduction

One of my earliest jobs in IT was in software testing. I discovered that developers and testers have separate communities, with separate techniques and bodies of knowledge. I also found that, in some companies, the developers had an antagonistic relationship with the testers: developers resented testers for being proud of poking holes in their hard work. In return, testers resented the slapdash and inconsistent way in which the developers had written and released the software. Of course, neither of these extremist positions was actually grounded in reality.

This chapter lays out a way of thinking about making software that puts developers and testers in the same position: that of wanting to make a valuable product. It then includes an introduction to the field of systematic software testing, as understood by software testers, and as apparently given little attention by developers.

A Philosophy of Testing

Imagine plotting the various dimensions of your software: the functionality, performance, user interface, and so on, on a multidimensional chart (for the diagrams in this section, I'll stick to two dimensions; even if you're viewing them on some mad future reader, my graphics tool doesn't support more than that).

The first thing to notice is that you can't draw a point on *Figure 6.1* that represents the "target" product to develop. The most important reason is that the target may not exist. Depending on your philosophical approach to software, there may not be a *true* collection of requirements that is universally understood to be the *correct* thing to build. Consider the people who are using the software as part of the system the software is supporting, so the "right thing" depends on those people and their interactions with each other. The thing you "should" build depends on the context and varies with time. (Manny Lehman wrote a more complete description of this philosophy, in which he describes software systems embedded in real-world interactions and processes as "E-type" systems (E for **Evolving**). In exploring the properties of E-type systems, he formulated eight **laws of software evolution**–http://en.wikipedia.org/wiki/Lehman's_laws_of_software_evolution. I find it ironic that these came to be described as laws as if they were intrinsic to nature, when the lesson is that there are no universal truths when it comes to software.)

What you *could* graph are many fuzzy blobs representing various *perceptions* of the software: what customers think it does, what customers think it *should* do, and what various members of the project team thinks it does. Then there's another blob, representing what the software *actually* does.

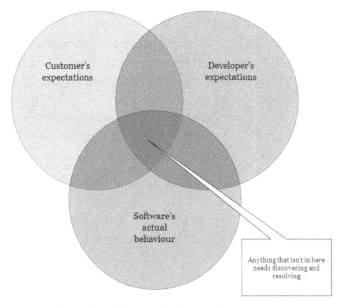

Figure 6.1: Software behavior Venn diagram

The behavior of a software system and the opinions different people have of what that behavior is or should be are different regions in the space of possible behaviors. Software testing is the practice of identifying these differences so they can be reconciled.

The various practices that comprise software testing can be seen, alongside some marketing and requirements gathering activities, as part of the effort to catalog these perceptions and the gaps between them. The effort to reconcile these different perceptions and to close the gaps is then not *solely* a debugging effort, implying that testers will find problems the developers missed. It's a whole-team effort where debugging is just one of the reconciliation activities. Marketing (changing the customers' perceptions to match the capability of the software), extra-sales engineering (changing the deployment environment to match that expected by the software), and other techniques are all ways to close these gaps.

With this mindset, testers are not working to "show up" developers; everybody is working to create both a valuable software system, and a common understanding of what that system does. The goal of testing is to identify *opportunities* for the project team to exploit.

Black and White Boxes

One thing that I've found can infuriate developers is when a problem report is written from a black-box perspective – the tester has reported a bug with no other information than what can be discovered through the user interface: "I tried this and it didn't work." I know it's infuriating, because I've been on the receiving end of these reports.

From the perspective outlined in the previous section, though, black-box test reports are the most valuable reports. (Here, "black-box" refers to the format of the test report, where the inputs to the software are described along with the difference between the expected and the actual output. In test *planning*, testers use the phrases "black-box" and "white-box" to refer to whether the software's source code was used in designing the tests; such tests are still likely to be executed via the software's interfaces.) Anything that doesn't work as expected via the UI represents one of the gaps that was described: a gap between the customer's perception of what the software does and the capability it actually demonstrates.

The reason it's often frustrating to receive this kind of report is that it can be incredibly difficult and time-consuming to replicate the reported issue and to isolate the cause. Often, this process takes longer than fixing the problem when it's been located; why are the testers giving you so much extra work when they could be using white-box techniques, using internal knowledge of the software, to test components in isolation and go straight to where the bug is?

This is another example of one of those perception gaps. Because we spend all of our time working with methods and functions that group instructions into sequences of 10 or so, the natural view the programmer has of the system is in terms of those instructions and methods. Black-box problem reports bear a strong resemblance to the old puzzle game of black-box, where you shine a light from one edge and see that it gets absorbed or deflected. You want to be thinking about mirrors and other features of the box's innards, but you're forced to infer them from what happens to the light beams.

The tester, meanwhile, is acting on behalf of the customer and therefore has no emotional attachment toward the guts of the system. The customers will think "I have *this* problem, and I believe the software can help me to solve it if I do *that*" – a naturally black-box view that only interacts with the external interface of the software. In other words, they (and the testers on their behalf) have no opinion on whether a particular method returns **true** or **false** when the parameter is **3**; they care whether the software's output is a useful solution to the problem expressed as its input. Remember that the tester is trying to find differences between the expected and the actual behavior; discovering their causes is something that only needs to be done once the team has decided a code fix is appropriate.

Shining Light on The Black-Box

Evidently then, if the effort of locating and diagnosing a code problem is only needed when it's decided that the code must be fixed, it's the programmer and not the tester who needs to go from a black-box problem definition to a root cause. Like it or not, it's the developer's responsibility to isolate the fault – whether or not the testers are able to help out.

Obviously, it would be possible to isolate the fault by going through the reproduction steps in the problem report, stepping through the code in a debugger from start to finish until the problem shows itself. That's neither very fast, nor very enjoyable though. It'd be much quicker to diagnose problems if you could hypothesize the likely cause and rapidly demonstrate whether or not that hypothesis is valid.

This is where component and integration testing become useful, but as part of a larger picture: knowing (or being able to find out) the conditions under which the various modules that comprise the whole system work successfully, and whether those conditions are being satisfied for each of the modules taking part in the buggy behavior.

Help in constructing these hypotheses can come from the software's behavior. A common device used in problem diagnosis is a configurable level of logging output: messages are tagged with differing levels of severity and users choose what levels get recorded in the logs. When reproducing a bug, the logging is set to show everything, giving a clearer view of the flow of the code. The downsides to this approach depend on the specific application but can include noise from unrelated parts of the software, and changes to the overall behavior if the problem is timing related.

Problem diagnosis also benefits from having a scriptable interface onto an application; for example, a command-line or AppleScript interface. The first benefit is that it gives you a second UI onto the same functionality, making it possible to quickly determine whether a problem is in the UI or the application logic. Secondly, it gives you a repeatable and storable test that can be added to a regression test suite. Finally, such interfaces are usually much simpler than GUIs, so only the code that's relevant to the problem is exercised, making isolation a quicker task.

Otherwise, going from observable behavior to likely cause is largely still a matter of intuition and system-specific knowledge. Knowing which modules are responsible for which parts of the application's external behavior (or being able to find out – see *Chapter 8, Documentation*) and reasoning about which is most likely to have caused the problem cuts down debugging time greatly. I therefore prefer to organize my projects along those lines, so that all of the code that goes into one feature is in one group or folder, and is only broken out into another folder when it gets shared with another feature. **Eclipse's Mylyn task manager**–http://eclipse.org/mylyn/start/ is a richer way of providing a problem-specific view of your project.

Test Case Design

Random, undirected testing (otherwise known as playing about with the user interface) is an inefficient way to test software. A long-established technique (documented in Myer's **The Art of Software Testing**–http://books.google.co.uk/books/about/The_art_of_software_testing.html?id=86rz6UExDEEC&redir_esc=y) seeks to cover all possible conditions with the minimum number of tests. For each input variable or state, the tester discovers the ranges of values that represent distinct conditions in the software. As an example, an age field may have the following ranges:

- [0,18[: child

- [18, 150[: adult

- 0[: too small

- [150 : too large

- NaN : not a number

The tester then tabulates these various ranges for all the inputs and creates the minimum number of tests required to exercise all of them. This is called **equivalence partitioning**: the behavior at age 36 and the behavior at age 38 are probably the same, so it's reasonable to expect that if you test one of them, the residual risk associated with not testing the other is small – specifically, smaller than the cost of also having *that* test.

In fact, testers will not quite produce the minimum number of tests; they will probably choose to pay extra attention to boundary values (maybe writing tests that use the ages 17, 18, and 19). Boundaries are likely to be a fecund source of ambiguity: did everybody understand the phrases "up to 18" and "over 18" to mean the same thing? Does the software use a rounding scheme appropriate to age in years?

Such a technique was first created with the assumption that the "true" behavior of a software system was to be found in its functional specification; that all tests could be derived by applying the above analysis to the functional specification; and that any difference between observed behavior and the specification is a bug. According to the philosophy of testing described at the beginning of the chapter, these assumptions are not valid: even if a functional specification exists, it is as much an incomplete and ambiguous description of the software system as any other. The technique described here is still useful, as ferreting out these ambiguities and misunderstandings is a part of the value testers bring to a project. It just means that their role has grown from verification to include being a (verbal) language lawyer.

Code-Directed Tests

Remembering that the phrase "white-box testing" has contextual meaning, I've chosen to refer to code-directed tests. This means tests that are *designed* with reference to the application's source code, however they're run.

When testers design these tests, they typically have one of two goals: either ensuring 100% statement coverage or 100% branch coverage. Maximizing branch coverage will yield more tests. Consider this function:

```
void f(int x)
{
    if (x>3)
    {
        // do some work...
    }
}
```

A tester who wants to execute every statement need only test the case where **x** is greater than 3; a tester who wants to execute every branch will need to consider the other case too (and a diligent tester will try to discover what people think will happen when **x** *is equal to* 3).

Because the tests are derived from the source code, which by definition is a format suitable for manipulation by software tools, tool support is right for code-directed test design. Plenty of platforms have tools for measuring and reporting the code coverage. There are even automatic test-case generators that can ensure 100% branch coverage; a good example is the **Klee**–http://klee.llvm.org/, symbolic virtual machine.

Testing For Non-Functional Requirements

In principle, testing the non-functional properties of a system should be the same as testing its functional behavior. You find out what the system does, what various parties think it should do, and compare those. In practice, non-functional requirements can be tacit (someone might want the system to work in a particular way, but they either doesn't know how to say that or considers it too obvious to make explicit) or defined in ambiguous terms ("the system must be fast").

The first step in addressing these problems is to get them into discussion, so testing these aspects of the software and reporting the results is a good idea. As an example, the customer might not have expressed any system requirements because they don't know it's important; a report saying "the application doesn't run properly on 32-bit systems and requires at least Service Pack 2" will uncover whether or not that's an issue, leading to a better mutual understanding of the system.

Automate All The Things

Testing software and writing software share the following property in common: it's not *doing* them that's beneficial, it's *having done* them. Having access to finished, working software is a useful thing, so a project that's in progress is only as valuable as one that hasn't started (although the in-progress one has already cost more). Therefore, as much of the testing procedure itself should be automated as possible to let testers get on with the more creative tasks of defining tests and discovering/reporting issues.

This automation starts with setting up the test environment into a known, initial state. Virtual machines are increasingly being used for this task (at least in server and desktop environments) because they offer a quick way to create an environment of known configuration into which the test harness and the software it's testing can be deployed. At the end of a test run, the state of the virtual machine is reset and it's ready to start again.

Automated driving of the software under test can be done through dedicated scripting interfaces, as already described, but these do not test the behavior of the UI buttons and widgets. Developers tend not to like automatic GUI driving tests as there's a finite chance the test will fail due to unimportant properties of the GUI changing, such as the location or design of a control. There are two things to notice here:

- The location and design of a control *are* important; if a test driver cannot find the same control between two versions of the software, there's a likelihood that customers won't be able to either.

- While there's a risk of such tests failing due to innocuous changes, if you drop the tests completely, then there's a risk that you'll ship undetected problems with the GUI. These conflicting risks must be resolved. The impact of the test failure scenario is that, on those occasions, when the GUI is updated, there will be a brief flurry of false negatives from the test suite until someone realizes what's happened and spends some time updating the tests. The impact of the broken GUI scenario is that your software *definitely* won't do what your customers expect, which will lead to dissatisfaction, low reviews, maybe loss of revenue, *and* someone will have to spend some time releasing a fixed version of the software. The second scenario seems a lot less desirable than the first, so accepting the cost of keeping the tests up to date is the better choice.

Automation is particularly helpful if you have a "smoke test" procedure for determining whether a build is stable enough to be subjected to further testing or treated as a release candidate. Going through the smoke test suite is almost the definition of repetitive drudgery, so give it to a computer to do. Then, developers can go back to planning and working on the next build, and testers can work on providing valuable tests. Additionally, automated smoke test suites will be faster than manual smoke tests, so the build can be subjected to greater rigor. You could go as far as to add all automatic tests to the smoke test battery, so that each build contains no known regressions over previous builds.

Some teams *allow a build to be deployed automatically*–https://github.com/blog/1241-deploying-at-github as soon as it passes the automatic tests.

Getting Someone Else In

Much of the literature on testing makes reference to the fact that an external tester has less emotional attachment to the software under test than the developer, will be more dispassionate in their evaluation of that software, and therefore will uncover more problems. The fact is that a developer *can* systematically test their own software, but the inclination to do so is often lacking (particularly as we tend to see writing code as the valuable thing we do, and everything else as overhead). Getting some form of external input, whether it's a third-party tester or a consultant to examine whether our own testing covered the relevant cases, is a valuable check on our work.

Notice that beta testers are *not* likely to provide such systematic reviews. Typically, a beta tester is an interested user who can be given access to the software for free while it's still under development. They are likely to approach testing in a random fashion, and to only use the parts of the software that are of interest to them. Beta testing is useful for discovering the gap between how you think software will be used and how you expect it to be used, but statistical techniques must be employed in analyzing reports from beta testers. The temptation to change something reported by one beta tester because "the customer is always right" is high but remember that the other **n-1** testers did not report the same problem, and that *none* of them has tested the alternative.

On one project I worked on, the thing we called "beta testing" was really customer environment testing. We gave the software to customers in the hope that their setups would be different from ours and might uncover problems that were configuration specific. Being large businesses, those customers did not actually test the beta versions on their real networks but in "different" environments set up expressly for testing. Therefore, the team still did not know whether the software worked in the customers' setups.

Getting external involvement is also useful when the testing procedures require specialized knowledge. Security testing, performance testing, and testing localized versions of the software are situations where this applies.

Other Benefits Of Testing

I have shown throughout this chapter that software testing has an important role to play in identifying the gaps between your software's actual behavior, apparent behavior, and expected behavior among the various people who interact with it. Additionally, I've described the benefits of using automated tests as a regression suite, so that a problem fixed once will be detected if it's accidentally reintroduced. There are other benefits that result from investing in testing your software, too.

Accessibility

Traditionally, in the world of software, accessibility (or a11y, after the eleven letters that have been elided) refers to making a software's interface usable by people with certain disabilities or impairments. Often, it's narrowly applied to considerations for just the visually impaired.

Indeed, an automated user interface test suite can improve the accessibility of an application. Some UI test frameworks (including **Apple's UI Automation**–http:// developer.apple.com/library/ios/#documentation/DeveloperTools/Reference/ UIAutomationRef/_index.html and **Microsoft's UI Automation**–http://msdn.microsoft. com/en-us/library/ms747327.aspx) use the metadata supplied for screen readers and other assistive devices to find and operate the controls on an application's display. Testing at this level ensures that the tests can still find controls that have had their labels changed or have been moved on the screen, which image-detection-based test frameworks have difficulty coping with.

Some developers who have difficulty arguing for making their products accessible on other a11y-grounds find that testing is a handy device for doing it anyway. In my experience, first the ethical approach is taken ("it's the right thing to do"), then the legal approach ("are we bound by the Disability Discrimination Act?"), then the financial approach ("we'd get more customers – ones that our competitors probably aren't selling to"). Even **vociferous promoters of accessible software** (http://mattgemmell. com/2010/12/19/accessibility-for-iphone-and-ipad-apps/) admit that the financial justification is shaky: *I'm not going to try to make a convincing commercial argument for supporting accessibility; I'm not even sure that I could*–http://mattgemmell. com/2012/10/26/ios-accessibility-heroes-and-villains/). Managers tend to love reduced cost and risk: automating user interface tests, then keeping them as part of a regression battery can provide these two reductions.

Structure

From unit tests to system tests, whatever level your tests are operating at, the object under test must be extractable from your application to execute in the test harness. This requirement enforces a separation of concerns: at each level, modules must be capable of operating in isolation or with external dependencies substituted. It also strongly suggests a single responsibility for each module: if you want to find the tests for the logging facility, it's easier to look in the "Logging Tests" fixture than the "Amortization Calculation (also does logging, BTW)" fixture.

Admittedly, such a rigorous separation of concerns is not *always* the appropriate solution, but it *usually* is until you discover otherwise. It will simplify many aspects of development: particularly the assignment of work to different developers. If each problem is solved in an entirely separate module, then different programmers need only agree on the interfaces between those modules and can build the internals as they see fit. If they need combining for some reason later, then the fact that you *have* tested them as separate standalone components lends confidence to their integration, even if you have to remove some of the regression tests to get everything to work.

I've seen this case primarily in optimization for performance. As I was writing the visualization for a particular feature, another developer wrote the functionality. Those pieces each worked in isolation, but the interface made them too slow. We took the decision to couple them together, which made them fast but introduced tight dependencies between the modules. Certain things that could previously be tested in isolation then required the other parts to be present; but we *had* tested them in isolation, so had some idea of how they worked and what was assumed.

7

Architecture

Introduction

The term "software architect" has become sadly maligned of late, probably as a result of developers working with **architecture astronauts**–http://www.joelonsoftware.com/items/2005/10/21.html who communicate through PowerPoint-Driven Development. Simon Brown has written a book called **Software Architecture for Developers**–https://leanpub.com/software-architecture-for-developers; check it out for a complete discussion of the responsibility of a software architect. The focus of this chapter is on the incremental differences between thinking about a problem as code and as architecture that supports the code. It's also about some of the things to think about as you're designing your application, when to think about them, and how to communicate the results of such considerations to other people on the team.

Non-Functional Requirements Are Essential

I'd almost go as far as to say that the *primary indicator of success* for an application architecture is whether it supports the non-functional requirements the customer has described. Anyone can, given enough patience and stubbornness, carry on gluing features together arbitrarily until all of the required functionality is present. However, making it do that coherently, in a way that combines desired attributes from the customer side (the NFRs) and the developer side (adaptability, readability, and the like) is where the art form of software architecture comes in.

So, what are these non-functional requirements? It's common to say that these are the "-ility" statements made about the software. It takes a bit of squinting to accept that, but it's roughly true:

- **Performance**: How is this an -ility? Is it speedability? Velocitility? Well, something like that anyway. It's important to understand what's meant by *performance*, as it has many different aspects. It could refer to the software's behavior with restricted resources, or large datasets. If we're talking "speed," that could be about the rate at which requests are processed, or the time to process any one request (measured in wall time or clock cycles, depending on which is more important). It could be an average, or under peak conditions. If it's an average, over what time is it measured? And is it the *mean* time or another average? Perhaps the *median*?

  I worked on one project where the performance requirements were described thus: the time and memory required to complete certain operations should be within 105% of the previous versions of the software. That's easy to measure, and whether the software has succeeded is unambiguous.

- **Compatibility**: What operating systems will the software have to run on? What versions? What other software components will it communicate with? Are there reasons to choose particular languages, environments, or third-party components?

- **Reliability**: What happens when there's some problem? Is there a failure, a recovery, or some restricted mode of operation? How much downtime can be accepted, over what period? Or maybe there are limits on how many users may be affected simultaneously?

- **Legal or regulatory requirements**: These can be requirements *not* to do things (such as don't give customer data to third parties) or mandates that the software *must* do something (such as keeping a record of any request from data).

- **Security**: Such a wide topic that many books have been written, including *one of my own*. Now, I'm sure security experts will get annoyed that I've lumped security in with "other" NFRs, but that's what it is. For most software, security is not functionality that the customer wants but a property of how they want that functionality to be delivered. Notice that while security isn't directly related to other requirements, such as compliance, it can be a prerequisite to ensure that other requirements are still satisfied in the face of subversion.

- **Usability**: This can cover a wide range of requirements: ease of use, obviously; but also what (human) languages should be supported, accessibility, design aesthetics, and so on. I mentioned usability, but usability by *whom*? The people who will be using it, of course; but is there anyone else who needs to be considered? Who will be deploying, installing, testing, configuring, and supporting the software? What usability requirements do those people have?

- **Adaptability**: What are the most likely variations in the execution environment or the (human) system that the software's supporting? There's no need to support those things now, of course, but an architecture that makes it easier to make those changes (without causing unacceptable costs now, of course) could be beneficial.

With a list like that, we can come up with a less hand-wavy definition of non-functional requirements: they're the *constraints* within which the product needs to provide its functionality – not the things it does, but the ways in which it must do them.

That's why a successful architecture *must* support satisfaction of the non-functional requirements. If the software doesn't remain within the constraints of its operation, customers may not be able to use it at all; in which case, the software would be a failure. To support these requirements, the software architecture needs to provide a coherent, high-level structure into which developers can build the app's features. The architecture should make it clear how each feature is supposed to fit, and what limitations are imposed onto the implementation of each component. In other words, the architecture should guide developers such that the most obvious implementation of a feature is one that conforms to the NFRs. Ideally, whenever a developer has a question along the lines of "where would I add this?" or "how should I make this change?", the architect (or even the architecture) should already have an answer.

When Should I Think About the NFRs?

The above discussion probably makes it seem that you need to get the architecture in place *before* any of the features are built, because the feature implementation must be constrained by the architecture. That's more or less true, though often you'll find that requirements for the app's functionality feed back into architecture decisions.

I find this iteration is best handled by a series of successively high-fidelity prototypes. ("Fidelity" here refers to the technical accuracy and functional completeness of prototypes; these are for architectural evaluation, after all. I'm not talking about the prototypes' applicability to UI testing, which is **a whole separate issue**–http://dl.acm.org/citation.cfm?id=223514.) The architecture is roughly defined and some of the features are roughly implemented; any identified problems are resolved and the design is refined slightly. This carries on until everything stabilizes, by which time the product is ready to ship.

There's a discussion on project methodologies in *Chapter 13, Teamwork*. Those who have read that, or a similar discussion, will realize that this sounds somewhat similar to the **spiral model of software development**– http://dl.acm.org/citation.cfm?doid=12944.12948, proposed by Boehm in 1986. The difference between that proposition and prototyping in stages as I practice it is the length of each iteration: days or weeks rather than the months to years Boehm was considering.

People who believe in the "build one to throw away" line are at this point picking up their mortified jaws from the floor. The problem with that line is actually getting around to throwing away the one to throw away. You *intend* to throw the first one away, but somehow it manages to hang around and end up in production. You may as well accept from the beginning that this is going to happen and write a prototype that isn't ready *yet* but will be at *some time*, supported by documentation that helps the team understand the gap between the prototype and production-readiness.

Performance in Low–Fidelity Prototypes

Tools for measuring the performance of an application are among some of the most capable developer tools available. Time profilers, memory managers, network packet inspectors, and others all help you to discover the performance characteristics of your application. But how do you do that when it isn't written yet?

You write simulations that have the expected performance characteristics. If, for example, you estimated that an operation requested over the network would take about 0.1±0.01s to complete, using about 4 MB of heap memory, you could write a simulation that allocates about 4 MB then sleeps for the appropriate amount of time. How many of those requests can the app's architecture support at once? Is the latency to complete any one operation acceptable? Remember to consider both the **normal and saturated cases**–http://queue.acm.org/detail.cfm?id=2413037 in testing.

This form of simulation will not be new to many developers. Just as mock objects are simulations designed to test *functionality* when integrating two modules, these simulations are the performance equivalent.

Security in Low-Fidelity Prototypes

Retrofitting a security model to an existing architecture can be intensely problematic. Finding all of the points where access control is needed (This is a key use case for aspect-oriented programming; access control can be inserted at the "join points" of the application's code), or where data should be inspected for different abuses is difficult when the data flow was designed without those aspects being considered. For critical security concerns, including access control and data protection, it's best to incorporate them in the design from the start.

That doesn't necessarily mean completely polishing their implementation; it just means making sure that even the early prototypes are capable of (even prototypical) protection. As an example, on one project I was involved in, we knew that the application needed to encrypt documents that were written to disk. The early versions of the app used a **Caesar cipher**–http://en.wikipedia.org/wiki/Caesar_cipher to do this – far from cryptographically sound, but sufficient for showing which files were being protected and whether anything was being written through another route. You can imagine doing the same for authorization, by ensuring that even stub functionality cannot be used by unauthorized people.

Reliability in Low-Fidelity Prototypes

You can easily explore how an architecture responds to failures by injecting those failures and observing what happens. In the *Performance* section in this chapter, I talked about having a stub network module that simulates the memory and time requirements of real network requests. Similarly, you could arrange for it to fail every so often and observe how the rest of the system copes with that failure. Some companies even inject random failures **in production**–https://github.com/Netflix/SimianArmy/wiki) to ensure that their systems are capable of coping.

Defer When Appropriate; Commit When Necessary

Working with successively refined prototypes means that the architecture becomes iteratively more complete; therefore, certain decisions become more "baked in" and difficult to change. Remember the notion presented earlier: that the architecture should always be ready to answer developer questions. This means that whatever the developers work on first are the things that should be solved first. But that's a tautological statement, because you can probably arrange the development work to track the architectural changes.

The best things to start with are the riskiest things. They might be the exploratory aspects of the product that aren't similar to anything the team has worked on before, they could be the parts that interface with other software or other organizations, or they could be the aspects that will potentially have the highest cost. These are the aspects of the application that will most likely change, and where change will be expensive. Dealing with these issues first means a high rate of change, early on in the project before the schedule and costs have become too well-established, rather than at the end, when people have expectations about when everything will be ready. In addition, changes made before much code has been written mean less code to rework.

There's an expectation management issue here. During the exploratory and experimental work, you have to be able to convince clients, managers, and anyone else who asks that the answer to "how long will it take?" is "I don't know; we're not sure what it is yet" and any progress that has been made so far is illusory. It might *look* like you've made a lot of progress, but most of it will be simulation code that doesn't really do what it looks like it does. On two separate projects I've led the development of, we've run into trouble where a stakeholder has based assumptions about the project's progress on seeing a prototype. It's not their fault; it's my responsibility to provide a realistic appraisal of the project's status on which they can base their judgements on how to proceed.

Justify Your Decisions

So, you've chosen the technology that will be used in a particular aspect of your application. Was that because it will lead to satisfying the customer's requirements with the least effort, or because it's the new shiny thing you've wanted to use since you went to that conference?

When someone asks why the team is using a particular language, framework, or pattern, a shrug of the shoulders accompanied by the phrase "right tool for the job" isn't going to be a very satisfactory answer. What is it that *makes* that tool right for the job? Does it satisfy some requirement, such as compatibility, that other alternatives don't? Is it cheaper than the alternatives? (Remember that cost is calculated holistically: a commercial tool can be cheaper than a free one if it significantly reduces effort and the likelihood of introducing bugs.)

You need to convince other people that the solution you're choosing is appropriate for the task at hand. Before brushing up on your rhetoric skills (which are indeed useful – there's a section on negotiation in *Chapter 13, Teamwork*, and a whole chapter on critical thinking), the first thing to do is to make sure that it *is* an appropriate tool for the job. Think about the different considerations people will have:

- The customers: Will this technology let you build something that satisfies all of the requirements? Will you, or someone else, be able to adapt the solution as our needs change? Can we afford it? Is it compatible with our existing environment?

- The developers: Do I already know this, or will I have to learn it? Will it be interesting to learn? Is using this technology consistent with my career plans?

- Management: Is this cost-effective? Is it actually the best solution for this project, or is it just something you've always wanted to learn? What's the **bus factor**–http://en.wikipedia.org/wiki/Bus_factor going to be? Can we sell this to other customers? Can we buy support from the vendor? Does it fit well with the capabilities and goals of the company?

If you can answer those questions honestly and your chosen technology still comes out looking like the best answer, well, I'm not going to say you won't need your skills of persuasion and negotiation – just that you'll make it easier to employ them.

But remember that negotiation is one of those tangos that requires two people. In **Metaphors we Live By**–http://theliterarylink.com/metaphors.html, Lakoff and Johnson propose that the way we think about argument is colored by our use of combat metaphors. Well, destroying your opponent with a deft collection of rhetorical thrusts is fine for the school debating society, but we all need to remember that we win at software by *building the best thing*, not by steamrollering dissenting arguments. It can be hard, especially under pressure, to put ego to one side and accept criticism as a way of collaborating on building better things. But it's important to do so: look back to the list of different concerns people have, think of any others I've forgotten to add, and realize that your opinion of what's best for the project only covers a part of the story.

When to Fix and When to Replace

A particular decision you often have to justify as a software architect is the choice of whether to continue using some existing code, or whether to throw it away and replace it with something else. Well, you rarely have to justify the decision to keep what you already have; you often have to justify its replacement.

This is as it should be. While it's satisfying – even calming – to think of leaving all that legacy cruft behind and starting on a greenfield implementation, there are good reasons to avoid doing so. The existing code may seem buggy and hard to understand, but your team has existing experience with it and probably knows where the problems and limitations are. The same cannot be said of the as-yet nonexistent replacement, which will probably bring its own difficulties and bugs.

It's important to realize now that this argument is not the same as the sunk-cost fallacy. That would be to argue that you shouldn't throw away existing code because of the time and resources that have already been spent on it; I'm saying that you should consider carefully whether the cost of developing something new is really lower than the cost of carrying on with what you've got.

It probably isn't in many cases. Here's a question: how many bugs will your replacement implementation have? What will those bugs be? How long will they take to fix? If you could predict that, you probably wouldn't leave those problems in, and you could also predict how long it'd take to fix the bugs in the existing implementation and compare the two. Experience has taught us, though, that predicting the quality of a piece of development work is really difficult. There is thus a probability that, while your new implementation will fix some bugs in the original (because you're conscious of those problems when you're developing it), it will introduce new problems, including regressions where the earlier version worked better than its replacement. You've got to factor that risk into your decision.

A significant shift in the economics of this situation occurs when the replacement is not something, you're going to build in-house but is an open source or commercial module you can use. In those cases, the cost of acquiring the software will be well-known, and the fitness for purpose could probably be investigated by examining the bug database or asking the community or vendor. The cost of integration, and the extent to which you'll be responsible for fixing problems (and the costs you'll incur if you aren't) are the remaining costs to consider.

Another thought on rewrites: while they're not clearly an advantage for the developers, they certainly aren't a benefit to customers. I've seen a number of applications where a new version is touted as being "a complete rewrite" and, as Danny Greg from GitHub said, this is not a good thing. If the new version of the software is a complete rewrite, then, to me as a customer, all it shares with the previous version is the name and the icon.

There's a risk that things I relied on in the previous version won't work as well, or at all, in the rewritten version. This is an excellent opportunity for me to evaluate competing products.

You're faced with a known, and well-understood code module, with some known problems. Using this is free, but you might have to spend some time fixing some of the problems to extend it to cope with your new project. The alternative is to spend a while building something that does the same work but has an *unknown* collection of problems. Your team doesn't have the same experience with it, though it might better conform to your team's idea of what well-designed code should look like... this month. Given the choice between those two things, and the principle that my code is a liability not an asset, I conclude that I'd rather choose the devil I know than the devil I don't.

Know When to Nitpick, And When to Leave It

One of the attributes of a good developer is being able to pick apart the small details of a problem. Developers are good at that because computers demand it; computers are really bad at inference, so you have to predict every little case that could happen, no matter how rare, and tell the computer what to do with them. Unfortunately, this attribute, if carried too far, turns programmers into **lousy conversationalists**–http://tirania.org/blog/archive/2011/Feb-17.html in all other fields, including other areas of software creation.

When you or someone else is designing the architecture for a software system, think of it as a low-fidelity proposal for the *shape* of the solution, not the actual solution. The answer to the question "how does this solve X?" is almost certainly "it doesn't – this is an early-stage prototype," so there's not even any point asking the question. You could demonstrate the answer by building the solution into the proposed architecture: if it works, you've built a feature; if it doesn't work, you've found something important. But often, you'll start by thinking that something isn't going to work and find out that it actually does.

Similarly, "why did you do it like *that*?" is not a useful question. If the person who did it like that didn't think that doing it like that was a good idea, they wouldn't have done it like that. Many developers don't like reading other programmers' code, and I think it's because *developers aren't taught how to critically analyze code well*–http://blog.securemacprogramming.com/2012/12/can-code-be-readable/. If you can't turn "what is *that*?" into a specific question about the proposed solution, don't ask.

This is not to say that criticism is bad or unwanted. Of course it's wanted – the architecture will benefit from the input of multiple people. But the feedback has to be at the *same level of abstraction* as the architecture itself.

In other words, the feedback must be in terms of the constraints placed on the solution and whether they can be met while providing the required features. Problems like "I can't see how errors from the `frobulator` interface would get into the audit component" are fine. Questions like "how does this degrade under ongoing saturation?" are fine. Suggestions like "if we use this pattern, then the database plugin can be interchangeable without much additional effort" are welcome. Comments along the lines of "this is useless – it doesn't handle the filesystem reporting a recursive link problem when you open a named pipe" can be deferred.

Support, Don't Control

Given the definition that architecture serves to support the application's features within the constraints of its non-functional requirements, we can describe the role of architect in similar terms.

What Does A Software Architect Do?

A software architect is there to identify risks that affect the technical implementation of the software product and address those risks. Preferably, before they stop or impede the development of the product.

That could mean doing tests to investigate the feasibility or attributes of a proposed solution. It could mean evangelizing the developers to the clients or managers to avoid those people interrupting the development work. It could mean giving a junior developer a tutorial on a certain technology – or getting that developer to tutor the rest of the team on the thing that person is an expert on.

What A Software Architect Doesn't Do

A software architect doesn't micromanage the developers who work with them. An architect doesn't rule by memos and UML diagrams. The architect doesn't prognosticate on things they have no experience of. Perhaps confusingly, the role of software architect bears very little resemblance to the profession after which it's named. If you want analogies with civil engineering, all developers are like architects. If you want to see the software analog to the builder, that's work done by the compiler and IDE.

Architects don't make decisions where none is necessary. They don't ignore or belittle suggestions that come from people who aren't architects either.

In one sentence

A software architect is there to make it easier for developers to develop.

8

Documentation

Introduction

The amount of documentation produced as part of a software project varies dramatically. Before digging in to when and how it's appropriate to document your code, I'll first define how I'm using the term.

Documentation in the context of this chapter means things that are produced to help other developers understand the software product and code, but that aren't the executable code or any of the other resources that go into the product itself. Comments in the code, not being executable, are part of the documentation. Unit tests, while executable, don't go into the product–they *would* be documentation, except that I cover automated testing in *Chapter 5, Coding Practices*. UML diagrams, developer wikis, commit messages, descriptions in bug reports, whiteboard meetings: these all fulfil the goal of explaining to other developers - not to the computer - what the code does, how, and why.

On the other hand, documentation prepared for other stakeholders, like user manuals, online help, and marketing material for your users, or project schedules and overviews for managers, will not be considered here. That's all important too, and if you need to produce it then you need to do a good job of it. But charity begins at home and saving someone time by helping them understand the code they're working on is definitely a charitable act.

Documentation Is More Useful Than You Might Think

A common reason given for not documenting code is that the *source code is accurate documentation*–http://www.codinghorror.com/blog/2012/04/learn-to-read-the-source-luke.html; that, while documentation can be created with errors in it or can become inaccurate as the software changes, the source is guaranteed to be both an exactly accurate *and* exactly precise description of what the software does.

If you assume that framework and compiler bugs don't exist, then this idea is correct: the source *is* complete and exact documentation of the software's behavior. The problem is, it's not always the most appropriate documentation to read.

Sure, source code is entirely accurate, but it's also at the lowest possible level of abstraction. If you've just been brought onto a project and need to get to grips with the unfamiliar software, reading each operation in sequence (once you've even worked out the correct sequence) is not the easiest way to proceed.

Even if you leave this point aside, there are still problems with using source code as your only source of information about the software. It does indeed tell you exactly *what* the product does. Given a bit of time studying, you can discover *how* it does it, too. But will the programming language instructions tell you *why* the software does what it does? Is that weird **if** statement there to fix a bug reported by a customer? Maybe it's there to work around a problem in the APIs? Maybe the original developer just couldn't work out a different way to solve the problem.

So, good documentation should tell you *why* the code does what it does, and also let you quickly discover *how*. It should provide the context at the expense of the details, whereas the source provides all of the details at the expense of making the context hard to discover. In other words, where the source code represents an exact plan to the virtual world you're creating, your documentation should be the **tourist's guide**–http://www.infoq.com/presentations/The-Frustrated-Architect (This idea was first presented, to my knowledge, by *Simon Brown*–http://www.codingthearchitecture.com), with maps, recommendations of places to go (and to avoid), and information about world history.

The Up-To-Dateness Problem

The other primary complaint about creating documentation other than source code is that, unless the docs are maintained alongside the source, they'll quickly go out of date; that reading documentation that's obsolete is worse than reading no documentation; and that effort that doesn't go into working code is effort wasted.

I'll address the second point first. The point of producing *any* form of developer documentation is to make it easier for developers to work with the software. Therefore, the cost of creating the documentation should really be weighed against the *opportunity cost* of not producing it. If the effort saved by letting developers get straight on with their work is greater than the time spent creating and maintaining the documentation, then it's worth doing. Conversely, if the trade-off doesn't work out, you need to decide whether to give up on that form of documentation for something more valuable or find a quicker way to produce it.

But what about the other issue – that obsolete docs are worse than no docs? There's some truth to that, in that being led in the wrong direction won't help someone find their way. It'll probably take much longer than you think, though, for this to become important. Remember that the documentation captures the high-level features: why (and to some extent, how) the code does what it does. Imagine you've got some documentation that is, whatever its completeness, current. Your very next commit isn't likely to change the frameworks used by your product, or the type of database it connects to, or even how it authenticates to a remote component. The product, at a high level, remains the same.

Just as city guides are still useful if a handful of shops or restaurants change what they offer, the tourist guide to your code can still be helpful when some of the methods have changed their behavior a little. The risk that documentation really is uselessly out of date is one that plays out over years, not days.

Automatically Generated Documentation

I talked in the last section about an economic trade-off associated with producing documentation: whether the cost of production is lower than the opportunity cost of not having that documentation available later. The balance can be tipped in favor of producing documentation in two ways: either by decreasing the cost of production or by increasing the value of the documentation.

The automatic generation of documentation from code—often called *reverse engineering* the documentation—is a tactic used to drive down the cost of production. The idea is simple: if developers can always create the docs at a moment's notice from the source code, they can always avail themselves of up-to-the-minute descriptions of how that code works.

Reverse engineering tools, which usually produce UML diagrams, a particular format of documentation discussed later in the chapter (To be clear, I'm not talking about tools that extract documentation embedded in code comments; you still have to write that form of documentation yourself), are good at providing high-level overviews of a project with some or all of the details elided. As an example, given a class definition such as a `.java` class or Objective-C `.h` and `.m` files, a reverse-engineering tool can highlight just the API methods and properties, as shown in the following figure:

StackOverflowCommunicator
- delegate : StackOverflowCommunicatorDelegate # fetchingURL : NSURL # fetchingConnection : NSURLConnection # receivedData : NSMutableData - errorHandler : Block - successHandler : Block
+ searchForQuestionsWithTag:(tag : NSString) + downloadInformationForQuestionWithID:(identifier : NSInteger) + downloadAnswersToQuestionWithID:(identifier : NSInteger) + cancelAndDiscardURLConnection + delegate : id <StackOverflowCommunicatorDelegate> + setDelegate (delegate : id <StackOverflowCommunicatorDelegate>) + dealloc - fetchContentAtURL:successHandler:errorHandler: (url : NSURL, errorBlock : Block, successBlock : Block) - launchConnectionForRequest: (request : NSURLRequest)

Figure 8.1: A UML class diagram

They say there isn't any such thing as a free lunch (some people say TANSTAAFL), and this is correct. On the one hand, it costs almost nothing to produce that class diagram. If you understand UML class diagrams (You also need to understand how I've chosen to bend the UML to make it better at representing Objective-C – the U stands for **Unified**, not **Universal**), it certainly gives a better overview of the class's API than diving through the source code and picking out all the methods. But because the diagram was produced from the source, and the source doesn't tell us *why* it is the way it is, this diagram can't enlighten its readers as to the whys behind this class.

Why does the API use delegate callbacks in one place and block callbacks elsewhere? Why use `NSURLConnection` rather than another class for downloading the content? Why are some of the instance variables protected, rather than private? You can't tell from this diagram.

In addition, you don't get much of an idea of *how*. Does it matter in what order the methods are called? Is it OK to call the cancellation method when nothing's in progress? Can the delegate property be `nil`? The diagram doesn't say.

So, yes, the automatic documentation was cheap. It removed information that was in the code but didn't provide anything additional. Having that brief overview is useful but it's unlikely that reverse-engineered documentation will solve all of your problems.

Analysis Paralysis

Taking what you learned about generated documentation, it might be tempting to turn the controls the other way round. If documentation with zero input effort doesn't provide much additional value, then maybe the more you increase the effort spent on creating documentation, the more useful it becomes.

Perhaps, to a point, this is true. However, the incremental value of adding documentation is asymptotic. In fact, no – it's worse than that. Create too much documentation and people can't even work out how to use *that* without some guide – some meta-documentation. Shovel too much in and it becomes harder to use the docs than if they didn't exist at all.

Notice that **analysis paralysis** (http://c2.com/cgi/wiki?AnalysisParalysis) isn't *directly* related to writing documentation; it's actually a flawed design methods. The interaction with docs comes when you dig into the problem. Analysis paralysis occurs when you're afraid to move away from designing a solution toward building it. Have you thought of all the edge cases? Is every exceptional condition handled? Is there a use case you haven't thought of? You don't know—and you don't want to start building until you find out.

Polishing your architecture documentation or class diagram is basically a complete waste of time. The best way you can find these edge cases is by building the thing and seeing what doesn't work—especially if you're writing unit tests to cover the corners of the API. You'll discover that a use case is missing by giving the software to your customer.

So, analysis paralysis, then, isn't a problem that falls out of creating documentation; it occurs when you *focus* on the documentation. Remember, at the beginning of the chapter, I said the docs were there to support the development of the code by helping the programmers. Your goal is your product: the thing your customers want to be using.

How to Document

The first couple of sections in this chapter were about the *whys* of documenting, what the benefits are, and why you might be in trouble if you do too little or too much. Now it's time to discuss the *how*, some of the forms of documentation that exist, how they can be useful (or otherwise), and how to go about making them.

Coding Standards

Most organizations with more than a couple of developers working together have a style guide or coding standard. This document explains the minutiae of writing code to create a "company style": where to put the brackets, how to name variables, how many spaces to indent by, and so on. If you haven't seen one before, the **GNU coding standard**–http://www.gnu.org/prep/standards/standards.html is very comprehensive. Indeed, one company I worked at required their code to conform to the GNU standard rather than writing their own: it already existed, covered most issues, and was easy to conform to.

Coding standards are great for ensuring that developers new to the project will write consistent code–particularly very novice programmers who may not yet appreciate the value of a single approach to layout, variable and method naming, and the like. (The value is that you're not surprised by the names of the variables, placement of expressions, and so on. The organization of the code gets out of the way so you can focus on the meaning of the code – perhaps in addition to why, how, and what, I should've added *where*.) For developers who are comfortable with the language they're using and its idioms, a coding standards document is a waste of time: they'll be able to *see* how you lay out your brackets from the code; they'll be able to adapt to your house style automatically, or at the very least configure their IDE to do it for them. As Herb Sutter and Alexei Alexandrescu put it in C++ Coding Standards:

Issues that are really just personal taste and don't affect correctness or readability don't belong in a coding standard. Any professional programmer can easily read and write code that is formatted a little differently than they're used to.

Sadly, many coding standards documents do not progress beyond those superficial features.

The parts of a coding standard that don't specifically describe how to lay out code are not useful. They're busy work for people who want to be in control of what other people are writing. Telling a developer "ensure all exceptions are caught" or "handle all errors" is not something that they'll take to heart unless it's part of how they work anyway. If what you want to do is to ensure programmers are catching exceptions or handling errors, then you need to find those who don't and mentor them on making it part of how they think about their work. Writing an edict in some document handed to them on day one isn't going to stay with them, even into day two.

An experienced developer who hasn't yet learned to handle all errors won't start just because a wiki page tells them to. An experienced developer who *has* learned to handle all errors, except the one they don't know about, won't discover that error through reading a document on coding standards. A novice developer who doesn't know how the error conditions arise is left none the wiser.

High-level goals such as "handle all errors," "log all assertion failures" (Which is probably the entry after "assert all preconditions and postconditions"), and so on are great for code review checklists. They're even *better* for automated code analysis rules. They don't belong in standards documents: no one will make those things a "standard" just because they read a bullet point demanding them.

> **Coding Standards And Me**
>
> As previously mentioned, I've worked at a company that used the GNU standards. I've also created coding standards for a developer team, at a time when all team members (myself included) were inexperienced at the language we were using.
>
> In the last 4 years or so, despite working for and contracting at a number of different companies, none has had documented coding standards. I haven't really missed it – the "standard" layout becomes "whatever the IDE does out of the box," and everything else is done by automated or manual review.
>
> So, would I recommend writing a coding standard? Only if the lack of a standard is proving problematic. Actually, it might be just as easy—though more passive-aggressive—to write a pre-commit hook that reformats code before it gets into your repository. Some IDEs (those from JetBrains, for example) offer this feature already.

Code Comments

There are a couple of platitudes that get trotted out whenever comments are mentioned:

Real programmers don't comment their code. If it was hard to write, it should be hard to understand and even harder to modify (from **Real Programmers Don't Write Specs**– http://ifaq.wap.org/computers/realprogrammers.html)

Any code should be self-documenting. (found all over the internet; in this case, on **Stack Overflow**–http://stackoverflow.com/questions/209015/what-is-self-documenting-code-and-can-it-replace-well-documented-code)

It should be obvious that the first quote is a joke, and if it isn't, read the referenced article. The second quote is not a joke, just sorely misguided.

At the time that you write any code, you're *in the zone*, mentally speaking. You're likely focused on that problem to the exclusion of all (or at least to the exclusion of many) others. You've been working on that particular problem for a short while, and on problems in that domain for quite a bit longer. So, of *course*, you don't think the code needs any comments. When you read the code, it fires off all those synaptic connections that remind you why you wrote it and what it's supposed to be doing.

Nobody else has the benefit of those connections. Even you, when you come back to the code later, do not have that benefit: memories that are not reinforced will *decay over time*–http://www.simplypsychology.org/forgetting.html. According to that link, memories fade from long-term recollection if they aren't consolidated.

With this in mind, comments are among the best form of documentation you can create because they provide a connection between two distinct forms of information. The information is the code and the prose comment, and the connection is proximate: you see both in the same place (that is, the source code editor in your IDE). If one doesn't remind you what you were thinking about when you produced it, its connection with the other will trigger some memories.

Recalling (pun somewhat intentional) the discussion from the beginning of this chapter, code tells you very quickly *what* software does, and with a little work tells you *how* it does it. There's no need for comments to retread that ground–you're already looking at something that gives you that information. (A quick reminder of how the code works can save an amount of reading, though. Or, as Fraser Hess put it by paraphrasing Frank Westheimer, A *month in the lab can save an hour in the library*– https://twitter.com/fraserhess/status/299261317892685824.) Comments should therefore focus on *why*.

Many people are put off comments by reading code that looks something like this:

```
//add 1 to i

i++;
```

When you're experienced enough at programming to know what the various operators in your language do, a comment like that is redundant line noise. If all comments were similar to this example, then there would be little point in competent developers reading comments–a situation in which it would indeed be hard to justify them writing comments. Obviously, not all comments *are* like that; indeed, the ones you write don't need to be.

If you find it hard to believe that anyone could ever need reminding what the **++** operator does, you probably don't remember learning programming, and haven't had to teach it either. The **Teaching H.E. Programming blog**–http://teachingheprogramming.blogspot.co.uk is a good overview of just how hard that thing you do every day is for people who don't do it every day.

The thing is that redundant comments are simply redundant. You read them, realize they don't help, and move on. This doesn't waste much time. It's worse to read comments that are mentally jarring: ones that actively stop you thinking about the code and make you think about the comment.

That joke that seems really funny in your head – don't write it down. It might work well on Twitter or in the company chatroom, but not in a code comment. Even if the person reading it thinks it's funny the first time, they probably won't if they have to stop grokking code every day for the rest of their career while they read that joke over and over.

While I was writing this book, someone asked on a Q&A website whether *there's empirical evidence for the value of comments in code*–http://programmers. stackexchange.com/questions/187722/are-there-any-empirical-studies-about-the-effects-of-commenting-source-code-on-s. More usefully, someone answered that question with references. One of the papers, **The effect of modularization and comments on program comprehension**–http://portal.acm.org/ft_gateway. cfm?id=802534&type=pdf&coll=DL&dl=GUIDE&CFID=278950761&CFTOKEN=48982755, is worth looking into in more detail.

Your first reaction may be to look at the date of this paper–March 1981–and decide that it can't possibly say anything relevant to modern programmers. But wait up. The article investigates how people (who haven't changed much in three decades) read (which also hasn't changed much) comments (written in English, which hasn't changed much) and code that is organized along different lines of modularity. Only the way we write code has changed, and really not by very much. This paper investigates code written in FORTRAN, a language that's still in use and not too dissimilar from C. It investigates code written with different approaches to modularity, a variation that's observed in modern code whether written using procedural or object-oriented languages. There's really no reason to dismiss this article based on age.

What they did was to implement a few different code solutions to one problem: a monolithic program, a modularized program, an over-modularized program (each "module" consisted of 3-15 lines), and one organized around an abstract data type. They produced two different versions of each; one had comments describing each module's functionality and the other did not. Interestingly, to remove other hints as to the operation of the programs, they made all variable names nondescriptive and removed any formatting hints.

Whether this represents as good a control as, for example, using a consistent (meaningful) naming and formatting strategy throughout all examples would be worth exploring. Forty-eight programmers were each given one version of the code and a quiz about its operation. They summarized their results as follows:

The comment results seem to imply that the comprehension of a program can be significantly improved with the addition of short phrases which summarize the function that a module is to perform. Contrary to the original hypothesis, it was concluded that comments were not significantly beneficial to logical module identification. Those working with the uncommented monolithic version seemed able to comprehend the program and understand the interaction of the parts as well as those working with the commented monolithic version. However, it seems that those working with the uncommented modularized programs found it more difficult to understand the function of a module and how it fit into the context of the program than those who were given the commented modularized versions.

This does not say "comments are good" or "comments are bad." It *does* say that a particular type of comment can help people to understand a modular program. Notice that it also says that *uncommented* modular programs are harder to understand than *uncommented* monolithic programs. Could this result have any relevance to the Dunsmore et al. study in *Chapter 5, Coding Practices*? Remember that they found object-oriented programs hard to understand:

The desirable design properties that lead to a connected system of loosely coupled objects also produce a system where it's difficult to discover the flow of execution; you can't easily see where control goes as a result of any particular message.

Literate Programming

Donald Knuth took the idea of comments recalling the programmer's thought processes much further with his idea of **Literate Programming** (http://www.literateprogramming. com). In a literate programming environment, programs are written as "webs" in which prose and code can be intermingled.

Programmers are encouraged to explain the thought processes behind the code they create, including the code implementation as part of the documentation. A hyperlinked tree of code references in the web is used to generate a source-only view of the web (via a tool called `tangle`), which can then be fed into the usual compiler or interpreter. Another tool, `weave`, converts the web into a pretty-printed readable document.

The purpose of this hyperlinked graph is to separate the structure required by the programming language (for example, the classes and methods in an OOP language) from the structure of your thoughts. If you're thinking about two different classes and how they'll interact, you can write the parts of the code as you think of them and tell the compiler how they should be ordered later.

Reading the web back later, the person who wrote it will remember why they made the decisions they did as the organization of the code matches their thought processes. Other readers will get insight into how the code evolved and why certain decisions were made: the key reasons for writing documentation.

I'm not sure whether literate programming is a style to adopt – I haven't yet built any large projects as webs. I've kicked the tires on LP tools though and it is a fun way to write software (but then I like writing prose anyway, as you can probably tell). I'm not convinced it would scale – not necessarily to large projects. If I'd known about CWEB when I wrote **Test-Driven iOS Development**–http://blog.securemacprogramming. com/2012/04/test-driven-ios-development/, I would have got it done quicker and with fewer errors. When the authors of **The Pragmatic Programmer**–http://pragprog. com/the-pragmatic-programmer/ wrote that book, they effectively re-implemented bits of LP to keep their manuscript in sync with their code.

The scaling I wonder about is scaling to multiple developers. If you find reading someone else's code style irksome, then wait until you have to read their unproofed prose. Of course, there's one way to find out.

Comment Documentation

While literate programming webs focus on the structure of your thoughts and documentation, letting the code fit into that flow, many other tools exist that retain the code's structure but extract and pretty-print comments into hyperlinked API documentation. (Doesn't comment documentation come under "comments," discussed above? Not precisely, as the formality and intention are very different.)

These tools–including Doxygen, Headerdoc, and friends–retain the proximity of the code with its documentation. As you're making changes to a method, you can see that its comment is right above, inviting an update to remain consistent.

I find it helpful to produce comment documentation for classes and interfaces that I believe other people are going to use. I don't normally generate pretty output, but that's something people can do if they want. I certainly appreciate that option where it exists and use the formatted documentation for another programmers' API.

Some static analysis tools, notably Microsoft's, warn about undocumented methods, classes, and fields. This leads to comments for the sake of their presence, without necessarily leading to a better standard of documentation. Well-formatted comments explaining that a method's purpose is "banana" and its return value is "banana" are rife.

Much of what is specified in comment documentation often includes restrictions on input values to methods ("the `index` argument must be greater than 0 but less than `count`"), when to call them ("it is an error to call this method before you have called `configure()`"), or expectations about the return value ("the object returned will have a `size` less than `2*count`"). These are candidates for being expressed as assertions (usually in addition to, rather than instead of, the documentation), or you could use a language that supports contracts.

Uml Diagrams

UML is a huge topic. Several books have been written on the subject. I'm not even going to try to replicate all of that, so here's the potted version, which also lets you draw analogies with other diagramming techniques:

A UML diagram is a view of some aspect of your code expressed in a manner that conforms to the rules of the UML. Any developer that understands those rules will derive the same information (Provided the diagram actually expresses enough information to be unambiguous, of course) from the diagram.

This means you can consider CRC cards, data flow diagrams, and other techniques to be covered by this section.

The first thing to notice is that it's possible to understand UML diagrams even if you don't know the UML. It's just boxes and lines, though sometimes the meaning of "box" is more precise than "thing" and the meaning of "line" is more precise than "joined to this other thing." Don't be put off by the idea that it's some complicated language with lots of rules you need to learn. That's only true if you want it to be.

Diagrams like these can appear in many contexts. I usually create them as quick sketches, on whiteboards or with paper and pencil (or their modern equivalent – the iPad and stylus). In these cases, the rules are not *too* important, but do increase the likelihood that another reader will understand the details on my diagram and that I'll create the same diagram twice if documenting the same thing.

It may be clear that diagrams produced in this way are for the moment, not forever. They might be captured via an iPhone photo "just in case," but the likelihood is that they'll never be looked at again. There's certainly no expectation that they'll go into some "*Project X Artefacts*" folder to be kept indefinitely.

The more effort you put into this sort of graphic, the more likely you are to want to keep it around. For something like a blog post or a diagram in a book, I'll usually use **Omnigraffle**–http://www.omnigroup.com/products/omnigraffle/), **dia**–https://live.gnome.org/Dia/, or something else that lets me use the shapes and lines from the UML but doesn't care about the rules.

I have also used tools that *do* care about the rules. One company I worked at had a site license for **Enterprise Architect**–http://www.sparxsystems.com.au), a tool that requires you to construct conforming diagrams and supports "round-trips" through the code. A round-trip means that it can both generate the diagram from the code (discussed earlier) and also generate stub code from the diagram. It could also respect existing code, not trampling over existing methods when adding new features to a class.

A few of the other teams made use of this extensively, maintaining the design of their components or applications in UML and implementing the behavior in generated C++ or Java classes. My team couldn't make use of it because the tool didn't (and, to my knowledge, still doesn't) support Objective-C. I therefore feel underqualified to talk about whether this is a good idea: my gut feeling is that it could be a good idea, because it forces you to think at a high level (the features exposed in the diagram) while designing, without getting bogged down in implementation details. On the other hand, different languages have different idioms and preferred ways of doing things, and those aren't readily expressed in a UML model. There's also some overhead associated with configuring the code generator to your team's liking–you still have to *read* its code, even if you don't have to *write* it.

Summary

Documentation is a good thing to have, at those times when you need it. It's useful for telling you why and how software does what it does, when the code can only tell you what it does with a little bit of *how* mixed in.

Maintaining documentation incurs additional cost and carries the risk that the documentation and the code could become unsynchronized. There are various ways to document code, and the preferred trade-off between effort and benefit can be found by experimentation.

Requirements Engineering

There may have been roughly an equivalent amount of thought over the last few decades into how to know you're building the right software as there has been into how to build software better. The software engineering techniques of the period 1960s-1980s explained how to construct requirements specifications, how to verify that the software delivered satisfied the specifications, and how to allow discoveries made while building and testing the software to feed back into the specification.

In the 1990s, methodologies arose that favored closer interaction between the users of the software and its builders. **Rapid Application Development** dropped "big upfront" planning in favor of quickly iterated prototypes that customers could explore and give feedback on. **Extreme Programming** took this idea further and involves the customer or a representative of the customer not only in appraising the product during development but in prioritizing and planning the project as it proceeds. (It's a bit of a simplification to call these 1990s ideas. Many of the concepts behind RAD and other methodologies had been around since at least the 1970s, and a systematic literature review could pin the ideas more precisely onto the calendar.

Nonetheless, it was the 1990s in which the ideas were synthesized into proposed systems for building software, and it was also the 1990s in which development teams started to use the systems and vendors created products to exploit their needs.)

In parallel with that story, the history of how software applications are presented to their users has also been evolving. The success of this presentation is evident in the way that successive generations of practitioners have distanced themselves from the terminology used by the previous generation. If attempts to make software usable had been seen to work, then people would be happy to associate themselves with the field. Instead, **Human-Computer Interaction** has fallen out of favor, as have **Human Interface Design**, **Computer-Supported Collaborative Working**, **Interaction Design**, **User Interface Design**, and so on. It'll soon be the turn of **User Experience** to become one of history's résumé keywords.

If the whole point of building software is to make it easier for people to do things, we should investigate what it is that people are trying to do and how to support that. Along the way, we can find out how to understand what *we* do, which can help us improve our own work (maybe even by writing software to do so).

Study People

Software applications do not exist in a vacuum. They are used by people; a system of people with existing goals, ideas, values, and interactions with each other (and yes, programmers, existing technology). The introduction of a new software product into this system will undoubtedly change the system. Will it support the existing goals and values or replace them with new ones? Will it simplify existing interactions, or introduce friction?

To answer these questions, we must have a way to measure that system of people. To do *that*, we must understand what questions we should ask about that system in order to support the things we want to learn and discover what it is we should measure.

Decide The Model

In *Chapter 6, Testing*, I had to start by deciding that the requirements of a software system did not arise as some fundamental truth about the universe but were based on the way the people who used the system worked with the world and with each other. Now imagine that you're trying to understand the requirements of an application such as Excel. Will you consider the needs of each of the millions of users individually? While this could lead to a higher-quality product (or products, if you resolve conflicting needs by producing different solutions), there are few, if any, companies that could afford to undertake the research involved, and even if they could, it would be difficult to profit from the resulting software.

It's much cheaper to pick a small number of representative users and design the software for them. Some teams pick actual customers, while others create "personas" based on hypothetical customers, or on market research. Whichever way it's done, the product will come to represent the real or imagined needs of those real or imagined people

User personas give the impression of designing for users, when in fact the product team has merely externalized their impression of what they want the software to be. It's easy to go from "I want this feature" to "Bob would want this feature" when Bob is a stock photo pinned to a whiteboard; Bob won't join in with the discussion, so he won't tell you otherwise. The key thing is to get inside the fictitious Bob's head and ask "why" he'd want that feature. Sometimes, teams that I've been on where personas were used nominated someone to be their advocate during discussions. This gave that person license to challenge attempts to put words in the persona's mouth; not quite the same as having a real customer involved but still useful.

At first glance, the situation seems much better for builders of in-house or "enterprise" software; find the people who are going to use the software and build it for them. There are still some important questions about this model of the software's environment. One clear problem is where you're going to stop. Does the team you're building for represent an isolated unit in the company with clear inputs and outputs, or do you treat the interactions between members of this and other teams as part of the system? How about the interactions with customers, partners, and other external parties? The article **Three Schools of Thought on Enterprise Architecture**–http://ieeexplore.ieee. org/lpdocs/epic03/wrapper.htm?arnumber=6109219 explores the effects of these boundaries on considering the systems involved.

Having decided on the scope of the system, are you designing for the specific people who currently comprise it or for more abstract concepts such as the roles that are occupied by those people? In either case, be aware of political biases entering into your model. Software designed according to a collaborative model of the interaction between a manager and their reports will differ from that modelled on the struggle between the oppressed workers and the exploitative bourgeoisie. Because the software will end up changing the system it's deployed into, such decisions will affect the way people work with each other.

You Shouldn't Necessarily Build What The Client Asks For

Discovering the requirements for any software application is hard, even if the people building it are going to be the people using it. In *Chapter 6, Testing*, I explored the notion that everybody has their own idea of what the software should do, and in *Chapter 7, Architecture*, the fact that some requirements are not made explicit. So, if you just asked everyone for a list of things the software should do and built that, it'd be rife with conflicts and probably wouldn't do everything that any one person wanted from it.

While it's an inaccurate way of finding out what software should do, asking people is one of the easiest and most accessible methods. You can interview people with either a directed questionnaire or an open-ended discussion, finding out what they think of the system of interest and hopefully teasing out some of those tacit requirements. You can also get a group of people together, as a round-table discussion or a focus group, to collectively discuss their needs and problems. Even when people are being helpful and answering your questions to the best of their abilities, there will be problems that come up with interpreting their answers. The thing they do is likely a specialist activity, and so is making software. Each of these disciplines will have its jargon and its accepted "common sense" knowledge; translating between those will be difficult. Everyone has their own version of what "everybody" who does their job knows and will probably not think to tell you about those things.

So, there's an art (or maybe a science; I don't think the industry has made its mind up yet) to looking past the direct answers to your direct questions, to find out both what questions you *should* have asked and what answers you would *never* have been given. This is where bespoke software (particularly so called "enterprise" software) has a chance to provide a much better experience than off-the-shelf software; you have the opportunity to observe what your users *really* do and to provide software that supports that, rather than offering something that supports their stated needs.

You need to remember too that *you* are the software expert, and your client is the expert at solving whatever problem it is that they solve. When they talk about the *problem* they are having, there is more information about how it should be solved than when they tell you about the *solution* they envisage. That's not to say that you shouldn't accept their suggestions; but you *should* remember that their expertise lies elsewhere and that your team probably has more experience of designing software. Obviously, if you're a start-up working on a developer tool, your team probably has *less* experience than your customers.

Avoid Asking What You Want To Hear

If you've got a pet feature, it's all too easy to drop it into a discussion of the proposed system when conducting interviews and focus groups with prospective users. The problem you then face is that it's easy for people to agree that said feature would be a good idea, even if it really wouldn't.

Firstly, you have to separate things that people think they would use from things that people *do* use. Consider whatever word processing software you use and think about all the features it has that you've never touched. When you bought the software, were you swayed by any of the discussions of those features in the marketing material? (The idea that word processors have more features than people use has been investigated by human-computer interaction researchers—https://www.cs.ubc.ca/~joanna/papers/GI2000_McGrenere_Bloat.pdf and while they found that some features go unused by some users, the users still know that those features are there and have some familiarity with their function. So, saying that these extra features are entirely without value is clearly a stretch; nonetheless, the default choice on whether we "should" incorporate a feature into a product is usually "yes" due to the feature matrix marketing described here.) Do you think the majority of other users do make use of those features? Would the software be worth as much if it didn't have those features? Given the choice between an application that does a thing and one that doesn't, people will often choose the one that does it even if they don't see a need for that right now. Particularly as, when you're gathering requirements, there's no other information to go on; without being able to see the two (currently hypothetical) applications, prospective users can't compare their usability, speed, quality, or other features, so the options really do boil down to "with" or "without."

Bear in mind, too, the tendency for people without a strong view on a statement to agree with it. This is known in psychological circles as the *acquiescence response bias* and needs to be taken into account when evaluating the results of questionnaires. An example is in order. Imagine that you wanted to build a "clean coder" IDE, but you want to find out whether anyone would use it first. You create a questionnaire asking respondents to rate how strongly they agree or disagree with these statements:

- A professional programmer writes unit tests.

- A good method has minimal loops and branches.

- Long, descriptive variable names are better.

Someone else wants to write a "stripped-down" IDE, harking back to the times when "real programmers didn't eat quiche" and just got their jobs done. (This is a tongue-in-cheek reference to the article **Real Programmers Don't Use Pascal**–http://www. ee.ryerson.ca/~elf/hack/realmen.html, which was itself a tongue-in-cheek reference to the book **Real Men Don't Eat Quiche**–https://bit.ly/2XjLjxw. That was itself satirical, but I've run out of cheeks into which I am willing to insert my tongue.) They create a questionnaire in which respondents rate their agreement with these statements:

- Time spent writing tests is time spent not adding value.

- A good method has as many loops and branches as necessary to provide a simple interface onto complex work.

- Typing is not the focus of programming; terseness is a virtue.

These questionnaires will yield different results; not necessarily entirely in opposition to one another but certainly each revealing a bias in favor of the higher end of their respective scales. This is the acquiescence response bias; each has asked what they wanted to hear and the respondents in each case have tended to agree with it. The two researchers should have each chosen a mix of questions from both lists to get a more representative survey.

Finally, bear in mind that telling your client "I think we should do it like *this*" will predispose them to that approach, due to a cognitive bias called **anchoring**–https:// www.sciencedaily.com/terms/anchoring.htm). Having *anchored* a particular feature or workflow in their mind, they'll prefer options that contain that feature or workflow even if it rationally appears worse than an unrelated alternative. You could end up privileging a suboptimal or costly design just because it was the first thing you thought of and blurted it out to your clients. It's best to leave options open early on so that you don't pit your own customers against better designs you create later on.

Understand The Problem Domain

As mentioned earlier, you and your team are the experts in making software, and the customers are the experts in the thing that the software will do. I've cautioned against using that distinction to build the software you want rather than the software that the customers need; should this be taken to mean that the software people stick to software and the customers stick to their problem domain?

No.

You need to know what you're building *for*, so you need to have some understanding of the problem domain. Yes, this is asymmetric. That's because the situation is asymmetric – you're building the software to solve a problem; the problem hasn't been created so that you can write some software. That's just the way it is, and compromises must come more from the software makers than from the people we're working for. The better you understand the problem you're trying to solve, the more you can synthesize ideas from that domain and the software domain to create interesting solutions. In other words, you can write better software if you understand what it is that software will do. That's hopefully not a controversial idea.

There are different levels on which this understanding can be implemented, relevant to different amounts of interaction with customers. *Chapter 5, Coding Practices*, described **Domain-Driven Design** and the ubiquitous language: the glossary of terms that defines concepts in the problem domain and should be used to name parts in the software domain, too. Needless to say, everyone working on the software should be familiar with the ubiquitous language and using it in the same way – it's not ubiquitous otherwise! The point of the ubiquitous language is to ensure that everyone–customers and software makers–means the same thing when they use technical or jargon terms. Therefore, it prefers jargon to be from the problem domain, so that non-software people don't have to learn software terminology, and it's expected that the terms pervade the software design and implementation and are not just used in customer meetings.

The ubiquitous language should be considered a starting point. Some methodologies, including Extreme Programming, require that the development team have a customer representative on hand to ensure that the development work is always adding value. These discussions need to be had at the level of the business, that is, at the level of the problem domain. (This is one of the reasons that programmers often get frustrated that the business doesn't schedule time for refactoring, development infrastructure, or "paying off" technical debt. The problem is that bringing these things up in the context of a business discussion is a mistake; these are internal details of what we do and how we work with each other and have nothing to do with business value or how we work with customers. If some refactoring work is going to make it easier to work on the software, then just do it and let the business see the results in terms of reduced costs.) This in turn means that at least one person is going to need to be capable of having a peer discussion about the problem at hand with the customer representative.

Uncover Tacit Requirements

This chapter has already covered the idea that you need to find out what customers need from their software that they're not talking about. But it's worth bringing up again, because the ubiquitous language may have ubiquitous holes.

Think of all the times you've been surprised at a question someone from outside the software field has asked about an application you're writing. Well, no, of *course* the app we made for the seven-inch tablet won't work on the three-inch phone. It's such a basic thing, it's not even worth mentioning, so why would someone ask it?

Now think about flipping that situation. What are the things that people in your problem domain think so basic that they'd never mention them? The things that a professor told them were "obvious" in a first-year lecture and they haven't questioned since? How are you going to get anyone to tell you about them?

As with pair coaching, this is a situation where acting like a petulant toddler can be to your advantage. Domain experts are likely to have particular ways of doing things; finding out *why* is what's going to uncover the stuff they didn't think to tell you. It'll be frustrating. Some things we don't have real reasons for doing; they're just "best" practice or the way it gets done. Probing those things will set up a cognitive dissonance, which can lead people to get defensive; it's important to let them know that you're asking because you're aware how much of an expert they are at this stuff and that you just need to understand the basics in order to do a good job by them.

Why the cognitive dissonance? Well, sometimes we just do things because "that's how they're done," rather than because there's any known value to that technique. We can find examples of this in the field of making software. Many developers (though, far from all) use version control. What are the benefits of doing so? Surprisingly, *no study can be found*–http://www.neverworkintheory.org/?p=451 that investigates that. However, many developers, myself included, will tell you that version control is important, you should be doing it, and can come up with benefits. Tell us "but there's no evidence for those benefits, so why not just stop?" and we'll get confused and angry, trying more vociferously to defend our position despite the problems with the argument.

You Shouldn't Build What Your Client Wants

At least, you probably shouldn't, anyway. Most of the time, they won't represent the majority of users, or even *any* of the users. This happens in pretty much every field of software:

- In-house software is usually commissioned by the IT department, but will be used by sales, engineers, finance, and other departments.

- Commercial software is usually driven by a product manager but will be sold to thousands (or more) of people. Even where you have a dedicated customer representative, they represent only one of many users. And, as with in-house software, the "representative" may still not be the ultimate user of the application.

- Even in a case where you're building bespoke software for a small team of people who are involved in the decision-making, a disproportionate number of suggestions will come from the more senior or more vocal users; with the worst case being that specific requests get filtered through the understanding of a senior manager before being summarized and presented to the development team.

What this means is that, in almost all situations, what your client wants is at best only a rough approximation to what would be in the best interests of the product (and therefore its user base, and presumably your bottom line). The trick to managing this is, of course, political rather than technical; you probably don't want to offend the people who *are* giving you input into the software requirements, especially if they're paying the bills. That means flipping the **Bozo Bit**–http://c2.com/cgi/wiki?SetTheBozoBit is out of the question. But if something's a bad idea, you probably don't want it in your app.

But what makes *you* sure it's a bad idea? Even if you are the user of the software you're writing, it's still one not-quite-representative user versus another. Yes, you may have more of an idea about platform norms and expected behavior, but that could also mean that you're conservative about brand new ideas because no other app works this way.

Resolving this conflict can be achieved with data. I discussed A/B testing and user acceptance testing in *Chapter 6, Testing*; those tools can be put to use here in discovering whether any given suggestion improves the software. It doesn't have to be expensive; in that, you don't have to build the whole feature before you can find out whether anyone wants it. You could try out a prototype on a whiteboard to see how people get on with it or build a very basic version of the feature to see how popular it is. Be cautious about trying to poll users to find out how popular a feature would be though: answering "yes" or "no" takes the same effort, but in one case they get a higher chance of getting a new shiny thing, whether they'd use it or not. The risk/reward calculation in responding to a feature poll is biased toward affirming the request, and we've already seen acquiescence bias means people tend to agree with whatever statement is presented to them.

When you've got the data, the conversation can start "that was a nice idea, but it looks like the customers aren't ready for it" rather than "I'm not building your bad feature." That's a much easier way to have an ongoing relationship with your clients. Unfortunately, it's not always an option; plenty of software is still built in secrecy, with no user engagement until 1.0 is nearly ready (or even later). In these cases, your imperfect customer proxies are all you've got and, like it or not, you have only their suggestions and your opinions to work with. You can still frame discussion around hypothetical other users (often called personae) to defuse any emotional feelings about challenging "personal" feature requests, but that's an imperfect rhetorical tool rather than an imperfect requirements tool. Application telemetry in the 1.0 release can tell you how people really use the features and help you prioritize future development, but that's too late for discussions about the initial release; and remember that it's the initial release that costs money while it's not paying for itself.

Human Factors In Software Systems

The thing about software requirements is that they don't exist. Or at least, they don't exist in isolation. The standard model of particle physics is based on the idea that there are fundamental particles called quarks, and that these combine into systems called *hadrons* (heavyweight particles including protons and neutrons) and *mesons* (middleweight particles important in high-energy interactions). Quarks are bound into these systems by *gluons*, the particles that carry the strong force. This model is generally accepted, even though no one has ever seen a quark or a gluon in isolation; they're always part of a hadron or meson.

Just as quarks and gluons have no existence on their own, so software on its own without users is meaningless, and software users without software have nothing to do. The whole represents a *socio-technical system* and it is *this* system that we are constructing and modifying with our software-building efforts. So, no view on software requirements is complete without a view of the effect the software will have on the politics, economics, social structure, and psychology of the people who will interact with it, and of how those people will affect the software.

I've had a theoretical grasp on this point for years. It was finally emotionally reified for me by **Robert Annett**–https://twitter.com/robert_annett *during a talk he gave on legacy software systems. The anecdote he told involved him walking through an office at the company he was deploying a new system at, talking with one of the people he'd be working with. As they left a room where around 20 data entry clerks were working, his new colleague said quietly "it's a shame really – when your new system comes online, we'll have to fire them."*

Sometimes, the pattern of sigils and words you feed to the compiler can have a real impact on real people, good or bad.

Economics

The economic side of this interaction is covered well by Barry Boehm in his 1981 book **Software Engineering Economics**–http://books.google.co.uk/books/about/ Software_engineering_economics.html?id=VphQAAAAMAAJ&redir_esc=y. His model for estimating the costs of software projects has not been generally adopted in the industry, but it does include what he calls "human relations factors," which can affect the cost of a software system and the benefits derived. It includes the "modified golden rule" for working with other people:

Do unto others as you would have others do unto you – if you were like them.

The point of the conditional clause is to remind programmers that not everyone wants to be treated like they enjoy solving software problems and can understand computer science concepts. Boehm argues that the costs and benefits of usability, of satisfying human needs, and of allowing users to fulfil their potential need to be considered in economic terms for a software project.

While surely better (or at least, more complete) than not reasoning at all about these factors, trying to find a dollar value for them is an early stage in their consideration. What I infer from it, and from similar arguments in information security and other fields (remember the discussion on the economic value of accessibility, in the *Chapter 6, Testing*) is that we either can't *see* or can't *justify* an intrinsic benefit of those properties, but would still like to include them in our decision-making. The fact that we're not willing to ignore them leads me toward the second explanation: we know that these things are valuable but don't have an argument to support that.

That's not to say that these defenses for human factors aren't useful; just that they aren't the apotheosis of debate. You can see how usability might be economically justified in terms of cost; more effort in designing usable software can pay off in making its users more efficient, and more satisfied. Satisfaction (linked to another of the factors – fulfilment of human potential) can lead to greater engagement with their work and higher levels of staff retention, reducing the HR costs of the organization. Satisfying human needs is what **Herzberg**–http://www.businessballs.com/herzberg.htm deems a *hygiene factor*: people must have their basic needs met before they can be motivated to pursue other goals.

Sometimes the trade-off in goals cannot reasonably be cast in economic terms. A good example is a game: if it had great usability, it'd be really simple so people would complete it quickly and then get back to work – an economic win. But people don't play games that are straightforward; they play games that offer them a challenge, whether that challenge be mental, dexterous, or something else. Therefore, the player's desire to be challenged, or to lose themselves in the game world, takes precedence, although it is difficult to see how to assign a monetary value to that desire.

Politics

The political side of software development can have an impact on how people think they are recognized, supported, empowered, and valued by the system in which the software is used and the wider system of interacting systems. Let's start this section by looking at a case study: a shared calendar application used in a business. On one team, everyone can schedule events on their own calendar, and the manager can see everyone's calendars. Additionally, the manager has a personal assistant who can schedule events for the manager in the manager's calendar.

The manager feels in a position of power, because they can see where everyone is and can strategically walk past their desks to see what they're up to at times when their reports should be there, because they don't have any meetings recorded. Additionally, the manager feels empowered because the mechanical work of updating the calendar software has been delegated to someone else, and delegation is a key activity for managers.

On the other hand, the other members of the team feel empowered because they can control the manager through the calendar software. If they do not want to be disturbed, they can create themselves a "meeting" and find somewhere quiet to work. They can work with the personal assistant to arrange for the manager to be in a meeting at a time when they want to have a team discussion without the manager's involvement.

This discussion about calendar software depends on an underlying model of the politics in the group using the calendar: I wrote it to rely on a *Marxist* model, exposing the struggle between the manager (playing the part of the capitalist) and the workers. Each group is represented by their own goals, which are, according to the model, inevitably in conflict. Stability is achieved by ensuring that conflicting goals do not come into direct opposition over a single issue.

Whether the people participating in this system are really engaged in the conflict presented in this model of the system – and whether individual participants would recognize that conflict or have a different perception of the system, is not captured within this model. It's an internally consistent story that has nothing to tell us about its own accuracy or applicability.

In designing software to be used by multiple people, the real politics of the system of people and our model of those politics will both shape the interactions facilitated by the software. Will the software support an existing distribution of power or will it empower one group at the expense of others? Is the political structure modeled on a coarse level (as in the managers/workers case above) or are the different needs and expectations of every individual in the system captured? Will the software enable any new relationships or break some existing relationships? Will it even out inequalities, reinforce existing inequalities, or introduce new ones?

These are complex questions to address but it is necessary to answer them for the impact of collaborative software on its users to be fully understood. As the anecdote earlier in this section shows, software systems can have a real impact on real people: the management of a large business may be pleased to reduce their headcount after deploying new software, to recoup development costs, and see it as the responsibility of those who are made redundant to find alternative employment. A charity with a remit to support local people by providing work may prefer to retain the workers and reject the software. Only by understanding the political environment can you be sure that your software is a good social fit for its potential users and customers.

Prioritizing Requirements

This section really reiterates what came before: you should be building software that your users *need* in preference to what they *want*. That's the ideology, anyway. Reality has this annoying habit of chipping in with a "well, *actually*" at this point.

It's much easier to *sell* the thing the buyer wants than the thing they really need. Selling things is a good opportunity to take, as it allows you to fund other activities: perhaps including the development of the thing that the customers still needs. But, well, *actually...*

...good marketing efforts can convince the customer that the thing they actually need is something they do in fact want. You can then shortcut all of the above discussion by making the thing people *should* be buying and convincing them to buy it. This is one of those high-risk, high-reward situations: yes, *selling people a faster horse*–http://blogs. hbr.org/cs/2011/08/henry_ford_never_said_the_fast.html is easier but the margins will not be as high and the success not as long-lived as if you invent the motorcar industry. As they say, profit is a prize for taking a risk.

So, how you prioritize building the software really depends on your comfortable risk level. You could get incremental low-margin gains by finding the things that people are definitely willing to buy and building those. This is the **Lean Start-up** approach, where you start with nothing and rapidly iterate towards what the data is telling you people want to buy. Or you could take the risk: build the thing you know people need, then convince them that it's worth the money. This is the approach that bears most resemblance to Steve Jobs' famous position: *It's not up to customers to know what they want.*

Is It Really "Engineering"?

There's an old quote that says anything where people feel the need to include the word "science" isn't a science. And, yes, the original author was talking about computer science. But perhaps we should be wary of the attribution of "engineering" to requirements engineering. Engineering is, after all, the application of science to the manufacture of artifacts, while requirements engineering is the application of social science (the warning is firing again!) to the business of improving a social system. Really, it's a transformation of some fields of social science (politics, economics, anthropology, ethnography, and geography) to other fields of social science (sociology and business studies) with some software created to effect the transformation. (Shortly after I finished writing this section, Paul Ralph submitted a paper to ArXiv describing **the rational and alternative paradigms**–http://arxiv.org/abs/1303.5938v1 of software design. The rational paradigm is basically the intuition-based version of requirements engineering: the software requirements exist as a fundamental truth to the universe and can be derived from careful thought. The alternative paradigm is the empirical one: the requirements arise as a result of the interactions between people and can only be understood through observation. Ralph's paper does a good job of explaining these two paradigms and putting them in context in the history of software design.)

This isn't to say that the phrase "requirements engineering" needs to be retired, because people know what it means and use it as a placeholder for the real meaning of the discipline. But maybe we need to think of this as a generational thing; that while to *us* it's called "requirements engineering," we remember to give it a different term with the people we teach; something like "social software".

10
Learning

Introduction

When you started doing this stuff, whether "this stuff" is writing iPhone apps, UNIX minicomputer software, or whatever future programming you meals-in-pill-form types get up to, you didn't know how to do it; you had to learn. Maybe you took a training course, or a computer science degree. Perhaps you read a book or two. However you did it, you started with no information and ended with... some.

It doesn't stop there. As Lewis Carroll said:

It takes all the running you can do, to keep in the same place.

He was talking about the Red Queen's race, but I'm talking about learning and personal development. If you stopped when you had read that first book, you might have been OK as beginner programmers go, but if the woman next to you in the library read another book, then she would have been a step ahead.

We live in what is often called a knowledge economy. Francis Bacon said, "knowledge is power." If you're not learning, and improving yourself based on the things you learn, then you're falling behind the people who are. Your education is like the race of the Red Queen, constantly running to keep in the same place.

Do as Much as You Can

There's no such thing as too much learning (though the real problem of "not enough working" can sometimes be found in proximity to a *lot* of learning). Not all education comes through formal settings such as training or university courses. (Indeed, much material from university-level computer science programs is now available for free through schemes such as iTunes U and Coursera. That can make for some interesting lunchtime reading, but I find I learn better when I've got the structure of a taught course and the pressure of a submission deadline. That said, you're not me and you might benefit from a more relaxed learning environment.) Reading a book, magazine article, or blog post in your lunch break can be very helpful, as can going to birds-of-a-feather developer meetings.

Bigger items such as training courses and conferences obviously involve a larger time commitment. There is, obviously, such a thing as "not enough working," and that's a balance you'll need to address. If you're self-employed, then you need to balance the opportunity cost (How much work will you be turning down by attending the course?) and financial cost against the benefits (How much better will you be after taking the course? How much extra work will you be able to get? What good contacts will you meet at the conference?).

Of course, if you're employed, this decision may be made for you by your manager. You can help the decision along if you know how the training course fits with the company's direction... But I'll leave that to the chapters 12 and 13 Business on and Teamwork respectively.

Don't Stick to Your Own Discipline

Every field has its champions and superheroes: the people with tens of thousands of followers, whose blog posts are always read and quoted and who speak at all the conferences. People look to these champions to analyze and direct the way their community works. Often, the leaders in one field will be contrasted with "them," the leaders in a different field: that iPhone programmer is one of "us," and the Android programmer giving a talk in the other room is talking to "them."

This definition of "us" and "them" is meaningless. It needs to be, in order to remain fluid enough that a new "them" can always be found. Looking through my little corner of history, I can see a few distinctions that have come and gone over time: Cocoa versus Carbon; CodeWarrior versus Project Builder; Mach-O versus CFM; iPhone versus Android; Windows versus Mac; UNIX versus VMS; BSD versus System V; SuSE versus Red Hat; RPM versus dpkg; KDE versus GNOME; Java versus Objective-C; Browser versus native; BitKeeper versus Monotone; Dots versus brackets.

Sometimes, it takes an idea from a different field to give you a fresh perspective on your own work. As an example, I've found lots of new ideas on writing object-oriented code by listening to people in the functional programming community. You might find that the converse it true, or that you can find new ways to write Java code by listening to some C# programmers.

You could even find that leaving the programmers behind altogether for a bit and doing some learning in another field inspires you – or at least lets you relax and come back to the coding afresh later. The point is that, if you focus on your narrow discipline to the exclusion of all others, you'll end up excluding a lot of clever people and ideas from your experience.

Put it into Practice

At various points in history, I've learned a collection of languages, of the inter-human and computer programming varieties. The only ones I can remember anything about are the ones I use all the time.

I expect the same's true for you. The reason I expect this is not that I believe everyone's like me, but that there's basis for it in theory. The **Kolb learning cycle**–http://www.businessballs.com/kolblearningstyles.htm says that there are four processes that form the practice of learning:

- **Concrete Experience**: Actually doing a thing.

- **Reflective Observation**: Analyzing how you (or someone else) did a thing.

- **Abstract Conceptualization**: Building a model of how things should be done.

- **Active Experimentation**: Just playing with the plasticine and seeing what comes out.

Not everybody goes through all of the items in the cycle, but most people start out somewhere and progress through at least a couple of the points, probably in the order presented (acknowledging that, as a cycle, it should be, well, cyclic). Therefore, almost everyone who learns something goes through either an experimentation or building experience: it's very hard to learn something without trying it out.

Perhaps more importantly, it's hard to adapt what you've learned to fit everything else you do if you don't try it out. An idea on its own doesn't really do anything useful; when it's put into practice, it becomes combined with other ideas and techniques and adds something valuable.

Collaborate and Share what you Learn

There are numerous benefits to sharing the things that you learn. The first is that everybody you share with will have had different experiences and can tell you how what you've learned applies (or doesn't) to their context. That insight can give you a more complete picture of what you learned, especially of where it might be limited. Conference talks and books are often delivered with a spin on being persuasive—not because the author is being disingenuous, but because the material will be more successful if you go away wanting to apply what you've learned.

Listening to other people who've found that what you want to do does (or doesn't) work in particular situations, then, can give you a more complete picture of a concept and its applications than just relying on the first source you discovered. In return, you'll probably tell the person you're talking to about *your* experiences and problems, so you both get to learn.

That's the real reason I'm keen on shared learning—everyone benefits. That includes the teacher, if you're collaborating in a formal learning environment such as a training course or a class. Even if you've got a lot less experience than the teacher, you'll have unique insight and ideas that are more useful out in the open than being kept quiet.

Publications such as *Communications of the* ACM frequently cover problems associated with teaching computing. Indeed, in the issue that was current at the time of writing, **two articles**– http://cacm.acm.org/magazines/2012/11/156579-learning-to-teach-computer-science/fulltext **articles**–http://cacm.acm.org/blogs/blog-cacm/156531-why-isnt-there-more-computer-science-in-us-high-schools/fulltext discuss a shortage of computer science teaching. I believe that to address such problems, we need to get feedback not from experts (who managed to make it through the initial learning phase – no matter how shoddy the resources available) but from neophytes. We need to get more feedback on what's currently making it hard for beginners to make progress, if we're to scale the industry and allow new colleagues to quickly get to the point of doing better than we do.

Of course, listening to newbies will work best if the newbies are talking to us; specifically, telling us what's going well and what's going wrong. A great way to encourage that is to lead by example. Unfortunately, it doesn't seem like this is popular. In the world of Objective-C programming, two great aggregators of blog content are **the Cocoa Literature List**–http://cocoalit.com and **iOS Dev Weekly**–http://iosdevweekly.com/issues/. Maybe I'm just getting jaded, but it seems like a lot of the content on both of those sites comprises tutorials and guides. These either rehash topics covered in the first-party documentation or demonstrate some wrapper class the author has created without going into much depth on the tribulations of getting there.

What we really need to understand, from neophytes to experienced developers alike, is actually closer to the content of **Stack Overflow**–http://www.stackoverflow.com than the content of the blogosphere. If lots of inexperienced programmers are having trouble working out how two objects communicate (and *plenty do*–http://stackoverflow.com/questions/6494055/set-object-in-another-class), then maybe OOP isn't an appropriate paradigm for people new to programming; or perhaps the way that it's taught needs changing.

So, this is a bit of a request for people who want to improve the field of programming to mine Stack Overflow and related sites to find out what the common problems are–trying to decide the experience level of any individual user can be difficult so organizing problems into "newbie problems" versus "expert problems" would be difficult. It's also a request for people who are having trouble to post more Stack Overflow questions. The reasons?

- Usually, in the process of crafting a good question, you end up working out what the answer is anyway. The effort isn't wasted on Stack Overflow; you can answer your own question when you post it, then everyone can see the problem and how you solved it.

- The reputation system (to a first approximation) rewards good questions and answers, so the chances that you'll get a useful answer to the question are high.

- Such questions and answers can then be mined as discussed above.

There are downsides, of course:

- Duplicate questions cannot easily be measured, because they're usually closed, and often deleted. Or people will find existing questions that cover the same ground (as they're supposed to, within the "rules") and not ask their duplicate. The voting system and view count have to be used as proxies to the "popularity" of a question; an inexact system.

- The voting system tends to reward received dogma over novel ideas or technical accuracy; upvoted answers are "popular," which is not the same as being "correct."

A better system for teaching programming would base its content on the total collection of all feedback received by instructors at programming classes ever. But we're unlikely to get that. In the meantime, Stack Overflow's pretty good. What I'm saying is that you shouldn't just share what you learn, you should share what you're stuck on too.

Opportunities to Learn

So, your training budgets used up, the conference you like was last month and won't be around for another year; is that it? When else are you going to get a chance to get yourself into the learning frame of mind?

All the time. Here are a couple of examples of how I squeeze a little extra study into life:

- I drive about an hour each way on my commute. That's two podcast episodes per day, ten per week.

- Once a week, my developer team has "code club," an hour-long meeting in which one member makes a presentation or leads a discussion. Everybody else is invited to ask questions or share their experiences.

- There's a little time at lunch to read some articles.

- I go to one or two local developer groups a month.

You don't necessarily need to deep-dive into some information in order to make use of it. Just knowing that it's out there and that you can find it again is enough to give it a space in your mental pigeonhole. When you've got a related problem in the future, you'll likely remember that you read about it in *this* article or made *that* note in Evernote. Then, you can go back and find the actual data you need.

Of course, conferences and training courses *are* great places to learn a lot. One reason is that you can (to some extent, anyway) put aside everything else and concentrate on what's being delivered.

Ranty aside

One of the saddest things to see at a conference is someone who's doing some work on their laptop instead of focusing on the session. They're missing out— not just on the content, but on the shared experience to talk about it with other delegates during the next break. It's not a good environment to work in because of the noise and the projected images, and they don't get anything out of the sessions either.

Rediscovering Lost Knowledge

You might think that, with software being such a fast-moving field, everything we're doing now is based on everything we were doing last year, with induction proving that there's a continuous unbroken history linking current practice to the "ENIAC girls" and Colossus wrens of the 1940s. In fact, the truth is pretty much the exact opposite of that; practices seen as out of date are just as likely to be rejected and forgotten as to be synthesized into modern practice.

As an example, I present my own experience with programming. I was born into the microcomputer revolution, and the first generation of home computers. Programming taught on these machines was based on either the BASIC language of the 1960s or using assemblers. The advances made by structured programming, object-oriented programming, procedural programming, and functional programming were all either ignored or thought of as advanced topics inappropriate to microprogramming. It wasn't until much later that I was introduced to "new" concepts such as 1973's C and had to come to grips with any form of code organization or modularity.

Armed with a history book, or a collection of contemporary literature, on computer programming, it's easy to see that I'm not alone in ignoring or losing earlier results in the discipline. After all, what is agile programming's "self-organizing team" but a reinvention of Weinberg's **adaptive programming**–http://dl.acm.org/citation. cfm?id=61465? Is there a clear lineage, or has the concept been reinvented? Is the "new" field of UX really so different from the "human-relations aspects" of Boehm's **software engineering economics**–https://dl.acm.org/citation.cfm?id=944370? As described in *Chapter 8, Documentation*, many developers no longer use UML; how long until UML is invented to replace it?

The Teaching Of Software Creation

My mitigation for the rediscovery problem outlined above could be that you undertake the heroic effort of discovering what's out there from nearly 70 years of literature, identify the relevant parts, and synthesize a view on software creation from that. That would be crazy. But in the short term, that's probably the only route available.

Like many people, I learned programming by experimentation, and by studying books and magazines of varying quality. This means that, like many programmers, my formative experiences were not guided (or tainted, depending on your position) by a consistent theory of the pedagogy of programming. Indeed, I don't think that one exists. Programming is taught differently by professional trainers and by university departments; indeed, it's taught differently by different departments in the same university (as I discovered, when I was teaching it in one of them).

There's no consistent body of knowledge that's applied or even referred to, and different courses will teach very different things. I'm not talking about differences at the idiomatic level, which are true across all types of teaching; you could learn the same programming language from two different teachers and discover two disjoint sets of concepts.

This is consistent with the idea of programming being merely a tool to solve problems; different courses will be written with solving different problems in mind. But it means there isn't a shared collection of experiences and knowledge among neophyte programmers; we're doomed to spend the first few years of our careers repeating everyone else's mistakes.

Unfortunately, I don't have a quick solution to this: all I can do is make you aware that there's likely to be *loads* of experience in the industry that you haven't even been able to make secondary use of. The effort to which you go to discover, understand, and share this experience is up to you, but hopefully this chapter has convinced you that the more you share knowledge with the community, the better your work and that of the community as a whole will be.

The particular material I learned from was long on descriptions of how operators work and how to use the keywords of the language, but short on organization, on planning, and on readability (There's an essay on what it means for code to be readable in *Chapter 11, Critical Analysis*); that is, on everything that's beyond writing code and goes into writing *usable* code. Yes, I learned how to use GOSUB, but not *when* to use GOSUB.

There's a lot of good material out there on these other aspects of coding. When it comes to organization, for example, even back when I was teaching myself programming, there were books out there that explained this stuff and made a good job of it: **The Structure and Interpretation of Computer Programs**–http://mitpress.mit.edu/sicp/full-text/book/book.html; **Object-Oriented Programming: an evolutionary approach**–http://books.google.co.uk/books/about/Object_oriented_programming.html?id=U8AgAQAAIAAJ&redir_esc=y; **Object-Oriented Software Construction**–http://docs.eiffel.com/book/method/object-oriented-software-construction-2nd-edition. The problem then was not that the information did not exist, but that I did not know I needed to learn it. It was, if you like, an unknown unknown.

You could argue that the organization of code is an intermediate or advanced topic, beyond the scope of an introductory book or training course. Or you could argue that while it *is* something a beginner should know, putting it in the same book as the "this is how you use the **+** operator" material would make things look overwhelmingly complex, and could put people off.

Firstly, let me put forward the position that neither of these is true. I argue from analogy with Roger Penrose's book **The Road to Reality**–http://books.google.co.uk/ books/about/The_Road_to_Reality.html?id=ykV8cZxZ80MC, which starts from fundamental math's (Pythagoras' theorem, geometry, and so on) and ends up at quantum gravity and cosmology. Each chapter is challenging, more so than the previous one, but can be understood, given an understanding of what came before. People (I included) have been known to spend years working through the book – working through the exercises at the end of each chapter before starting the next. And yet, it's a single book, barely more than 1,100 pages long.

Could the same be done for computing? Could a "The Road to Virtual Reality" take people from an introduction to programming to a comprehensive overview of software creation? I'll say this: the field is *much* smaller than theoretical physics.

Now, here's a different argument. I'll accept the idea that the field is either too big or too complex to all go into a single place, even for a strongly motivated learner. What's needed in this case is a curriculum: a guide to how the different parts of software creation are related, which build on the others, and a proposed order in which to learn them.

Such curricula exist, of course. In the UK, **A-level computing**–http://www.cie.org.uk/ qualifications/academic/uppersec/alevel/subject?assdef_id=738 doesn't just teach programming, but how to identify a problem that can be solved by a computer, design, and build that solution, and document it. Now where do you go from there? Being able to estimate the cost and risk associated with building the solution would be helpful; working on solutions built by more than one person; maintaining existing software; testing the proposed solution... These are all things that build on the presented topics. They're covered by *Postgraduate courses in software engineering*–http://www.cs.ox. ac.uk/softeng/courses/subjects.html; there's some kind of gap in between learning how to program and improving as a professional programmer, where you're on your own.

And these curricula are only designed for taught courses. Need the self-taught programmer be left out? (Some in the field would say, yes; that programming should be a professional discipline open only to professionals–or at least that there should be a designated *title* available only to those in the know, in the way that anybody can be a nutritionist but only the qualified may call themselves dieticians. Some of these people call themselves "software engineers" and think that software should be an exclusive profession, like an engineering discipline; others call themselves "software craftsmen" and use the mediaeval trade guilds as their models for exclusivity. I will leave my appraisal of those positions for later. But for now, it's worth reflecting on the implicit baggage that comes with *any* description of our work.)

There are numerous series of books on programming: the **Kent Beck signature series**–http://www.informit.com/imprint/series_detail.aspx?ser=2175138 on management methodologies and approaches to testing, for example, or the **Spring Into**–http://www.informit.com/imprint/series_detail.aspx?st=61172 series of short introductions.

These published series are often clustered around either the beginner level or are deep and focus on experienced developers looking for information on specific tasks. There's no clear route from one to the other, whether editorially curated by some publisher or as an external resource. Try a web search for "what programming books to read" and you'll get more than one result for every programmer who has opined on the topic–as Jeff Atwood has written about it more than once.

Building a curriculum is hard – harder than building a list of books you've read, and you'd like to pretend you'd read, then telling people they can't be a programmer until they read them. You need to decide what's really relevant and what to leave aside. You need to work out whether different material fits with a consistent theory of learning; whether people who get value from one book would derive anything from another. You need to decide where people need to get more experience, need to try things out before proceeding, and how appropriate it is for their curriculum to tell them to do that. You need to accept that different people learn in different ways and be ready for the fact that your curriculum won't work for everyone.

What all of this means is that there is still, despite 45 years of systematic computer science education, room for *multiple* curricula on the teaching of making software; that the possibility to help the next generation of programmers avoid the minefields that we (and the people before us, and the people before them) blundered into is open; that the "heroic effort" of rediscovery described at the beginning of this section needs be done, but only a small number of times.

Reflective Learning

Many higher education institutions promote the concept of **reflective learning** analyzing what you're learning introspectively and retrospectively, deciding what's gone well and what hasn't, and planning changes to favor the good parts over the bad. Bearing in mind what we've seen in this chapter – that there are manifold sources of information and that different people learn well from different media, reflective learning is a good way to sort through all of this information and decide what works for you.

This is far from being a novel idea. In his book **The Psychology of Computer Programming**–http://www.geraldmweinberg.com/Site/Home.html, Gerald M. Weinberg describes how some programmers will learn well from lectures, some from books, and some from audio recordings. Some will–as we saw when discussing the Kolb cycle–want to start out with experimentation, whereas others will want to start with the theory. As he tells us to try these things out and discover which we benefit from most, he's telling us to *reflect* on our learning experiences and use that reflection to improve those experiences.

Reflective learning is also a good way to derive lessons from your everyday experiences. I have a small notebook here in which, about 4 years ago, I wrote a paragraph every day based on the work I did that day. I thought about the problems I'd seen, and whether I could do anything to address them. I also thought about what had gone well and whether I could derive anything general from those successes. Here's an example entry:

*Delegated review of our code inspection process to [colleague]. Did I give him enough information, and explain why I gave him the task? Discovered a common problem in code I write, there have been multiple crashes due to inserting **nil** into a collection. In much ObjC, the **nil** object can be used as normal but not in collections, and I already knew this. Why do I miss this out when writing code? Concentrate on ensuring failure conditions are handled in future code & get help to see them in code reviews. Chasing a problem with [product] which turned out to be something I'd already fixed on trunk & hadn't integrated into my work branch. What could I have done to identify that earlier? Frequent integrations of fixes from trunk onto my branch would have obviated the issue.*

You don't necessarily have to write your reflections down, although I find that keeping a journal or a blog does make me structure my thoughts more than entirely internal reflection does. In a way, this very book is a reflective learning exercise for me. I'm thinking about what I've had to do in my programming life that isn't directly about writing code, and documenting that. Along the way, I'm deciding that some things warrant further investigation, discovering more about them, and writing about those discoveries.

11

Critical Analysis

Introduction

During your professional career, people will tell you things that aren't true. Sometimes they're lies, intended to manipulate or deceive; sometimes they're things that the speaker believes (or perhaps wants to believe), but on closer inspection don't pass muster; sometimes people will tell you things that *are* true, but irrelevant or of limited use, to persuade you of their position.

Who will be telling you these things? You've probably already thought of marketing and salespeople, desperate to get you or your company to take their product and win the commission. Speakers at conferences could do it too, trying to convince you that the technique, style, or strategy they're promoting is applicable to your situation in addition to theirs. The website for that new language you want to try out may be making exaggerated claims. Your manager or teammates may be trying a little too hard to sell you on their way of thinking.

There will also be plenty of occasions on which people tell you things that *are* true. Some of these could be surprising, especially if **common sense**–http://rationalwiki. org/wiki/Common_sense tells you the opposite is true; some of these could be suspicious; some you might be willing to accept without debate. Though there's no harm in questioning the **truthiness**–http://en.wikipedia.org/wiki/Truthiness of things, even when they are indeed true.

Critical analysis is about studying arguments to determine their well-formedness. In this context, an "argument" is a collection of statements affirming a particular position; it isn't a verbal sparring match between two people. An argument is well-formed if it contains some premises and reaches a conclusion logically derivable from those premises. Notice that such an argument is *well-formed*, not *correct*: the argument could rely on contested knowledge or the premises could be unsound for some other reason. Nonetheless, uncovering the rhetorical techniques and fallacies, if any, present in an argument can help you to understand the arguer's position and why they want you to agree with their conclusion, in addition to helping you decide whether you can agree with that conclusion.

Criticism Is Often Uncritical

"You're wrong." I hope that even without the information presented in the rest of this chapter, it's clear that the statement at the beginning of this chapter is not a well-formed argument. A fragment of a conclusion is presented (I'm wrong, but about what? This argument? Everything? Something in between? Is it my position that's wrong, or am I ethically abhorrent?), with no premises or deduction.

Criticism has come to mean expressing a negative opinion on some matter, but that's not the sense in which it's used here. The phrase "critical analysis" uses a more academic definition of the word critical. In this context, to be critical means to analyze both the pros and cons of an argument, to understand it in terms of the particular rules of argument formation, and to *discover* whether you find the conclusion to be agreeable. Many online discussions can be found that are entirely uncritical; the people taking part have decided on their positions in advance and are trying to find ways to more forcefully present their case and undermine the other.

Being faced with this sort of response can be frustrating. There's no value to be had from reading the counter argument; it's not critical, so it doesn't tell you *why* the other person disagrees with you. It's easy to take such responses personally though (on which, more later), and to get upset or angry at the person (or imagined person behind an online pseudonym). It's these factors that have led a minority of bloggers to switch off comments on their sites. It's easier to present an uninformed or uncritical argument than a well-thought-out one, therefore a large number of comments on the internet are of this unhelpful type.

Please do not be part of that problem. Read to understand, not to reply. If you're left with problems, try to formulate a rational explanation of why the argument presented did not discuss those problems. If it's still unclear after doing that, then by all means post your explanation. Both of you can probably learn from it.

How to Form an Argument?

Rather than describe how to analyze an argument, I'll explain how to construct one. It follows that critical analysis is the exploration of whether an argument contains high-quality versions of the features described here, linked coherently to support the conclusion or conclusions of the argument.

Though they need not be presented at the beginning of an argument (and indeed may not be explicit at all), any argument depends on a collection of assumptions or premises. These are statements accepted as true for the purpose of exploring the subject of the argument. The validity of any assumption depends on the context; in any field, some things are considered uncontested knowledge while others are contested. An example of uncontested knowledge in computing could be the features and operation of a universal Turing machine; the facts were documented and proven mathematically in the 1930s and are generally agreed to represent a sound base on which the rest of computer science is built. The assumption "Java is a useful language to teach beginners" would be considered contested knowledge, being far from universally accepted.

Such a contested assumption would need to be supported by external evidence that readers or listeners could evaluate to decide the validity of the assumption. In academic fields, acceptable evidence is usually restricted to reviewed literature. Indeed, it's possible to find papers that support the Java assertion made in the previous paragraph. In an academic argument, uncontested knowledge is roughly equivalent to "statements that are found in textbooks."

Almost tautologically, software creation practiced outside universities is not an academic discipline. There's little dependence on the formalities of academia and great reliance on personal or shared experiences. As a result, argument based on authority ("Martin Fowler says...") or on personal opinion ("I have found...") is often used to justify contested knowledge. In the latter case, the assumption could be presented as an intermediate conclusion: it follows from its own set of premises and is then used as input into a successive argument. Arguments outside those used in critical analysis textbooks are frequently built on chains of intermediate conclusions, combined with other premises to reach the eventual goal.

Arguments based on opinion or experience are easily, though not particularly usefully, undermined by the existence of people with differing opinions and experiences. Where these bases are used, the scope of the experience and the reasons for drawing particular opinions should be given as justification for reaching the stated conclusion.

The conclusion itself should be a position taken as a result of reasoning from the assumptions and intermediate conclusions. That is to say, it should be related to the premises; if you feel the need to confuse matters by introducing unrelated facts, then your argument is not particularly strong. The logical process of going from the premises to the conclusion, though potentially complex, should ideally be mechanistic; a "leap of faith" is inappropriate, and any lateral or otherwise devious steps should be explicit. Essay-style arguments are usually expected to reach their conclusions via deductive rather than inductive reasoning; appeals to analogy for example would be considered inappropriate. Practically speaking, as a programmer, you're more likely to be examining a sales pitch or a request from a customer than an academic essay, so the "rules" will be a lot looser.

The conclusion doesn't need to be the final part of the argument's presentation. Some writers open with the conclusion, to challenge the readers and get them thinking about how the argument might proceed, a technique also used in oral presentations of arguments. Occasionally, the conclusion comes after a bare-bones form of the argument, then further support is given to make the conclusion more compelling. In any case, the conclusion is often reiterated at the end of the argument; after all, it's the part you want to stick most in the minds of the readers or listeners.

Forms Of Fallacy

This section takes the form of a catalog, of sorts. It's not going to be complete and won't take a formal approach to describing the catalog in the same way that, for example, *Design Patterns* deals with its catalogue; a complete catalogue of fallacies would be at least as long as the rest of this book. A formal and consistent catalog would require planning.

Post Hoc, Ergo Propter Hoc

Translated, this means "After this, therefore because of this." Given two events, X and Y, the argument goes:

First X, then Y. Y was therefore caused by X.

This is a form of inductive reasoning that does not necessarily hold. Here's an absurd example:

The light turned red, and the car came to a halt. Red photons exert a strong retarding effect on cars.

In this case, there *could be* a causative relationship, but it is not as direct as the argument proposes.

Fundamental Attribution Error

Person P did X. Therefore, P is a moron.

This is also called correspondence bias. People often understand the situational basis for actions they take, but ascribe actions taken by others to their innate personalities. Here's a good example for coders to consider: if I take a shortcut, I'm being pragmatic, because of the pressures of the current project/iteration/whatever. If *you* were to take the same shortcut, it's because you don't understand sound software development principles.

Argument from Fallacy

This is a subtle one, but one that's quite easy to find in online discussions once you know about it:

Argument A says that X follows Y. Argument A is fallacious. Therefore, X does not follow Y.

Just because an argument contains a fallacy, it does not necessarily follow that its conclusion is incorrect. Consider this concrete example:

Isaac Newton's law of gravitation says that when I drop an object, it will fall to Earth because of a force called gravity. Einstein showed that gravity is in fact caused by the curvature of space-time. Newton was incorrect; therefore, the object will not fall to Earth when I drop it.

In fact, for pretty much every situation where Newton's law of gravity would predict that an object would fall to earth, so would Einstein's general relativity; and the object would indeed fall to Earth. Neither of these models would be in use if their predictions were not valid in certain scenarios, even though the *reasons* they give for the results they predict may not be what *actually* happens.

Continuum Fallacy

The continuum fallacy is one of the more frequently encountered fallacies in online arguments, particularly on media like Twitter, where the length of any statement is limited. The fallacy is to declare an argument incorrect because it is not satisfied in a particular condition. Going back to the example of gravitational theories, a continuum fallacy counterargument to Newton would be "Newton's **Law of Gravitation** does not predict the precession of Mercury's perihelion, therefore no result of Newton's Law has any value." In fact, within human-scale interactions, Newton's Law is very valuable; it gives reasonably accurate answers that are easy to compute. Einstein's theory is more general, giving answers consistent with Newton (and observation) at human scales *and* successfully predicting Mercury's motion. But Newton's significant baby need not be thrown out with the bathwater.

Here's a theory I have on the prevalence of the continuum fallacy in programmer discussions: our programming activities *train* us to look for and cover edge cases. Computers are, in the ways that most programmers use them most of the time, incapable of inductive reasoning. When dealing with a computer, then, a programmer must look for any situation that has not been discussed and explicitly state the results of meeting that situation. This training can lead to continuum fallacies in human interactions, where the programmer applies the same keen sense of edge-case detection to statements made by other people that were implicitly scoped or otherwise depended on induction in their correctness.

Slippery Slope

If X, then Y. Y, then Z. Z, then dogs and cats living together, mass hysteria.

A slippery slope retort is a popular rhetorical device for undermining an argument. If it's well-constructed, then the individual steps will each look plausible, though they actually represent successive continuum fallacies, or subtle straw-man variants on what was actually proposed. The end result will be absurd or, to the arguer's mind anyway, highly undesirable.

Begging the Question

This term has a specific meaning in the jargon of critical thinking, which is separate from its casual use as "an argument that raises an obvious question." Formally, an argument begs the question if it is made valid by accepting the conclusion as an implicit assumption: X, therefore X. Theological arguments sometimes beg the question; consider **this argument**–http://rationalwiki.org/wiki/Begging_the_question):

The order and magnificence of the world is evidence of God's Creation. Therefore, God exists.

The first statement is only true if you assume that God exists to have created the "order and magnificence of the world"; so, the argument is simply "God exists because God exists."

Appeal to Novelty

This is also called "argumentum ad novitatem" and says that something that's newer is better just because of its novelty. It's common to see in discussions of which technology is "better," particularly in vendor marketing material: our product is newer than the competitor's product, which means it must be better (This fallacy underpins the *completely rewritten from the ground up*–http://blog.securemacprogramming. com/2013/04/on-rewriting-your-application/ software product marketing position).

It doesn't take more than a few seconds of thought to construct questions that circumvent ad novitatem fallacies: just think about what would *actually* make one of the options a better choice. If you need relational, table-based storage, then a new NoSQL database would be worse than an RDBMS, despite being newer, for example.

Appeal to the Person

More commonly known by its Latin name, argumentum ad hominem, this fallacy takes the following form:

P says X. P is [an idiot, a communist, a fascist, smelly, or some other undesirable property]. Therefore, not X.

Leaving aside interpersonal arguments, it's common to see ad hominem arguments deployed in software architecture justifications. "We're not using that, because it's from [Google, Apple, Microsoft, Apache, and so on]" is the tech-industry version.

Is there any substance underlying this position? "We're not using that, because it's from Apple and Apple don't offer the support terms we need" could be a good argument. "We're not using that, because it's from Apple and I don't like them" might not be.

Further Reading on Arguments

This has been a brief overview of the critical analysis of arguments, telling you first why I think it's important, then giving a little information about what's involved. Many more eloquent writers than I have bent themselves to this task, so there are good resources to recommend for exploring this topic further.

Rational Wiki–http://rationalwiki.org/wiki/Main_Page is mainly a website for debunking pseudoscience, crank claims, and biased presentation of the news. It has a comprehensive section on logic, argument, and fallacies. **Less Wrong**–http://lesswrong.com has a similar scope, and finally, the Skeptics Stack Exchange–http://skeptics.stackexchange.com Q&A site features community-scored arguments in support or refutation of a wide variety of positions on different topics. (Refutation means constructing an argument against a presented point of view; *repudiation* means to deny the truth of an opposing argument without justification. However, both words are commonly used to mean repudiation, and depending on the historical meanings of words this is itself *a form of equivocation*–http://en.wikipedia.org/wiki/Etymological_fallacy.)

Debates and Programmers

Having just concluded the previous section with a footnote on the dangers of the etymological fallacy, it's time for another "there's a specific meaning to this word" section. While debating is commonly taken to mean two or more people expressing different views on the same topic, debates usually have rules dictating the forms in which arguments are presented and either a way of choosing a "winner" or of reaching a consensus view on the topic.

A specific example of a debating system with rules (which also has the benefit that I'm familiar with it) is the Oxford-style debate. The debate's topic is defined by a motion, in the form "this house moves to [X]." The audience votes on whether they are for or against the motion (or they can abstain). Two speakers, or teams of speakers, then present arguments, one in favor of and one in opposition of the motion. Unlike essay-style arguments, rhetoric and appeal to emotion are important parts of the presentations.

After the two presentations, a moderator directs a question-and-answer session with questions asked by the audience. After this, speakers give short closing presentations, then the audience votes again. The debate is "won" by the side that swings the vote in its favor (so, if 5% of the audience opposed the motion before the debate and 7% opposed it afterward, the opposition could win despite the majority either abstaining or being for the motion).

The skills practiced in a competitive debate are of course mainly the construction of persuasive arguments, with the interesting twist that you could be required to debate the position you don't agree with. That's not easy, but it does lead to a deep exploration of the topic and questioning the reasons that you disagree with the assigned position.

As explored in **The Leprechauns of Software Engineering**–https://leanpub.com/leprechauns, a lot of programming practice is based on folk knowledge (or common sense) that turns out to have a shaky evidential basis. Now, we know from research in human-computer interaction that a **satisficient**–http://www.interaction-design.org/encyclopedia/satisficing.html solution–one that isn't optimal but is "good enough" to get by–allows us to get our work done. Isn't it worth questioning these satisficing approaches to building software, and trying to find optimal approaches instead?

Debates would be good vehicles for such questioning, because of the equal weight given to supporting and countering a motion. Someone would be responsible for identifying problems or weaknesses in the folk knowledge and presenting a compelling argument to knock it down. As a *gedankenexperiment*, could you construct an argument opposing the motion "this house moves to make **version control mandatory**–http://www.neverworkintheory.org/?p=457 on all software projects"?

Software as Essays

Remember, in *Chapter 8, Documentation*, that I said code only tells you *what* the software is doing; it's hard to use it to interpret *how* it's doing it and impossible to discover *why* without some supporting material. You also have to think about *who* is doing the interpreting; understanding the written word, executable, or otherwise, is a subjective process that depends on the skills and experiences of the reader.

You could imagine an interpretation in the form of an appeal to satisfaction: who was the author writing for, and how does the work achieve the aim of satisfying those people? What themes was the author exploring, and how does the work achieve the goal of conveying those themes? These questions were, until the modern rise of literary theory, keyways in which literary criticism analyzed texts.

Let's take these ideas and apply them to programming. We find that we ask of our programmers not "can you please write readable code?" but "can you consider what the themes and audience of this code are, and write in a way that promotes the themes among members of that audience?" The themes are the problems you're trying to solve, and the constraints on solving them. The audience is, well, it's the audience; it's the collection of people who will subsequently have to read and understand the code. This group can be considered to be somewhat exclusive; just as there's no point writing code for features you don't need, there's no point writing it for an audience who won't read it.

We also find that we can no longer ask the objective-sounding question "did this coder write good code?" Nor can we ask, "is this code readable?" Instead, we ask "how does this code convey its themes to its audience?" The mark of readable code is not merely how the code is structured; it's how the code is interpreted by the reader. It's whether the code convinces the reader of the author's implicit argument, "this is what the code should do."

In conclusion, then, a sound approach to writing readable code requires authors and readers to meet in the middle. Authors must decide who will read the code, and how to convey the important information to those readers. Readers must analyze the code in terms of how it satisfies this goal of conveyance, not whether they enjoyed the indentation strategy or dislike dots in principle.

Source code is not software written in a human-readable notation. It's an essay, written in executable notation. The argument is that the code as presented is the solution to its problem. But the code must both *solve* this problem and *justify* the solution with coherent and rational explanations.

12

Business

Introduction

This chapter is a bit like the Roman god, Janus. Janus was the gatekeeper of heaven and had two faces. One of Janus' faces looked forward and the other backward; his name survives in the month January – looking forward to the new year and backward to the year that has passed.

This chapter similarly has two faces: one looks outward, from the perspective of a developer to the business that this person finds themselves interacting with; the other looks inward, from the perspective of the business to the developer. To keep things exciting, the narrative changes between these positions more than once.

"But I'm self-employed," I hear some of you saying. You still engage in business activities. You might have to justify your work to your client rather than your manager, but the concepts remain the same.

Even if you're a junior developer with plenty of levels of management above you, it still pays to understand the business you're in and how your work fits into the company's goals. Reasons for this begin with the cynical: you'll probably be expected to take a "bigger picture" or strategic view of your work to progress up the pay scale. But it's also going to be helpful; if you know what the business pressures are, you can understand why management is coming up with the suggestions and rules that they are.

If you *are* a junior programmer, this is likely to be the biggest change that helps your career progression (and, unfortunately, was one I learned the hard way). If all you see is the code, then all you see in management decisions is people getting in the way of writing code. They actually have different pressures, different inputs, and different experiences, so it's unsurprising that those people have come up with different priorities. Understanding that is the first step towards empathizing with their position and becoming a more valuable member of the team.

Evaluate Risks Dispassionately

On any project, there are things that could go wrong. Are you being realistic about them? What are the things that *have* gone wrong on projects you've worked on before? Did you consider the risk of those going wrong this time around? Did you think about how you might control the things that led to them going wrong?

According to some researchers in the field of disaster response, there are *five considerations in risk estimation*, leading to five different ways to get risk management wrong:

- Incorrect evaluation of probability (usually presented as optimism bias – the false belief that nothing can go wrong)

- Incorrect evaluation of impact (again, usually assuming, optimistically, that the damage won't be too great)

- Statistical neglect (ignoring existing real data in forecasting future outcomes, usually in favor of folklore or other questionable heuristics)

- Solution neglect (not considering all options for risk reduction, thus failing to identify the optimal solution)

- External risk neglect, in which you fail to consider factors outside the direct scope of the project that could nonetheless have an impact

Project Risks

Reminiscence of my experience making—and then failing to meet—estimates leads me to believe that ignoring risks leads to unmet schedule expectations more often than underestimating the time required to do the work. In other words, "oh I thought this would take 3 days but it took me 5" does happen, but less frequently than "oh I thought this would take 3 days and it did but I was taken off the project for 2 days by this other thing."

Techniques such as **the velocity factor**—https://resources.collab.net/agile-101/agile-scrum-velocity and **evidence-based scheduling**—http://www.joelonsoftware.com/items/2007/10/26.html) try to account for both of these impacts by comparing estimated completion time with actuals and providing a "fudge factor" by which to multiply subsequent estimates.

Assuming that both scheduling failures and external interruptions follow a Poisson distribution, that fudge factor should be roughly correct (given infinite prior data as input, which might be tricky to arrange). But then if that assumption's valid, you could just build a Poisson model (such as, as Spolsky suggests in the above link, a Monte Carlo simulation) to guess how the project will go.

Business Risks

At time of writing, the world of the Twitter client author has just been changed by updates to **Twitter's Developer Rules of the Road**—https://developer.twitter.com/en/developer-terms/agreement-and-policy.html. The company is limiting the number of client tokens any app can have before discussing their case with Twitter. They're also strongly discouraging (as they have done before) the standard "Twitter client" product category, suggesting that developers avoid developing that sort of product.

It's clear that, for a Twitter client app, Twitter is a single point of failure. Indeed, at a technical level, the service still occasionally suffers from short outages. But it's also a single point of failure at the *business* level—if they don't want to support what you want to do, there's little chance of it happening on their platform. It's not like you can point to how much you've paid them and would continue to pay them; the platform is free to developers and users alike.

Are there any companies or platforms that could similarly pull the rug out from under your business? What's the likelihood of that happening, and what will you do either to avoid or to react to it? What competitors do you have, and how does their behavior affect your plans? What patents might your work infringe on? And, in these days of cloud computing, how important is the San Andreas Fault or an Atlantic hurricane to your business?

Operational Risks

Operational risks are defined as risks arising from the potential for an organization's internal processes to fail. Perhaps your data recovery plan isn't resilient to losing your main office: that might be an operational risk. A salesperson failing to store a customer's information in the CRM, leading to a missed follow-up call and therefore a lost sales opportunity, is also an operational risk.

Of course, some level of operational risk is acceptable. Internal processes do not generate any profit, so gold-plating them means sinking a lot of cost in return for smaller losses rather than greater income. This is, in my experience, the ultimate end for utility and commodity companies, where getting something wrong is a bigger danger than any external factors. Internal processes will ossify as operational risks are removed, pushing costs up as reduced prices squeeze the margins from the other side.

Bad management decisions can also be classed as operational risks, as they represent internal processes of a sort.

Other External Risks

Are there regulatory risks to your business? Many software companies, particularly those in social networks and mobile apps, are starting to find that **California's Online Privacy Protection Act**–http://www.pcworld.com/article/2018966/california-sues-delta-airlines-over-app-privacy-policy.html is relevant to their work, even though they aren't necessarily based in California (Apple and Google, their exclusive distributors, *are* based in California).

Which rules or laws could change that would affect what your company does? Are those changes likely to happen? How would you have to modify what you do to take the new regulations into account, and are you prepared for that?

Is your pricing correct? If you reduced your price, you would increase unit sales; if you increased your price, you would increase revenue per sale. Which is the best route to take? Is your current price optimal? Michael Jurewitz, then of Black Pixel, wrote **a series of detailed posts** on this topic, using one particular model of software pricing:

- http://jury.me/blog/2013/3/31/understanding-app-store-pricing-part-1
- http://jury.me/blog/2013/3/31/understanding-app-store-pricing-part-2
- http://jury.me/blog/2013/3/31/understanding-app-store-pricing-part-3
- http://jury.me/blog/2013/3/31/understanding-app-store-pricing-part-4
- http://jury.me/blog/2013/4/1/understanding-app-store-pricing-part-5-pricing-kaleidoscope

Career Risks

That thing you're doing now. Yes, that thing. Eww, no, not *that* thing; the other thing. Will you still be doing it in 10 years?

Here's a hint: the answer's probably "no." Not *definitely* no, but probably no. Here's what I was doing in 2002:

- Learning condensed matter physics and particle physics

- Waiting for the success of desktop Linux

- Teaching myself Objective-C programming

- Coding in Perl and Pascal

Of those, it's only really Objective-C that's at all relevant to what I do now; maybe I pull Perl out once a year or less. (Of course, many people *are* still waiting for desktop Linux, so maybe I just quit too easily.) So, of the things you're doing now, which will still be around in 10 years? Which will be recognizably the same as they currently are?

And what are you doing about that? Of course, education is part of the solution; there's *Chapter 10, Learning*, in this book. But this section's about dispassionately evaluating risks, and that's important too: put aside what you *want* to be doing in 10 years' time. Sure, you *could* focus on writing iOS apps in Objective-C in 2022, just as you *could* be focused on writing Mac Carbon software or Palm Treo apps in 2012.

Will what you're doing now still be important then? Will it have been replaced by something else? If so, will it be from the same vendor? Even if it still exists, will there still be enough money in it for you to support yourself? And if the answers are no: what will you do before it happens?

Dealing with Risks

It's possible to get paralyzed by indecision: should we proceed before we have understood and controlled *all* the risks that could be faced by the company? That mentality won't be very profitable; essentially, profit can be seen as a return on taking risks.

You can decide what risks are important by evaluating their likely costs. Some people do this in a currency unit (that is, dollars it'll cost to recover from this happening times the probability of it happening in a given time period); others do it in abstract units such as high/medium/low likelihood and impact. Either way, the outcome is a list of risks ranked by importance, and it's easy to choose a low watermark, below which you just accept any risks.

Acceptance (or "sucking it up") is a very cheap way to deal with a risk. Other ways include:

- **Withdrawal**: Remove any likelihood and impact of a risky event occurring by refusing to participate in the risky activity. Withdrawing from the activity certainly mitigates any risk very reliably, but it also means no possibility of gaining the reward associated with participation.

- **Transference**: You can opt to transfer the risk to another party, usually for a fee: this basically means taking out insurance. This doesn't affect the probability that our risky event will come to pass but means that someone else is liable for the damages.

- **Countermeasures**: Finding some technical or process approach to reduce the risk. This means, of course, one or more of limiting its likelihood or the expected damage. But think about deploying these countermeasures: you've now made your business or your application a bit more complex. Have you introduced new risks? Have you increased the potential damage from some risks by reducing others? And, of course, is your countermeasure cost-effective? You don't want to spend $1,000 to save $100.

Personal Experience

Being mainly experienced in writing iOS apps, Apple is of course a single point of failure in my work. If they change the platform in ways I can't adapt to, I'll be out of luck: but I don't think that's very likely. They've shown (and said at their developer conferences) that they plan to iterate on their current platform for the foreseeable future.

On the other hand, they can and *do* reject applications that are inconsistent with their submission guidelines. My approach here has been twofold: firstly, to use the process countermeasure of planning apps that aren't obviously inconsistent with the guidelines. Secondly, transference: I don't sell any of the software I make myself, but sell development services (whether as an employee, consultant, or contractor) to people who themselves take on the risks associated with getting the products to market.

Find Out What You Need to Know, And How You Can Know It

True story: I thought about opening this segment with the Donald Rumsfeld "there are the known knowns" quote. It didn't take long to find that he wasn't the first person to say that: here's Ibn Yamin, taken from the *Wikipedia entry for the Rumsfeld speech*– http://en.wikipedia.org/wiki/There_are_known_knowns:

One who knows and knows that he knows... His horse of wisdom will reach the skies.

One who knows, but doesn't know that he knows... He is fast asleep, so you should wake him up!

One who doesn't know, but knows that he doesn't know... His limping mule will eventually get him home.

One who doesn't know and doesn't know that he doesn't know... He will be eternally lost in his hopeless oblivion!

The thing is that, had I not looked this up, I could've confidently attributed that idea to Rumsfeld. "Aha," thinks I, "I've shown an example of thinking I know what I'm doing when I really don't. This is classic **Dunning-Kruger Effect**–http://rationalwiki.org/wiki/Dunning-Kruger_effect."

Then, of course, ready to find and cite their Ig Nobel-winning paper, I spied the Darwin quote at the linked rationalwiki page:

Ignorance more frequently begets confidence than does knowledge

In each of these cases, armed with an idea of what I wanted to say, it only took one web search to find:

- A claim (that I could verify) that the idea was earlier than I imagined; which also served as...

- ...a reminder that I don't know everything about what I'm writing.

It's really *that* easy to go from "thinking you know what you're talking about" to "realizing you don't know very much." That means it's probably best to assume that you don't know very much; particularly, if you're facing a new challenge you haven't dealt with before.

The way I like to help along this realization when I'm planning is to spend about 5 minutes with an outline tool such as **OmniOutliner** or **iThoughts** HD, just writing down questions that are relevant to the problem at hand. Even that small amount of work gives me a plan for later research, and the humility needed to follow it up.

What You Discover May Not Be to Your Liking

Sometimes, you'll look at the results of the research you've done and realize that things don't look promising.

Perhaps there aren't as many customers for your product as you first assumed, development is going to be harder, or you've found a competing product you didn't know about before. Perhaps the task you estimated would take 2 days is going to take longer than a week.

You need to decide what you're going to do about that. The *worst* way to do this is by ignoring the problem: you're relying on luck or on faith to get you through. You're cleverer than that; you can think of a plan to overcome the problem.

Personal Experience

One of the first software projects I worked on had a team of three developers, none of whom had much experience with the technology we were using, and two of whom (myself included) didn't really have much experience of anything.

As we progressed with the project, we found that it was taking us longer than we planned to deliver each build and that the builds were very buggy. We convinced ourselves that we could make up for it in the *next* build each time, even though this would mean coming in *under* schedule (something we hadn't demonstrated we could do), *and* at sufficient quality (ditto), *and* finding time to fix all the existing bugs.

Eventually, our manager had to stop us and point out that for every day of new work we were doing, we were adding 3 days of bugfix work. In other words, the project would never be finished if we didn't change what we were doing.

Contrast that with a project I worked on very recently. Looking at the plan, it was clear that some parts of the software would put significant computational load on the target hardware, and there was a real risk that the full functionality couldn't be delivered because it wouldn't run at an acceptable speed.

I therefore wrote these parts of the application *first*, leaving the standard data-handling parts until later. Sure enough, within 3 weeks, we'd found that there were observable performance problems and we couldn't continue until we'd found a way to address them.

It worked out that this pushed the schedule out by over a week – in other words, the project was delayed. But because we'd been open about this being a potential problem, had identified it, and addressed it as early as possible, this impact could be handled and didn't cause any great friction.

Other books have covered this ground; a good place to go for an alternative discussion is the *pivot or persevere* section in *Chapter 8, The Lean Startup by Eric Ries*—http://theleanstartup.com/book.

How to Interview A Programmer?

I've been on both sides of job interviews for technical positions. I've seen both success and failure (on both sides: my own success rate is currently at around 2/3, where I count a job that I left after 2 months as a failure). This isn't the definitive guide to running an interview, or to being interviewed, but it's a good guide to what interviewers should be looking for. As a result, it's also a good guide to what interviewees can assume interviewers are looking for. How meta!

Bear the Goal in Mind

The goal of an interview is to find out—often in only an hour or so—whether you could work with the person you're talking to daily without one of the two of you going insane. Some people phrase this as whether you could spend 8 hours trapped in an airport with just the interviewee to talk to. Imagine that, but 5 days a week for the next 2 years.

Find out enough about their technical skills to decide whether they were lying on their CV. You don't need to probe them on the depth of their skills beyond that; if you didn't think their CV expressed enough relevant experience for them to be good at the role, you wouldn't have invited them in for an interview.

This focus on the interpersonal side is especially true of interviews for interns, graduates, and other positions where you don't expect applicants to bring much experience to the table. In these cases, you *can't* rely on technical questions to carry the interview—almost by definition, the best candidate will probably be unable to provide many answers. Rather than making candidates uncomfortable by showing how much more you know than them, make them comfortable and find out whether they'll be good people to work with.

The Interview's There for Both of You

When I was a fresh graduate, I assumed that the purpose of a job interview was to put on my best suit (My *only* suit, at the time) and convince other people to let me work for them. I now know this not to be true, though I still encounter people who behave in this way. I feel that either the real purpose of an interview is being kept secret or careers services don't think people need to be told about it.

The real purpose of an interview is to find out whether you want to work for that company. Is the interviewer—who will most likely be your colleague or supervisor—someone you'd want to work with? Is the job actually what was advertised? Does it still seem interesting? Do they mention all sorts of extra responsibilities that weren't in the advert? Are the people you're talking to enthusiastic about the company? Where is the business going over the time you envisage being there, and beyond? Do you like that direction? Will you get the freedom and/or supervision that you need?

If you treat the interview as an advert for your ability to fit in with the hirer's needs, then they'll end up with someone who doesn't actually work as they claimed in the interview, and you'll end up with a job you don't know much about.

What If You Could Avoid Hypothetical Questions?

Whichever side of the interview you're on, avoid questions that investigate what would happen if some conjectural situation came to pass. The answer is always the same.

Q: *What would you do if you had a tight deadline?*

A: *Whatever the perfect employee would do.*

Q: *What would you do if a colleague came to you needing help?*

A: *Whatever the perfect employee would do.*

Or, from the other position:

Q: *What would you do if Google moved into this business?*

A: *Whatever the perfect company would do.*

Q: *What would you do if your main competitor suddenly introduced a huge killer feature?*

A: *Whatever the perfect company would do.*

You will not find out anything useful by asking these questions. You'll discover how the person opposite you pictures the land of milk and honey; this may be interesting if you're into armchair psychology but is ultimately not going to tell you what would *actually* happen in such situations.

Instead, try to discover what *did* happen when those situations occurred.

Q: *What did you do the last time you had a tight deadline?*

A: *I shouted at my colleagues, told my manager everything was fine, and quit work the day before the build was due.*

Q: *How did the company react when Google brought out a similar product?*

A: *The executive team cashed in their stock options. Then they closed R&D to focus on our core business.*

Admittedly, these answers are not as pleasant as the first ones. But they're more specific, more indicative of real behavior, and therefore of what would likely happen should these situations ever arise again. Ultimately, these are better things to discover.

Don't Try to Prove the Other Person Is Stupid

If you've ever been in the Q&A period at the end of a conference talk, you know that it attracts a certain type of person. There'll always be a question that goes–though this wording is changed to make it sound like a question–"I know more about this than you." This is poisonous to the atmosphere of the gathering: the asker looks rude, the answerer is wrong-footed, and the audience learns nothing from the interaction – apart from maybe to avoid working with the person who asked the question.

Now consider what happens if you're in an interview and manage to teach the other people in the room not to work with you. You'll potentially miss out on either a good job or a good candidate, depending on which side of the desk you're sitting.

It's fine–nay, **required**–that different people on a team think and know different things. If you have two people on a team who both bring exactly the same knowledge and opinions, one of them is redundant. This was told to me by a former manager of mine. Needless to say, I disagreed in order to remain employable.

You may know something the other person in the interview doesn't, but you shouldn't crow about it. Instead, you should discover what the other person does when faced with a lack of information. There will be more on this topic in the section on *working with business partners*.

Personal Experience

My first job out of university included, among other things, managing a heterogeneous Unix network. When I started in that job, I asked my manager, John, for feedback about the interview (you should always do this, whether or not you were offered the job).

The interview was a setup that's turned out to be quite common in my experience: I sit on one side of a desk with a few people (the hiring manager, an HR person, and a technical expert) across the way. A "novel" feature was a UNIX workstation sat between us, which had two monitors and two keyboards.

Apparently, the one feature of my interview that stuck in the panel's mind was when I was asked a question that I didn't know the answer to. None of the other candidates knew either; I don't remember the exact question, but it had something to do with getting a list ordered by time of all of the hard links to a particular file on a filesystem.

When I said I didn't know how to do it, the technical guy could've easily rushed to demonstrate how much better at UNIX he was than me, but he didn't. He, like the other interviewers, did nothing. While I mumbled something I was thinking about and sweated into my shirt collar, I pulled the stunt that made my interview memorable and helped me to get the job.

I typed `man ls` *into the Terminal. The interviewers could see that I typed* `man ls` *into the terminal, because they had a monitor on the workstation too. They could see that I didn't know what I was doing. They could also see that I wanted to know what I was doing, and I knew how to attack this problem.*

The interview moved on before I solved the problem, but the interviewers discovered what they wanted because they didn't stop to point out how clever they were.

Be Transparent and Honest with Your Business Partners

I don't just mean "business partners" as people with whom you entered into business, or even other companies with whom you have a partnership arrangement. I mean everybody you work with in order to get the project completed: you should treat all of these people as peers, whose help you need, and who need your help in order to deliver a quality product to your customers. If you want their respect, honesty, and help you need to be respectful, honest, and helpful to them.

Currently, this sounds like the sort of hackneyed non-lesson in working with others that has remained unchanged for the last few thousand years: "do as you would be done by." But bear with me; there's more science to it than that.

Have you ever described someone, or heard someone described, as "clueless"? They "just don't get it"? You've probably experienced the **correspondence effect**–http://en.wikipedia.org/wiki/Fundamental_attribution_error, a well-studied effect in social psychology. If *you* make a suboptimal decision, it's because of the deadline pressure, compromises to incorporate other people's requirements, and other local problems. If *someone else* makes a suboptimal decision, it's because they're an idiot. Interestingly, they believe that *their* mistakes are due to the situation they find themselves in, and that *your* mistakes come about because *you* are the idiot.

Perhaps neither of you is the idiot. Perhaps both of you are trying to do your best at reconciling conflicting needs and pressures. Perhaps your opinions on what to do next differ because you have different information about the problem, not because one of you is a genius and the other a moron.

That's why transparency is key. If you proclaim "we should do this" or even "we *will* do this" with no supporting information, you leave the other people in the conversation free to conclude *why* you think that – free to get it wrong. Alternatively, you could say "here's the problem as I see it, this is what we want to get out of solving it, and here is the solution." Now your colleagues and partners are left in no doubt as to why you believe in the approach you present, and you've set a precedent for how they should present their views if they still disagree. The conversation can focus on the problems facing the project, not the imbeciles around the table.

> **An Aside On Persuasion**
>
> Framing an argument in this way is a well-known rhetorical technique. First, people identify themselves as facing the problem you describe, so that when you describe the benefits of a solution, your audience agrees that it would help. When you finally present your proposed solution, people already know that they want it. *Nancy Duarte's talk at TEDxEast*—https://www.duarte.com/presentation-skills-resources/nancys-talk-from-tedxeast-you-can-change-the-world/ goes into more depth on this theme.

Of course, people may still disagree with your conclusions and the reasons you reached them. Listen to their arguments. Ask why (if they didn't already tell you). Remember that this is software development, not a high school debating club: you "win" by creating a great product that satisfies a business problem, not by ensuring that your argument is accepted over all others.

Choose Appropriate Technology

As the last sentence of the previous section says, the goal here is to satisfy a business need. If that business need isn't aligned with your current favorite platform or shiny toy, you have to decide which you want to pursue. The best choice for the business – and, therefore, for your role in it as a developer – is the one that achieves the goal with least effort and fewest difficulties or compromises.

Of course, "effort" can include training – a short (and usually fixed length) effort needed to get developers and others up to speed with some new technology. But then "effort" also includes maintenance and support – ongoing costs that build up over the lifetime of the product in the field. This is sometimes ignored when estimating a project's cost, as the project ends on the ship date, so maintenance is somebody else's problem. That's a false economy though; the maintenance cost of a project is very much the problem of the project team.

Aside: Opportunity Cost

No cost analysis is complete without a measure of "opportunity cost." The opportunity cost of an activity can be thought of as the answer to the question "what will we miss out on doing if we're doing this thing instead?"

So, the actual cost of an activity includes the direct costs (equipment, staff, and so on required) and the opportunity costs; there may also be other negative aspects that are considered "costs."

On the flip side, the benefit includes more than simply the money made from a sale. It can include "defended income"—existing customers who do not switch to a competitor as a result of doing the work you're planning. Other benefits can include improved reputation or market position.

This has all been a bit Economics 101, but for people who work with exact numbers all day, it's important to remember that a full cost/benefit analysis does not simply involve subtracting money out from money in.

Factoring opportunity costs into maintenance work causes multiple hits. There's the direct cost of fixing the problems; there's the opportunity cost to your development team, as you must take on less new project work while you're fixing the maintenance problems; and then there's the opportunity cost to the customers, who lose time working around the problems and deploying the maintenance fixes. I'll stop short of quoting *how much* more expensive maintenance fixes are; *I've made that mistake before–* http://blog.securemacprogramming.com/2012/09/an-apology-to-readers-of-test-driven-ios-development/.

Another way to look at this technology choice consideration is a quote I heard from **Jonathan "Wolf" Rentzsch**, though he certainly isn't the original source:

All code you write is a liability, not an asset.

There's a good discussion of the quote at *Eric Lee's blog* on MSDN–http://blogs.msdn.com/b/elee/archive/2009/03/11/source-code-is-a-liability-not-an-asset.aspx. If your favorite platform would mean writing more code to solve the problem than using some other, then selecting that platform would mean taking on a greater liability. We have a phrase to describe the problem of doing work to solve a problem that's already been solved, one that we use mainly when *other* people are guilty of this: *Not Invented Here*.

All of this means that, to some extent, you have to put your personal preferences aside when designing a software system and choosing the technology that will go into it. But that isn't a bad thing; it's a chance to learn even more.

Manipulation and Inspiration

In the previous section, I touched on rhetoric and persuasion. As in any collaborative activity, these are great tools when used judiciously and dangerous weapons at all other times.

My opinions on business issues are all based on a philosophy of playing a long game. That's why I argue for choosing the right technology even if that means retraining or going slower in the short term for other reasons. If the end result is a better product, you'll have a more satisfied team, happier customers, and more repeat business and referrals.

In relation to persuasion, the long game is epitomized by inspiring people to follow your path, not manipulating them to do what you want. What's the difference? To me, inspiration is about showing people that what you propose is the best option. Manipulation is pejorative, convincing people to follow some course despite the shortcomings to them or to others.

Manipulation often means running the risk of getting "caught out," as your mark discovers the true reason behind your ruse or the pitfalls it entails. You then end up having to hide or play down these issues, until your manipulative example becomes degenerate with or even more expensive than doing the right thing.

Worked Example: An App Store Sale

Let's look at this distinction between manipulation and inspiration by examining the case of selling an app in one of the mobile app stores.

The usual approach to selling apps is to charge a one-off cost on initial purchase, as is the case with boxed software. This could suggest a manipulative approach to sales; we want to get someone as far as buying the app, but don't care what they do after that. Indeed, updates to the software are usually distributed for free, so perhaps we'd prefer it if they never used the software after purchase.

The manipulative take, then, would be to put minimal effort into building the product, and more work into describing its features and benefits on the product page. People will see our effusive description of the app and will be all too happy to pay for the download. By the time they've realized that the product page is a lie and the app isn't as good as we claimed, we won't care because we've got their money.

One big problem with the above approach is that it only works for a short while. In the longer term, customers will talk to each other. They'll read the reviews of the app in the store and on other websites, and they'll discover that the app isn't all that we claim. We're going to have to convince the reviewers to write good things about the app.

We could try paying them off ("astroturfing" – the practice of creating fake grass-roots support) but that doesn't scale well; besides, it still leaves the possibility that unwanted "honest" reviews outside our control will be published.

Another way to get good reviews is to create a good product. If people genuinely enjoy using the thing, then they'll gladly tell other people how good it is. Now our victims^Wpotential customers will see the reviews left by other happy customers and will want a piece of the action. Success! We've tricked people into buying our app, and all we had to do was... make a great app.

It's not just in interactions with customers that this tension between short- and long-term benefits can arise – in fact, it will happen anywhere and everywhere in life. It's good to keep your trade-off thermostat somewhere towards the long-term end of the scale, because (hopefully!) your career will long outlast your current project.

It's with this in mind that I come back to the subject of this section: favoring inspiration over manipulation. You don't want your reputation as you go into your next challenge to be based on the sour taste people experience as they remember working with you on this one.

But you *do* need people to see the project and its challenges from your perspective, and you *do* need the help of other people to get everything done. This is where the inspiration comes in. Inspiration should really be about stimulating other people, not about cajoling them. If what you want to do is beneficial for everyone involved, it shouldn't take any special tricks to make other people want to do it too. The details on how to do that are best left to *Chapter 13, Teamwork.*

You Don't Need to Be A Founder to Be A Programmer

Thanks to **Rob Rhyne**–http://twitter.com/capttaco *and* **Saul Mora**–http://twitter.com/casademora *for inspiring this section in their NSBrief interview.*

As software developers, we live in a great time to start your own business. One person, working with a few freelancers and using some online services, can get an app out in a few months with very little outlay. Success stories abound of programmers who've quit working for "the man" to "go indie" – in other words, to start their own software company.

> ### An aside on confirmation bias
>
> One reason that there are so many success stories from small business founders is that the failures don't get invited to give talks. In fact, some people claim that *9 out of 10 new businesses fail within a year*—http://www.gardnerbusiness.com/failures.htm, a number corroborated by my accountant. Because that's not news, and not interesting, it doesn't get reported; so, we only hear about the successes. There's more on biases and fallacies in *Chapter 11, Critical Analysis.*

But it's not for everyone. Some people (myself included) prefer to let other people find the customers and do the marketing, and to get on with writing the software. It's not just the greater focus of salaried development that can be appealing. A well-run company can offer a more structured environment, with clearly defined goals and rewards. Some people thrive on the chaos of running a business, while others want observable progress in becoming a better programmer.

There are plenty of jobs around, in many countries, for people who want to write software for a company. Even through recent recessions, people were still hiring programmers. The opportunities–and rewards–are there for those who don't want to start their own business.

> ## My story
>
> I've been doing this development thing for a while, now. I've worked for large and small companies, been self-employed as a contractor, and run my own consultancy business. Both of these independent ventures were "successful," in that I made enough money to support my lifestyle and got both new and repeat business. Once I'd tasted the indie life, why did I go back?
>
> It's at least partially for the reason of structure explained above. I like knowing what's expected of me and working to improve myself against that standard. I found that running my own business, the goals (at least in the first year, which is as far as I got on each occasion) are too short-term: either find a customer or complete their project. I just didn't know what I was doing well enough to set and work towards long-term goals.
>
> Another reason is that I'm too gregarious. I really enjoy working with other people – both of the indie jobs I tried involved a lot of working at home or telecommuting, which didn't provide the human contact I needed. It's possible when you're self-employed to hire other people or rent office space in a shared environment to solve this problem. I couldn't afford to do that in my city.

So, if you want to start your own business, that's cool – you should give it a go. Good luck! But if you don't, or if you try it and it isn't for you, there's no problem with that. Many people (again, I include myself here) are happy being career programmers.

13
Teamwork

Introduction

Unless I've completely failed at writing convincingly for the last hundred-and-something pages, you should have the impression that software is a social activity. We work with other people to produce software, and the value system that we share as makers of software shapes the software we make. We give (or sell) our software to other people to use, and that shapes the way they see themselves and work with each other. Software can reinforce existing bonds or create new ones, but it can also destroy or reduce the importance of existing connections. Professionally speaking, the bonds our software has influence over that are closest to our experiences when writing code are with the team that we interact with every day.

This chapter discusses these bonds: how we work as a team, how our colleagues work with us, and the benefits and tensions that can occur.

Focus versus Interruption

We've heard the clarion call. We've heard how programmers need to get *in the zone*– http://www.joelonsoftware.com/articles/fog0000000068.html in order to get their best work done, and that it's hard to enter the zone. We've heard that a simple phone call or chat from a friend is all it takes to exit the zone, but that getting back in can take 15 minutes. So why doesn't everyone work from home? If having other humans around is so poisonous to productivity, why does *any* business even bother with the capital expenditure of an office?

Because, while a good person works well on their own, two people working together can be *awesome*. Let me describe the day I had prior to writing this paragraph. I didn't really get much done in the morning, because a colleague asked me about memory leaks in the code he was working on and I helped him with that. This solved his problem much faster than he would've solved it on his own.

So, I only really got about an hour of time "in the zone" before lunch, and it didn't go so well. I made a bit of progress on my problem, but then hit a problem where a simple change to add new behavior broke the stuff that already existed. I couldn't work out why that was. Anyway, it was then lunchtime, so we went to get a sandwich and I described the problem to my colleague. Before we got to the sandwich shop, we'd already agreed what the problem was and what I should do to solve it, which worked first time when I got back to my desk.

The point of this anecdote is that, had we both been left "in the zone," we could undoubtedly have worked faster: up to the point where we could not individually solve our problems. We would've more efficiently failed at our jobs. As it was, having the possibility to work together let us pool our knowledge, even though it meant each of us getting taken out of "the zone" at some point.

I've worked in various environments. In my first job, I had an office to myself–albeit one where one of the walls was the lift shaft and the whole shebang was underground. (In fact, this office had previously been the bunk room for on-site **Digital Equipment Corporation** engineers maintaining the computer that came a few before the systems I was responsible for. Either they were very heavy sleepers, or they turned the lifts off during the night shifts.) Since then, I've worked in cubicle spaces, open-plan spaces, and in my house. I know what it's like to be "in the zone": but I also know what it's like to be banging your head up against a wall when you can't solve a problem and have no one to ask about it. I know what it's like to work for 10 hours straight on a really interesting problem, and what it's like to be told after 5 minutes that the company already has a solution you could use. I know what it's like when the guitars over in the corner are beckoning, and what it's like to feed off the energy of a handful of other engrossed and motivated people sat nearby.

The fact is that "the zone" is not always relevant, as the case example above shows. You may want to enter "the zone" to do some research from books or the internet, but then it'd probably be helpful to get some input from other people to compare their experiences and opinions with what you learned. "The zone" is helpful while you're coding, but only if you know or can work out what you're supposed to be doing. If the problem is at all difficult, talking it over with other people will be more helpful.

A final point here: humans are *"an intensely social species"*–https://thoughteconomics. com/ and the best environments for entering "the zone"–working from home or in a secluded area–are the worst for having shared social experiences with our colleagues. Some of us are lucky enough to be able to fill our social requirements with interactions among friends or family outside of work, but for more extroverted people who prize continual social contact, working in solitude can have a negative impact on mental health.

So, working alone in conditions conducive to solitary work is sometimes useful but can be emotionally unstimulating. Working with other people can be rewarding and beneficial, but also distracting and frustrating. How do we balance these two aspects? An approach that's commonly employed is the "headphones rule." Headphones on: I'm concentrating. Headphones off: feel free to talk to me. A variant of the headphones rule is the **duck of productivity**–https://www.youtube.com/watch?v=oBw cKdnUgw&index=11&list=PLKMpKKmHd2SvY9DLg_Lozb06M2MLcNImz&t=38s).

In my experience, enforcing the headphones or duck of productivity rule is difficult: people on both sides of the headphones feel it's rude to ignore friends and colleagues regardless of headphone status. Changing the social rules of the whole team can be hard. One group I worked in came up with a much simpler rule that's easier to work with: if I'm in the office, then I'm here to talk to everyone else and get some collaboration done. If I'm anywhere else (the canteen, a meeting room, at home, a coffee shop nearby), then I'm getting work done on my own.

Where the balance needs to be drawn varies based on the individual; therefore, the optimum approach for a team to take depends on the people who comprise the team. More gregarious people will want to spend more time working with others, so having a policy where people who want to work uninterrupted stay at home will isolate them.

One of the more general zone-related techniques I've come across is based on very lightweight time tracking. This calls for a kitchen timer (or an app – or, if you're in a hotel and enjoy annoying receptionists, wake-up calls) to be set for 25 minutes. During those 25 minutes, focus on your problem. If someone wants help, ask if you can get back to them after the time's up. At the end of those 25 minutes, take a short break, answer any interruptions that came up, and plan to enter the next 25 minutes. If you absolutely need to work on something else, it's suggested that you abort (rather than pause) the work period and start again when the opportunity arises.

An important observation regarding this technique is that it's OK to not be in a timed stretch if you're taking a break or helping someone else: both important parts of your working day. You might only manage one or two 25-minute bursts on some days, but at least you get to control the trade-off between "the zone" and all the other things you have to do.

I've only used this technique for a short while, but I've found that it does help to improve focus. Initially, I was surprised by how long a 25-minute stretch can seem to last! As I write that, it seems absurd, but it shows how much I was allowing distractions such as social networks to get in the way of my focus.

Remaining focused even for as long as 25 minutes needs support from both your environment (the subject of the next section) and your tools. One iPad app that I worked on could only be tested on tethered iPads, as a third-party library was not supplied for the simulator. It took about 30 seconds to *Build and Run* or to launch any unit tests – plenty of time for me to be distracted by email or Twitter. I also found that my ability to stay disciplined tails off after lunch; I still get work done, but I'm much more likely to carry on working into the breaks or stop in the middle of a stretch.

Working Environment

Your interactions with your colleagues are a small portion of the collection of experiences and inputs that make up your entire working environment. Unsurprisingly, the best environment is no less personal than the best trade-off between solitary and team working; the best I can do here is describe what's worked for me and some of the things you could consider to reflect on your own environment.

Firstly, if you're working somewhere that expects a "standard" desk layout with no decoration or personalization, that's just not a very healthy environment at all. People like to decorate their environments to *express their individuality*–https://www.colorado.edu/cmci/academics/communication. A homogeneous workspace may be good for ensuring the facilities manager's magnolia paint does not get stained but does not allow employees any creative freedom. Constraining the creativity of our software makers is not good for making creative software.

The 1999 edition of Peopleware–https://books.google.co.uk/books/about/Peopleware.html?id=eA9PAAAAMAAJ&redir_esc=y has a lot to say about working conditions. I arrived into working life too late to see the full-height cubicle farms they complain about (though I have, of course, seen *Tron and Office Space*), but other aspects of their discussion of office setups are still relevant.

A couple of places I've worked in have had those huge **Voice-over-IP** desk phones with all the buttons, redirect options, switches, and so-on that the conn in **Star Trek** first introduced to human-machine interaction. An early discovery of mine was that no one knows how to operate those phones, which means that you have plausible deniability for any of your actions, should you need it. Find the manual online and locate the one mute/divert button you need, then work peacefully. When someone complains that they were trying to phone you:

1. Apologize for having hit the wrong button when you were trying to divert calls to your mobile phone.

2. Suggest that email or some other asynchronous communication is a better way to reach you.

Two important features of work environments for me are bookshelves and whiteboards. Even when I work from home, I have a whiteboard and marker to hand for quick diagramming – quite a small one that I can hold up to the Skype camera if I need to. Not having a whiteboard can have a deleterious effect on the rest of the workspace. One office I worked in only had whiteboards in the meeting rooms, so we grabbed dry markers and drew diagrams all over the (cheap, white, fibreboard) bookshelves. We soon found that the ink was really hard to clean off; but having ruined the bookshelves there was no reason to look back. Diagrams quickly became palimpsests as new "art" was drawn over the older stuff that couldn't be erased.

I mentioned earlier that my first office was underground. A literature review of the *effects of natural light on building occupants*–http://indoorenvironment.org/effects-of-natural-light-on-building-occupants/ found that people feel better and, as a result, perform better in environments with natural lighting. This result doesn't just apply to workers; students and even shoppers are affected. As DeMarco and Lister observe, there's no excuse for building a work environment where some people don't have access to a window. People who think it's impossible to give everyone a window need to look at the way hotels are designed.

Prioritizing Work

Most people who make software will have more than one thing they are working on at any time. The choice could be between different tasks on one project, tasks on different projects, and other work such as preparing presentations, responding to emails, and so on.

Some people like to capture all of these tasks in a big review system such as **GTD** (http://www.davidco.com/) so that, at any time, they can review the outstanding tasks in their current context and choose one to work on next. A much simpler approach I was taught by the human resources department at **Sophos** (http://www.sophos.com), who got it from President Eisenhower, was to draw four quadrants indicating the urgency and importance of tasks.

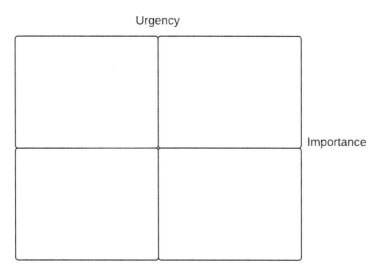

Figure 13.1: The Eisenhower Matrix

Now think about the tasks that are currently pending and put them into these quadrants. Anything in the top-right quadrant is both important and urgent, so probably needs to be done soon. Anything that's important but not urgent doesn't need to be done *yet*, and anything that's urgent but not important doesn't need to be done *at all* – or at least not by you.

A large amount of a programmer's work is prioritized by other agents anyway, which means that, much of the time, it's clear what you should be working on next. Later in this chapter, we'll examine some software development methodologies designed to allow the whole team to decide what they're working on. (In one of my rare rages against the establishment, I'm going to call them "patterns for software project management" rather than "methodologies." The latter word is used—alongside "paradigm"—in so many contexts as to be ambiguous. I saw Barbara Liskov give a talk reflecting on her work on data types where she used "methodology" to mean an overall software design approach: so object-oriented, structured, procedural, and so on are all "methodologies" at the same time that Waterfall, Scrum, and so on are.)

Tell Experts What Needs to Be Done

In other words, don't tell experts what to do. The more cynical of them will do what you tell them. That doesn't sound so bad, until you realize that *they* are the expert and are doing it out of spite. Neal Stephenson expanded upon this idea in his novel **Cryptonomicon**–https://books.google.co.uk/books/about/Cryptonomicon.html?id=Lw-00wTgBy8C&redir_esc=y:

The extreme formality with which he addresses these officers carries an important subtext: your problem, sir, is deciding what you want me to do, and my problem, sir, is doing it. My gung-ho posture says that once you give the order I'm not going to bother you with any of the details—and your half of the bargain is you had better stay on your side of the line, sir, and not bother me with any of the chickenshit politics that you have to deal with for a living. The implied responsibility placed upon the officer's shoulders by the subordinate's unhesitating willingness to follow orders is a withering burden to any officer with half a brain, and Shaftoe has more than once seen seasoned noncoms reduce green lieutenants to quivering blobs simply by standing before them and agreeing, cheerfully, to carry out their orders.

And it's not just fictional military figures who talk about this. General George S. Patton:

Never tell people how to do things. Tell them what to do, and they will surprise you with their ingenuity.

There are two sides to this. One is that the other person probably knows more about what you're asking than you do: OK, so you're a great programmer, but when it comes to graphic design, user interaction, documentation, translation, marketing, or any of the other things that go into building software, there are likely to be people out there who can handle it better than you. Your best option is to find one of them, outline the goal, and leave them to it.

The other issue to be aware of is that leaving someone else to it is a *lot* easier than taking control, because there's a lot less work involved. Once you get into the officer-marine relationship described in *Cryptonomicon*, you have to give *every* order because it becomes an expected part of the interaction that you *will* give every order. It's a lot quicker, and you get better results, to just say "this is the problem that needs solving" and let someone who's good at solving that problem assume responsibility.

So, the central trick to delegation is relinquishing control of the delegated task. That means the fundamental thing to learn is *trust*; not so much trusting the other person not to have messed it up but trusting yourself to have found the person who won't mess it up and to have communicated the problem to them clearly.

Working with Junior Programmers

Less-experienced programmers are just a special case of experts – they're experts-in-training. The above rules about dealing with experts apply, so let them know what needs doing, make sure you did that clearly, and let them get on with it.

The clarification aspect is the part that needs the most examination. Remembering *Chapter 10, Learning*, you'll find that different people learn in different ways. Some approach a new problem via experimentation, some by reading about concepts. *Diagrams help a lot of learners.* In my experience working as the senior developer on a team, it's important not to accidentally invert the expert-customer relationship, because then you get back into a micromanagement situation. Let the junior ask questions; indeed, encourage them to ask questions, but act as an oracle and not as a lecturer.

Having made yourself available while they're working, have a little retrospective when they've done the task. Try to avoid "I wouldn't have done it like that"—that's just an offensive statement of the obvious. No matter how experienced or skilled the other person is, you would've done it differently. The key question is not whether they've done *your* work but whether they've done *good* work. Find the things that work and call them out. Ask why the junior did them like that and reinforce those decisions. Find the things that don't work, ask why they did them like that, and discuss the issues. Focus on the *issues*; don't talk about the *quality of the work* (or the integrity of the worker). Your role as a teacher is to help the learner to build a generalized mental model of what they want to do.

A little aside on the subject of different ways of learning: I once found that body language gives you some great clues about how people think about their problems. I was working with a junior programmer and felt that I was not communicating very well. This programmer would solve the problems I posed, but often with some details missed out or not in the way I (thought I) had described.

Then, in one discussion, it struck me. When I'm describing a software system, I describe it spatially: my hands make boxes and circle shapes and I move these shapes around as messages or data flowing through the software. When the other programmer described them, his hands stayed flat and moved from top to bottom as he explained the steps. I was drawing diagrams; he was listening for lists! I switched to explaining problems by listing the features and found that details stopped disappearing between the two of us.

Working with Managers

There are two (almost opposing) interpretations of the word "manager" as it applies to the work context. The conservative view is of the manager as the controlling force in charge of a group of people. This manager's position is seen as ensuring that their reports do the work expected by the business, and by extension, don't do anything unexpected.

The liberal view is the manager as leader or enabler. This manager's role is to ensure that their reports have the resources they need to get their work done, free from distractions that the rest of the business (or its customers and suppliers, and so on) might impose.

In this section, I'm going to leave the political models aside and discuss the general idea of working with the person you have to report to. If you're a self-employed programmer, you don't have an *explicit* manager. You may still find, from time to time, that certain people fill similar roles; I know some independent developers who contract "business mentors" to act in a coaching and advisory capacity. In some cases, the social structure in which you work as a consultant or contractor may see you reporting to a specific person in the business you're supplying to. "Manager" will do as shorthand for all of these people.

Take a look back over what I've said about working with experts: you should tell them *what* needs doing, not *how* to do it. You should expect your manager to know and understand this, and in return, of course, you should act like the professional expert that you are. Really, the manager's task is as an *adaptor*. In one direction, they're taking the business goals and strategies and adapting them into *tactics* – into things that can be done *now* to improve the strategic position. In the other direction, they're taking your problems and concerns and adapting them into things the business can do to alleviate or remove those problems.

The best managers I've worked with seem like they could do the second part of that context-free. It's about *coaching*; not about taking on the hard parts of your work. By countering every question, we ask with a question of their own, they force us to introspect, to diagnose our own problems, to suggest, and to evaluate our own solutions. They don't remove our *responsibility* to tackle the problems ourselves, even if they do accept the responsibility (and the authority) for implementing the solutions at times.

That appearance of context-free management may not be entirely realistic. In a questionnaire completed by about 80 developers, *Jeremy Leipzig*–http://arxiv.org/abs/1303.2646v1 discovered that developers felt their relationship with their manager was easier if the manager came from a technical, rather than a business, background.

My hypothesis is that this is a communication issue, and thus has an effect on the first part of management (adapting the business's needs into things we need to do). Every group has its specific language, its *argot* of jargon and slang terms. Computing is certainly no stranger to that (I imagine an Ubuntu forum and Mumsnet would react very differently to discussions about "zombie children," for example). It can be hard to see when you're immersed in it, but this language creates a social inequality: the in-crowd who understand the jargon and the out-crowd who don't. If your manager is not part of the in-crowd, it's possible that you both struggle for terms in which to explain things and identify them on some level as "not one of *us*."

In *Chapter 9, Requirements Engineering*, I identified how the use of a ubiquitous language can help everyone to understand how the software you're writing solves the problems that the customers need it to. Now, we find that a ubiquitous language has *political* benefits, too: it makes you all part of the same team. (One company I worked in managed to create silos of employees by devising a project code name. Often, these are fun little names chosen to both describe the whole project in shorthand, and to give everyone a sense of belonging, like having a team name. In this instance, the company didn't provide a central glossary of what all the projects were named and what they did. This reinforced the feeling of "us and them" *inside* the company: you either were a member of the elite group who knew what "Merlot" meant or you were not.) Consider it your responsibility to find some linguistic common ground with your manager, even if you have a computer science background and they have an MBA. You'll find it easier to remember that you're both on the same team that way.

A final thought on working with managers that's really about professional ethics: over the last few years, I've found that managers don't like hearing bad news. It's a whole lot worse though if they *don't* hear the bad news and discover it for themselves, later. Being honest and alerting people to things going wrong early leads to some awkward conversations, but ultimately, you'll be respected more than if you pretend everything's going well up until the moment of disaster. I shouldn't have let myself get into a position of experience on this one, but I have, so you don't have to.

Patterns of Software Project Management

Over the last five decades, there have been numerous different ways to run a software project proposed and practiced. Over the last decade, I've been exposed to a few of them. Which will work for you depends on the team you're working with and the expectations of the people you're working for.

Waterfall

My first experience of a "death march" was on a waterfall project. The product manager wrote a document explaining the requirements of the new product. These were prioritized using 1-3 (with 1 being "we'll probably finish these in time," and 2-3 taking up space on the page). Then, the lead developer wrote a functional specification, explaining what each of the controls in the product would be and how each of them would fulfil a requirement from the first document.

Given the functional specification, the lead developer (not necessarily the same one as mentioned previously) would estimate how long it'd take to build, and the lead tester would estimate how long it'd take to test. Then, the ship date was the day after that work ended! Having built and tested the thing, documentation could write a manual, translation could translate the whole lot, then it'd be beta tested, and finally, marketing could write a new website and it would all get launched with beer and nibbles in the office atrium.

I should stress that the death march was not a *result* of following the waterfall process. The death march was the result of an inexperienced team, poor communication and collaboration, and an unclear vision of what the business or the customers thought the product should be.

The waterfall process did make it harder to *react* to these problems, though. Limited visibility in the usual running of the project meant that most people involved had an idealized view of how the project *should* be progressing and treated that as reality. They didn't have a view of how the project *was* progressing because that feedback was neither requested nor provided: come back when you're ready to enter the testing phase. The expensive change-control procedure, involving sign-off from senior managers who weren't involved with the usual running of the project, made it hard or even *undesirable* to react to eleventh-hour feedback. Unfortunately, the twelfth hour resembles the twelfth much more than it does the first.

In *Test-Driven iOS Development* section in *Chapter 5, Coding Practices*, I tried to paint the waterfall as a historical quirk that doesn't hold any relevance for modern developers. This isn't really true. If you're doing contract or agency work, the customer will often have a mental model that goes something like:

1. I tell you what app I want.

2. You build the app.

3. Maybe we have a phone call every week, so I know you're still alive. If you send me a prototype, I might suggest moving a button or changing a word.

4. You put the app on the store.

5. I retire to a cocaine-soaked mountain complex.

You can dispel that myth. In fact, you probably should: if you get more feedback from your client, they'll feel more engaged, and enjoy the process more. They'll also end up with the product they *wanted*, not the one they *asked for* months ago. And if you *ask* for feedback from the client, they'll give you *that* feedback instead of the stuff about the buttons and words.

Scrum

I've seen multiple projects run in multiple ways all named "Scrum," which is why I call these things patterns rather than rules. Most have had the following in common:

- Short iteration lengths with work planned only for the upcoming iteration

- Frequent feedback to the whole team on how work is progressing on the current iteration

- Acceptance or rejection of the previous iteration's work at the end

- Some form of retrospective on what to learn from the previous iteration

None of these things is in itself contentious and looking at the problems identified with my waterfall project above, we can see the benefit of frequent feedback, measurement of quality, and particularly of learning from our mistakes as quickly as possible. But the implementation often leaves people scratching their heads or updating their CVs.

Take the "frequent feedback" point as an example. This is often embodied in the stand-up meeting. Does everyone actually stand up? If someone's late, do we wait or proceed without them? How long is it going to take (my record being an hour and a half, in a team with 16 developers who obviously only took 5 minutes each)? Do I actually need to know everything that comes up in the meeting? Why are you asking every day whether I've finished the thing I told you would take a week? (Actually, this one's my fault. I don't think that estimates are worth anything if they represent more than half a day of work. If I think something's going to take more than that, then I probably don't know what's involved and should find out before you start relying on my guesses.) Are minutes taken? If I want clarification on something do I ask now or after we've disbanded?

The thing is, despite these differences in approach, things tend to actually happen. Stuff gets done and you can see it getting done because you've got a feel for what everyone is doing. I tend to think of Scrum as the closest thing you'll get to **Agile software development**–http://www.agilemanifesto.org/ in an organization that still wants close managerial oversight, though in most situations I've encountered it doesn't quite match *the principles*–http://www.agilemanifesto.org/principles.html.

Lean Software

Lean software isn't really a way to run a software project, so much as a description of a principle of organizing software projects with some Japanese words thrown in to help sell the MBA textbooks. Indeed, it's one of the 12 agile principles linked above:

Simplicity--the art of maximizing the amount of work not done--is essential.

That's really all that Lean is (plus the textbooks). Focus on doing the valuable thing (solving the customer's problem) and not on doing the invaluable things. Work out what you're doing that doesn't have value and stop doing it.

Interestingly, and probably because we enjoy doing it, we sometimes forget that writing software *doesn't* have value. Yes, *having* software that has been written does, but actually writing it costs money. Maybe we should be focusing more on reusing software or even on finding the thing that already exists that our customers could be using instead of a new bespoke product. The community of people promoting the lean idea have created *five principles*–http://www.lean.org/WhatsLean/Principles.cfm:

- Identify value to the customer

- Eliminate any steps in the business chain that aren't adding value

- Create a smooth flow of the remaining steps, ending in delivering value to the customer

- Each step should pull its valuable input as needed from the upstream step

- Iterate over the above

So far, so reasonable, although I know that I (along with a lot of you, I imagine) think it sounds a bit too businessy-MBAey. Therein lies the danger. This collection of values is actually *at an appropriate level of abstraction*, and it's *us* who are thinking too much about what we *currently* do, rather than whether it's useful. If you try to recast the above in terms of writing code, you get something like:

- Identify that writing code is valuable

- Eliminate the meetings and other things that stop us writing code

- Write a load of automation stuff so that code is automatically delivered to the next people in the chain

- Manage a **Kanban board**–https://en.wikipedia.org/wiki/Kanban_board

- Iterate over the above

This is useful for improving the efficiency of *writing code*, which will almost certainly make developers happier and incrementally improve processes. But it doesn't help identify whether the most valuable thing to do is to write code; in fact, it actively hinders that.

Anchoring Bias and Project Management

A last thought on running a software project for this chapter. The previous section explained that if we think about a process too much in terms of what we already do, it becomes harder to question whether *that* is worth doing at all. It turns out there are other problems associated with thinking about things – not that I'm suggesting anyone should stop.

There's a factor in decision-making called **anchoring**–http://www.skepdic.com/anchoring.html, in which people tend to fixate on a piece of information presented early in making later judgements. Anchoring is the reason infomercials ask you "How much would *you* pay for this? $100?" before telling you the price is $10. You probably don't expect the price to be $100, but it's given you an *anchor* that will set your further expectations.

Related to this is the **social anchoring**–http://dictionary-psychology.com/index.php?a=term&d=Dictionary+of+psychology&t=Social+anchoring factor. People are inclined to vote the same way as the herd. There's a great demonstration of this, devised by **Solomon Asch (1951)**–http://www.simplypsychology.org/asch-conformity.html. Eight "participants" are asked which of three lines is the longest; the first seven are stooges who all choose the wrong answer. Asch found that only 25% of the (actual) participants never conformed to the group and gave the wrong answer.

This is a genuine question, because I don't think it's been researched: what effect do these anchoring biases have on software projects, and what can we do to correct for them? Does giving people wireframes or other prototypes anchor their expectations and make them desire products that are like the prototypes? Do games like *Planning Poker* inadvertently anchor estimates to the number thought of by the first person to reveal? Might we accidentally bias estimates by discussing unrelated numbers in meetings ("I hope we can get this done in 45 minutes... Now, how many story points is this feature")?

Bias bias

An unfortunate phenomenon is the **Bias Blind Spot**–https://dataspace.princeton.edu/jspui/handle/88435/dsp013j333232r, in which we more readily report biases in another people's reasoning than in our own. A problem with drawing attention to cognitive biases such as the anchoring bias above is that, being aware of the bias, we're now in a position to identify *other people* relying on the bias, and to believe that *we* are immune from it because we know about it. This is not true. Being aware of it will not stop us from applying the bias: analyzing, detecting, and correcting for the bias in our own work and decisions will do that. There is *Chapter 11, Critical Analysis*, in this book.

Negotiation

You need to negotiate with other people. OK, if you're selling a consumer app, you probably don't negotiate with your customers: you set a price and they either pay it or go elsewhere. But that doesn't mean negotiation is limited to people dealing with terrorists and kidnappers. You might want to convince the rest of your team that it's worth rewriting some component, or that a feature you want to build should go into the product. You might want to ask your manager for more responsibility. Perhaps you want a vendor to fix a bug in their software, or a supplier to give you a preferential discount. In any of these cases, you'll need to negotiate. (L looked up the etymology of "negotiate" in the Oxford American Dictionary. Apparently, it comes from the Latin "otium" meaning leisure, so "neg-otium" is "not leisure" or, in other words, business. That's got nothing to do with this book but it's really interesting, so I wanted to share it.)

A sure-fire way to lose at negotiation is to ignore the other person's position. So, you want time to rewrite that server component in *FluffyMochaGerbilScript*, and your manager is saying no. Is that because your manager is a bozo who just doesn't get it? Are you the only person who can see the world as it really is?

No. That's the fundamental attribution error again (refer *Chapter 12, Business*). It's a common enough problem, but if you find yourself thinking that you're talking to an idiot, you're probably just talking to someone with different problems to solve. Perhaps they're worried about a rewrite introducing regressions: what can you do to prove that won't happen? Maybe they know that the company will be taking on some extra work soon, and the time you think you've got for the rewrite doesn't really exist.

The most reliable way to find out what the other person's concerns are is to ask, because the fundamental attribution error works both ways. While you're thinking that they just don't get clean code or craftsmanship or this week's buzzword, they're thinking that you don't get that this is a business that needs to make money and can't support the whims of a highly-strung developer. One of the two (or more) of you will need to be the one to break the stalemate by sharing what they know and asking what the other person knows. It could be you.

I find it's easy to get too emotional in the first discussion, particularly when it's a change to a project I've been working on for months and exhaustion has set in. For me, the best thing to do is to take a break, think about how we could meet in the middle, and come back to the discussion later. Just introspecting and wondering what the other person's position is goes some way to reconciliation, but the **empathy gap**–http:// en.wikipedia.org/wiki/Empathy_gap means that isn't foolproof. I'm likely to assume that the other person is being rational, underestimating the importance of emotional factors in their decision. But wait, I stepped back from the conversation because I was getting *too* emotional. It's likely that the other person is making decisions based on visceral factors too.

Empathy

The previous section made it clear that successful negotiation relies largely on *empathy*: being able to see what's driving the people you're talking to and identifying how to present your proposed solution in a way that addresses their concerns and satisfies their needs and desires. Let's look in more depth at how that works.

The Effect of Mood on Collaboration

You can probably anecdotally describe the effect that your mood has on how you work with others. I know that when I get grumpy, I value isolation and will bark at people who interrupt me, trying to avoid getting into conversations. This probably means I'm less likely to listen to other opinions and to either contribute meaningfully to discussions or to learn how to do my own job better. I'd rather do the wrong thing on my own than accept help when I'm in that mood.

In a column called "Mood"–http://cacm.acm.org/magazines/2012/12/157887-moods/ fulltext in Communications of the ACM, Peter J. Denning investigates the ways that mood can affect our interactions with each other, even transmitting mood socially between members of a team. He notes that when everybody is positive, collaboration is easy; when everybody is negative, the outcome is likely to be bad so it's best to avoid what will most likely become confrontational.

It's when people are in mixed moods that outcomes are hardest to predict. Will the negative person or people feed off the optimism of others, or will they resent it? How can you best help to improve the mood of negative people?

There are some high-level patterns in the overall moods of groups. Bruce Tuckman described four stages of development in the establishment of a team:

- **Forming**: The team does not exist yet; it is a collection of individuals. Each is seeking acceptance, so the team does not tackle any big or divisive problems. People work independently for the most part.

- **Storming**: The individual preferences and opinions of each member of the team come into conflict. The team learns what the differences and similarities between its members are, which it is willing to accept, and which cause problems. The group begins to discover where it is willing to be led and how.

- **Norming**: Through a combination of agreements and compromises, the team decides how to resolve its conflicts, what its goals are, and how it will work towards them.

- **Performing**: Having collectively agreed upon the team's norms, the members become more efficient at working within the team framework.

You can often work out someone's mood by the language they use. An example from Denning's column involves asking team members why they think a recent release of their product was poorly received. One person exhibits a sense of wonder and curiosity:

...I would love to interview our customers and find out what was behind their reactions. I am certain I will learn something that will help improve our software.

Other shows signs of confusion and resentment:

I also don't know what the heck is going on. But I do know those customers are jerks...

Language cues can provide information about what mood someone's in, which can inform your choice on how to engage with them.

Language and Introversion

Language also tells you about someone's personality. One scale along which psychologists often grade personalities is how introverted or extroverted someone is. Introverts gain energy from being alone, finding interaction with other people tiring or overwhelming. Extroverts gain energy from being with other people.

Introverts use more concrete phrases—http://www.bps-research-digest.blogspot.co.uk/2012/11/introverts-use-more-concrete-language.html, and less abstraction, than extroverts. In describing photos of people interacting, introverts were more likely to stick to facts ("the woman is pointing to the right, and has her mouth open"), whereas extroverts were more likely to infer reasons for what the photos depicted ("the woman is angry and is shouting at the man").

Being able to detect features of someone's personality can go a long way toward empathizing with them, as you can start to predict how they might react to situations or events. Language is a useful tool for this; and one it's easier to get people to engage with than a psychometric test like the Myers-Briggs Type Indicators.

Knowing What Level to Talk and To Listen At

So, extroverts are more likely to use abstract language than introverts, but there are other reasons people may discuss issues at differing levels of abstraction. You need to bear these in mind too, to get the most out of interactions with your team.

What role does the person you're talking to have? If you're discussing a bug with a fellow coder, then the weird thing you saw where the property was set on the view but then it didn't update because it was reset by a different thread is *totally* on topic. It's likely to interest your colleague, they'll have relevant experience to bring to bear, and they'll want to learn what the problem was in case they see a similar thing in the future.

If you're talking to the business development manager at your client's company, they *may* not be so interested. Of course, that's not necessarily true... but it's likely. They're probably more interested in whether the bug has been fixed, when they'll receive the fix, and whether the bug will impact anything else in the product.

As a courtesy to you, the business development manager probably isn't going to go into the intricacies of their contract with your company and the gnarly clause about how your boss has to fax them a copy of the company's business insurance policy every year. They expect the same courtesy in return. Similarly, your customer wants to hear about why they might want to buy your thing, not about how you completely rewrote it in *SuperFluffyAwesomeSquirrelNode*.

Even in discussions with fellow developers, there are times when the details matter and times when they don't. As we've seen, your colleague's mood can have an effect on their receptiveness: maybe don't go into a discussion about how much better your approach to database retrieval is than theirs when they're feeling apathetic or resigned.

Situation has as much (or more) of a role to play than personality or emotion, too: if someone's in the exalted "Zone" working on a complex problem, they probably don't want to listen to your opinions on the relative merits of the `pre-increment` and `post-increment` operators, fascinating though they may be. (If you actually *have* opinions on the relative merits of the `pre-increment` and `post-increment` operators and want to share them, please do send them to `/dev/null`.)

Shared Language and Shiny Buzzwords

Any social group has its *argot* – its special words and phrases that speed up communication between the cognoscenti. (Argot has another meaning: the secret language used by groups to protect their conversations from eavesdropping. In this sense, cants and rhyming slang/back slang are argots. We'll stick with the jargon sense for this book.) Think about what the word "tree" means; now think about what it means in a computer science context. That meaning is part of the argot of computer scientists.

In a sense, jargon terms define group boundaries because they're exclusive. If you haven't learned the buzzwords in one context, you aren't included in the conversation among people who have. So, while jargon facilitates conversation among those in the know, it also keeps people who aren't in the know from understanding that conversation; it's a cause of inequality and division.

It's important to realize that, sometimes, subsectors, companies, or even teams within companies develop their own slang phrases that are slightly divergent from even the slang used within their industry or sector. One company I worked at used "train" to describe a collection of semi-independent projects that were all due to be released together, where other project managers might use the word "program" instead.

My first few months working in the telecoms sector involved being bombarded with three letter acronyms (TLAs). When I asked what they meant, people would usually expand the acronym... when I asked what they *meant* they'd look at me as if I'd wondered just what these "phone" things we're selling are for. Immersed in the world where your argot is spoken, a new hire will quickly pick up the lingo. A customer or supplier may not have the capacity or desire to do so, however, so may just be confused or misinformed when you use them.

Confused or misinformed suppliers and customers should be avoided. Suppliers and customers (along with colleagues) should not feel *excluded* either, but jargon use can have that effect. If you realize which parts of your language are slang developed in your industry, field, or team, you can know when using them will help discussions and when it will hinder conversation.

14

Ethics

Introduction

The movement of developers – neophytes and experienced alike – to the iPhone with the launch of its app store has been *likened to a gold rush*–http://www.adweek.com/news/technology/inside-iphone-app-gold-rush-98856. Few people would hold the California gold rush of 1849 up as a shining example of humans behaving with humanity, though.

Selfish drive for profit broke up existing communities: three-quarters of adult men in San Francisco left the city during the rush, excited to find new deposits of gold to exploit. They even destroyed other communities, coming into conflict with the Native Americans in the region as they dug up the land the indigenous people inhabited. Paranoid self-protection led to rule of the mob and uncommonly harsh punishments for crimes of property: hanging was a common consequence for those thought to have stolen gold from another.

So, is the gold rush an acceptable model for today's programmers? Are we free to seek the highest financial income, whatever the cost to others – friends and strangers alike? Should we be *every coder for themselves*, or do we need to work together with fellow programmers and non-programmers alike? Is mob rule acceptable or is there a code of conduct we should be expected to follow?

Examples of Ethical Codes

Plenty of professions have their codes of ethics (The discussion of whether programming is a "profession" will take place in the next chapter). Indeed, the **Online Ethics Center** (http://www.onlineethics.org) has plenty of examples, case studies, and discussions. Rather than trawl through those, I'll focus on a couple from the computing field.

The Association of Computing Machinery's **code of ethics and professional conduct–** http://www.acm.org/about/code-of-ethics is a short document, comprising 24 ethical imperatives members are expected to follow: one of which is that membership of the Association is contingent on abiding by the other imperatives.

The code is both technology and practice agnostic, as it should be written at the level of abstraction of an entire industry's career lifetimes. Briefly, the four sections say:

- Respect other people and their property, do no harm, work to make humanity better

- Be up to date with what's going on in the profession, help others to stay up to date, and work to what the profession currently believes to be the highest standards and best practices

- Ensure that others in and affected by your organization are protected by these same standards

- Abide by and promote the code

Unsurprisingly, the *British Computer Society–*http://www.bcs.org/category/6030 has very similar ethical principles. Though their code is organized differently, it covers all the same points that the ACM's does.

I don't feel the need to add anything to either code; each sets out some principles that the organization aspires to and would like to see in its members. Discussing whether something should be added or removed is a big topic, but let's leave these codes as they are for now. The questions remaining are: how should we *interpret* these codes, and *should* we apply them?

Application of The Ethical Code

Abiding by some code of ethics is more expensive than ignoring it. The ACM code tells us to "Honor property rights including copyrights and patent": obviously, it's cheaper to steal someone else's copyrighted work than to build an equivalent work. Examples could be found for the other moral imperatives in the code.

Legal systems work, broadly speaking, by introducing a cost of non-compliance so that rational actors should also be abiding actors. This is an example of removing an *externality*, discussed in *Chapter 15, Philosophy*, of this book. If stealing the copyrighted work is going to cost the thief in legal fees, damages, and lost reputation, the other route becomes attractive.

For most of us making software, the legal framework we operate in doesn't directly apply to our actions. Laws exist covering data protection, and certain fields are strongly regulated (principally, life-critical systems such as control software for medical devices). For the most part, software makers are free to act as we please, subject to market forces. This is largely the result, ironically, of groups including the ACM lobbying for self-regulation in the software sector. They want an ethical code but wouldn't like it if the courts could enforce it.

Also, for the most part, software makers are *not* members of bodies such as the **BCS (British Computer Society)** so don't have the threat of expulsion for failing to comply with the ethical code. And finally, it's not obvious that ethics or morality enter into the hiring process either (though, once you're working for a company, their human resources department should be charged with ensuring that the whole company acts according to that company's ethical principles). I have certainly never been asked in an interview whether I've ever acted unethically. I've been asked what I know of Perl, and how I interact with other people on a team, but never whether I've failed to respect the privacy of others.

So, where does the obligation to behave ethically come from, if it's going to introduce additional costs?

One answer is that there *are* costs associated with acting unethically, albeit not direct financial ones. Acting outside of one's principles exerts an emotional cost, of which individuals can only pay so much.

This concept of emotional cost is already used in relation to network security policies. It's well understood that when users are asked to comply with security policies, the tasks usually involve *additional mental effort*–http://hal.archives-ouvertes.fr/docs/00/69/18/18/PDF/Besnard-Arief-2004--Computer-security-impaired-legal-users.pdf beyond taking the easy, but insecure, approach. If this mental cost gets too great, then users might decide not to pay it, taking the easier, non-compliant route. This still has some mental effort in terms of the anguish involved in knowing that they are violating their employers' trust, and the fear that they might get caught out. This anxiety could cause distractions in their other work or they could even leave their job rather than work against their own principles.

There are, additionally, reputation costs to unethical actions, as suppliers or customers may choose not to do business with companies or people they perceive to be unethical and may prefer to do business with those whose values align closely to their own. As described above, this is not really an *overt* input into the way the software marketplace works; that doesn't mean it's not a factor at all.

This reputation factor is a large input into the golden rule (here, supplied in Boehm's modified version): do unto others as you would have them do unto you if you were like them. This can build into a reciprocal and valuable network of people and organizations acting in support of their mutual values and interests. And *that* can make working ethically more efficient and easier than the alternatives.

Ethical Ambiguities

It's always easier to model the world as a system of exclusive choices: this is good, that is bad; this is right, that is wrong; this is fast, that is slow. Unfortunately, such a model can quickly be found to have too many limitations. Different ethical principles all-too-readily come into conflict. Part of our responsibility as members of society is to identify and resolve these conflicts (after all, if ethics were a simple application of rules, we would've got a computer to do it by now).

Let me provide an example from my own experience. I was offering advice to another programmer about applying and interviewing for new jobs, when this person told me about an interview they had attended. They described feeling that the interview had been discriminatory on the basis of candidates' ethnicities, which is clearly in breach of any professional ethics system. Referring to the ACM's code, this breaks imperative 1.4: Be fair and take action not to discriminate.

Some people would react to this by suggesting that I "blow the whistle," calling out the company's discriminatory practices publicly and moving, if their employees are members of a professional body, to have them black-balled by that association. Not so fast, though! To do so would mean applying my *own* unfair standards: privileging one side of a story without hearing and evaluating the other. It would also mean going public with the tale of the interview that I had been told in confidence, which breaks the ethical imperatives to respect privacy and confidentiality (1.7 and 1.8 in ACM's code).

In the end, I decided to recommend to the person who'd told me about this that *they* should lodge a complaint about the interview, and that I would support them in that. Regardless of whether you agree with that specific outcome, you can see that situations exist in which there is no clear "ethical" way to behave. Having an ethical code that you are aware of, can describe (even if only to yourself), and can relate to what you do is important. Looking to others for guidance and assimilating their advice is important. Knowing the "one true way" to act is best left to Taoism.

In fact, there really is no one true way. Ethical imperatives are *normative*: they arise from the shared beliefs and values of the people interacting together, defining actions they consider acceptable (appropriate behavior, if you will) and those they do not. What's ethical now may not be considered so in the future, and vice versa. What's ethical to one group of people may not be considered so to another group.

This change in ethical norms over time can be seen in the practice of psychology. After the post-WW2 war crimes trials disclosed the cruel experiments carried out on prisoners by the Nazi regime, psychologists accepted the need for a professional set of ethics and code of practice to govern their experiments. The first such rules were published as **the Nuremberg Code**–https://history.nih.gov/research/downloads/nuremberg.pdf in 1949.

Notice that the code says nothing about child subjects (or "participants" as modern psychologists would say). Indeed, the question of child participation has been answered in different ways in different countries and at different times. When Albert Bandura conducted his famous **Bobo doll experiment**–http://www.simplypsychology.org/bobo-doll.html into childhood imitation of aggression, the parents involved would've known that their children were involved in an experiment, but the children could not have known. In modern experiments, it is likely that the children themselves would need to be made aware that they are participating in an experiment. Indeed, even **primate research**–http://digitaljournal.com/article/343702 can involve voluntary participation – considerations not made when the Nuremberg Code was created.

Respecting Privacy

A problem that's been at the forefront of ethical debates in the software industry for at least the last couple of decades, and will likely remain at the forefront for at least another decade, is the use or misuse of personal data. In a quest to drive adoption, many software vendors have ended up distributing their software below cost and gaining revenue by collecting data about their users to sell to advertisers and other aggregators.

This practice of selling user data could be seen as unethical, as it may break the imperative to honor the privacy of others. This is especially true if the user did not give informed consent to sharing the data; if the user is a child who did not understand the implications of sharing the data; or if the information gathered is more than the minimum required to support the sharing activity.

Because this is such a large and immediate problem that is continually being raised and discussed both in the tech press and the corridors of power, I applied the privacy imperative to personal data sharing and came up with the "Don't Be a Dick" guide to data privacy (Wil Wheaton deserves credit for popularizing the phrase "Don't be a dick," known in some circles as Wheaton's Law):

- The only things you are entitled to know are those things that the user told you.

- The only things you are entitled to share are those things that the user permitted you to share.

- The only entities with which you may share are those entities with which the user permitted you to share.

- The only reason for sharing a user's things is that the user wants to do something that requires the sharing of those things.

It's simple, which makes for a good user experience. It's explicit, which means culturally situated ideas of acceptable implicit sharing do not muddy the issue.

It's also general. One problem I've seen with privacy discussions is that different people have specific ideas of what the absolutely biggest privacy issue that must be solved now is. For many people, it's location; they don't like the idea that an organization (public or private) can see where they are at any time. For others, it's unique identifiers that would allow an entity to form an aggregate view of their data across multiple functions. For others still, it's conversations they have with their boss, mistress, whistle-blower, or others.

Because the guide mentions none of these, it covers all of these – and more. Who knows what sensors and capabilities will exist in future smartphone kits? They might use mesh networks that can accurately position users in a crowd with respect to other members. They could include automatic person recognition to alert when your friends are nearby. A handset might include a blood sugar monitor. The fact is that, by not stopping to cover any particular form of data, the above guideline covers *all of these* and any others that I didn't think of.

There's one thing it doesn't address: just because a user wants to share something, should the app allow it? This is particularly a question that makers of apps for children should ask themselves. However, children also deserve impartial guidance on what it is a good or a bad idea to share with the innerwebs at large, and that should be baked into the app experience. "Please check with a responsible adult before pressing this button" does not cut it: just don't give them the button.

Epilogue

Of course, the picture I drew of the gold rush at the beginning of the chapter was deliberately one-sided. As people realized that they could only make tiny amounts of easily obtainable gold from single-person techniques such as panning, they started to work together. This collaboration – with the new social structures and rules attendant – led to technological advances in hydraulic mining, extracting both gold and useful minerals.

15

Philosophy

Introduction

As the manuscript for this book came together, I realized that a lot of the content was based on a limited and naive *philosophy* of software creation. I was outlining this philosophy as it applied to each chapter, then explaining what the various relevant tasks were and how they fit into that philosophy. Here it is, written explicitly and separately from other considerations in the book:

Our role as people who make software is to "solve problems," and only incidentally to make software. Making software for its own sake is at best a benign waste of time and money, or at worst detrimental to those exposed to it. Our leading considerations at all times must be the people whose problems we are solving, and the problems themselves.

If this were the 1970s, you might call that *new age* claptrap. These days, you'd probably just think of it as the kind of nonsense you get in those self-help books about becoming a better manager; perhaps I should've left software behind for management consultancy by now. But it's only by agreeing on the philosophy of a discipline that we can decide what work represents a valuable contribution. Consider how the philosophy of science has changed over the millennia (The discussion here is based on a talk given by my first manager, John Ward, at Oxford University's Department of Physics.).

In ancient Greek civilization, any conclusion that you could construct a logical argument for could be accepted as scientific fact. So, women had fewer teeth than men, and wood could combust because it was made of heavy earth and light fire, and the fire wanted to escape to the heavens. These things were accepted as true because people thought about them and decided that they were true.

Over the next few centuries, the face of science changed. Richard P. Feynman was likely paraphrasing the French philosopher-priest Buridan when he expressed the belief that "the test of all knowledge is experiment"; a viewpoint that, by Feynman's time, had already spent centuries working its way into society's philosophy of science. At the time of the foundation of the Royal Society, if a respectable person presented evidence for something in the correct circles, then it was true: this is how we knew that sea monsters existed, because gentlemen had sailed to the Americas and reported seeing them. If someone of repute had seen something, then it must be there.

In the twentieth century, Karl Popper argued for a falsification philosophy of science: rather than looking for evidence that a theory is true, accept it weakly and look for evidence that it is false. This is the approach that scientists take today. All of this is not some grand history presented to show progress toward our current, enlightened state. The accepted philosophy of science could change again at any time. The reason for presenting this anecdote is to show that what's considered good science, or bad science, or worthwhile science, is *situated* within the prevailing philosophical view (in addition to other considerations, including ethics). By analogy, if anyone wants to argue that there is such a thing as *good* programming practice, or bad practice, or worthwhile practice, they must do it, whether explicitly or implicitly, with reference to a particular philosophy and system of values.

In this concluding chapter, I want to bring the whole book together by examining the role of and inputs into a holistic philosophy of software construction.

Software as A Pursuit

Is making software (for money – we'll leave hobby aside) a profession? Is it a craft? Is it a science? An engineering discipline? An art form? A social science?

It's easy to refute the idea of professional programmers. Professions are marked by an educational barrier to entry: you can't be a self-taught lawyer or architect, for example. The education ensures that (prospective) practitioners are aware of the institutional body of knowledge and code of ethics – things that are absent from the "profession" of programming. Certain organizations, such as the *Chartered Institute for IT*–http://www.bcs.org/ and the **Association for Computing Machinery**–http://www.acm.org are trying to cast it as such but represent a minority of practitioners.

We have professional-style conferences; these cater to a small minority of practitioners, frequently featuring sales rhetoric and self-promotion alongside (or instead of) problem-solving workshops and technical presentations. There is no professional closure: you cannot be disbarred from writing software if you disregard the ethics of doing so. The ethics of programming were discussed in *Chapter 14, Ethics*, and were found to be largely absent.

A further difficulty with organizing software as a profession: as I described in the *Chapter 10, Learning*, the teaching of programming is far too haphazard to represent the transference of a core body of knowledge. In recommending a curriculum for university computing courses back in 1968, the ACM drew a thick line between academic computer science and computing as practiced in the wild. Even in the *latest version of the curriculum*–http://ai.stanford.edu/users/sahami/CS2013/, professional standards and ethical implications are only a small part of the training a *Computer Science* course would offer. (At time of writing, curriculum 13 was still in draft status.) People who complete CS degrees undoubtedly have good knowledge of the workings of a computer, but one could argue that this is a necessary, though insufficient, input to be a novice programmer.

The extent to which software practitioners treat our work as a profession has, then, always been varied. It is also largely à la carte. The practice of writing software is not a profession and would not survive professionalization over a short timescale. Almost everyone who currently calls themselves a programmer would be excluded from the profession until they had taken some appropriate training, unless there were some way to get "grandfathered" in, which would undermine the value of being a member of a recognized profession. The sudden collapse in the availability of "licensed" programmers would either cripple businesses or see them using existing, unlicensed practitioners legally or otherwise. Imagine, for example, that the BCS managed to secure protected nomination for the profession in the UK. Would UK-based companies wait until their programmers were chartered professionals before proceeding with their IT projects, or would they sack the now-underqualified employees and outsource their work abroad?

Could programming, then, be an art form, or a craft or trade that combines artisanal capability with some technical knowledge? In the book *The Computer Boys Take Over*, Nathan Ensmenger makes a compelling argument for this position. He observes that, while there is a significant corpus of technical knowledge and computer science that *can* go into programming, many programmers have only a partial understanding of this corpus. They augment their technical knowledge with self-taught patterns – things that experience tells them have worked before and will work again. Any programmer or team of programmers builds up a local domain of craft knowledge, with the result that the craft of programming varies from context to context.

Ensmenger also notices that the programmer is responsible for mediating "between the technological and social architectures of the organization." He concludes that this combination of artisanal craft with scientific knowledge and social integration makes the programmer not a professional, but a technician. He also observes that the rhetoric of professional programmers is one of fluid boundaries: programmers will talk about their work as science, engineering, *or* art, depending on who is listening. Bear this in mind throughout this discussion – both to appraise the various positions that are described and to analyze my own conclusions for signs of Humpty-Dumptyism:

'When I use a word,' Humpty Dumpty said in rather a scornful tone, 'it means just what I choose it to mean—neither more nor less.'

The **Software Craftsmanship movement**–http://manifesto.softwarecraftsmanship. org/ uses language that's firmly rooted in mediaeval trade schools. Adherents talk of apprenticeships and journeymen (and, to carry on an earlier reference, of shoes and ships and sealing-wax; of cabbages and kings.), though parallels with the guilds of middle-age Europe (and the exclusivity they practiced, on a par with professional institutes) tend not to be drawn. Focus is on community interaction, on learning from the experiences of others and synthesizing a new approach to the craft by combining those experiences.

While it appeals to centuries of tradition, software craftsmanship is very clearly a direct response to and retreat from the profession of "software engineering," or maybe from a straw man idea of it. The foreword to Pete McBreen's *Software Craftsmanship* asks:

Is software engineering appropriate for projects of less than 100 developer-years? Is the specialization inherent in software engineering a good idea? Can software development even be expressed in engineering terms?

The answer, as far as McBreen is concerned, of course turns out to be "no"; apprenticeship, practice, and self-organized teams are preferred here. Software engineering may be suitable for building space shuttle software, McBreen tells us, but fails the producer of shrink-wrap commercial software or in-house line of business applications. Such applications need the personal touch, and a good programmer would understand not only the technical details of software construction, but the artistry required to make a bespoke piece.

What that *doesn't* address, though, is whether the software craftsmanship movement actually promotes software making as a *craft*, or whether it's as much a straw man as the version of engineering discussed in software engineering. The image of the mediaeval craft is as much one of exclusivity and division as that of the professional trade. Master craftsmen would be members of a guild that controlled the practice of the craft (and the dissemination of its secret techniques) in a given region. Other than the guild members, only the apprentices would be allowed to practice (and then only in the limited fashions enabled by their masters). Anyone who had finished their apprenticeship would be booted out to become a "journeyman," taking odd jobs as they traveled to find a town that wasn't already under guild control, where they could set up shop, or until they could submit a "masterpiece" and become a member of the guild.

That members of the craftsmanship movement in software see this exclusivity as appealing is evident. The **Software Craftsmanship Manifesto**–http://manifesto. softwarecraftsmanship.org makes this point in both explicit ways:

we have come to value [...] a community of professionals.

...and implicit ways:

we have come to value [...] well-crafted software.

The second example is quite subtle, but what *is* "well-crafted software"? It's such a woolly phrase that the only way to get a definition would be by joining the guild of professionals; that is, by submitting to the masters.

Robert C. Martin likes to take this divisive approach to the language of software by defining "professionals" as those who exhibit desirable qualities, and "unprofessional" as those who do not:

- *Legacy code is not inevitable when programmers behave professionally*–https:// twitter.com/unclebobmartin/status/298762801164451840

- Here is a *minimal* list of the things that every software professional should be conversant with (from **The Clean Coder**–http://www.amazon.com/The-Clean-Coder-Professional-Programmers/dp/0137081073, *Chapter 1, emphasis original*)

- Professionals know they are arrogant and are not falsely humble. A professional knows their job and takes pride in their work. A professional is confident in their abilities and takes bold and calculated risks based on that confidence. A professional is not timid. (*The Clean Coder*, Chapter 1)

The language used here automatically creates a division among programmers: those who conform to Martin's ideal are "professional," and everybody else is, well, something else. Unprofessional? Amateurish? Not a programmer? It *also* creates a division between professional programmers and those they work with. Managers and customers had best not dare question how we're working – we're working *professionally*. (Brad Cox, in his book *Superdistribution: Objects as property on the electronic frontier*–http://virtualschool.edu/mon/Superdistribution/, makes the same point about the division between programmers and non-programmers, so it already existed when he was writing in 1996. He says, tongue in cheek, "The role of customers, and especially of managers, is to stand out of the way, checkbook in hand, admiring the brilliance of this programmer's skill and devotion to his craft.")

The craftsmanship movement asks whether software is *really* a professional engineering discipline, and in answering "no" promotes many of the same ideals and divisions as the software engineering movement or of any regulated profession.

I would like to pose a different question: is programming *really* a social science? To what extent should a programmer know the social, interpersonal side of software construction? Much of the content of this book has focused on the collaborative nature of programming: documentation, management, teamwork, and requirements engineering are all examples of things programmers do that are for or with other people. I would argue, then, that there are few situations in which a programmer can get away *without* those skills. The remaining sections in this chapter look at the practice of making software through the lenses of various branches of the social sciences.

An Economic Philosophy of Software

Direct Economic Factors

Software products are often created or extended as fixed-duration projects. The estimated cost of the project is compared against the estimated revenue generated, and if the balance is favorable then the project is given the go-ahead. Advanced project funders will consider *protected revenue* (how many customers will not jump to a competing product if this feature is added) and *opportunity cost* (what work could we be doing if we decline this work), factoring those into the decisions about the project.

I mentioned Barry W. Boehm and his book, **Software Engineering Economics**– http://books.google.co.uk/books/about/Software_engineering_economics. html?id=mpZQAAAAMAAJ&redir_esc=y in *Chapter 9, Requirements Engineering*. He introduced the idea of human economic factors; assigning a dollar value to the satisfaction (or otherwise) the software would bring to its users, for example. I'll come back to that in the next section, on *Externalities*, but for the moment, bear in mind that the expected human economic factors are considered in the *project* cost.

So, strangely enough, the *maintenance* costs are considered a part of the project economics in Boehm's COCOMO model. Remember from Lehman's Laws of E-type software that the deployment environment evolves, and the software system must evolve to keep up with it. In Boehm's model, this evolution is accounted for in an entry in the project's costs.

This maintenance costs fudge seems to be an indicator that something is wrong with the way we're budgeting for software. Some evolutionary changes (feature additions) must be accounted for as explicit projects, their costs explicitly calculated and balanced against projected income. Other evolutionary changes (maintenance fixes) are just considered a necessary risk of writing software, the costs of which are absorbed into the calculations of writing new features.

Are new features always bigger and more expensive than bug fixes? No. Do bug fixes always cost us money, and never attract or protect income? No. Are new features sometimes snuck into maintenance? Yes. Are bug fixes sometimes held off until new project releases? Yes. Then why aren't they budgeted together?

It could be for ethical reasons: perhaps programmers feel that maintenance problems are mistakes they should own up to and correct free of charge. But remember that one of Lehman's Laws says that the satisfaction derived from software will decay as the *social environment* involves. Not all bugs *were* bugs at the time of writing! You cannot be apologetic for work you did *correctly* before a change in the environment.

To me, this suggests a need for a nimbler economic model; one that treats any change equally regardless of whether it's a bug fix, feature addition, or internal quality cleanup. Forget what we've *already* spent and made on this product (for that way lies the sunk-cost fallacy), what will the *proposed* change cost? What will it get us? How risky is it? What else could we be doing instead? What alternatives do we have?

Externalities

The above questions only consider the *direct* economic impact of making software. There are other factors; factors that have some form of cost or benefit but that don't have a tangible effect on the price or revenue of the work. In economics, these are called *externalities*.

Externalities can be positive or negative, but they can also be personal rather than relating to a company and its work. Software making as a career has all sorts of externalities, in terms of benefits and costs, to being a programmer that aren't reflected in our salaries. Let's consider externalities that affect both the individual as well as the business.

Open source software is a positive externality for many businesses. Many companies in the software industry take components or systems that have been published freely and incorporate them into their own products or provide "value-added" services such as support. These companies receive value from the open source software without having to pay for creating that software. As an example of open source software as an externality, the cost of writing OpenSSH doesn't factor into the price of macOS X, although OpenSSH is a component of that system.

The picture for individual programmers is less clear. Leaving aside micro-ISV developers for a moment, who's personal and business goals are often tightly coupled, a career programmer applying for a job might be asked to produce a portfolio of open source projects that they have created or contributed to. I infer from this that *having created* open source software has a positive effect: it improves our reputation and the likelihood that we will be hired. On the other hand, *the act of creating* open source software can be negative: if you don't do it as part of your job, then you're effectively increasing the amount of work you do without any direct compensation.

Bugs are negative externalities. Software companies often either price their work according to market forces if they're selling to consumers or based on a day-rate for the initial project if they're selling to a client business. In neither case is the subsequent cost of maintenance factored into the selling price; it's going to be a reduction in profit compared to the same product requiring no maintenance. Customers themselves do not factor bugs into the (economic or psychological) cost of *using* software. As argued by David Rice in *Geekonomics: the real price of insecure software*—http://books.google.co.uk/books/about/Geekonomics.html?id=k6cRhfp2aWgC, customers often only have the feature checklist to go on when evaluating a software product and cannot tell anything about its quality. But the quality costs; you pay testers, you triage bug reports, you monitor support channels for problems, and you work on the fixes.

Some organizations run hackathons or hack days, in which people usually form teams to produce a software-based solution to some challenge, with the winners getting a prize. These hack days can have a positive career effect in that some employers might value contributing to hack days as evidence of community involvement, and they give the opportunity to "sharpen the saw" and try new skills or tools. On the other hand, spending even more time working (especially the all-nighters required at some hack days) will have a bad effect on your health, which is a negative effect.

Finally, consider whether all of the work that goes into making a software product is even reflected in the label price. If you double the amount you spend on producing a user guide, does the price go up? Probably not. The same goes for localization: you get a larger pool of potential customers, but for the most part you wouldn't be able to raise the price. That shows that, to your customers, localization is an externality: a benefit of localized software but not one that changes how much they pay.

Companies can factor the value they place on externalities into their decisions by internally charging for them or even passing the costs or savings onto customers: a simple example is that some agency companies will charge less for a project if they're allowed to co-brand the resulting product. The association of the agency's brand with the product and the possibility of that driving future work is a positive externality. Passing savings onto customers—that is, reducing costs when there are positive externalities—is obviously more palatable to them than passing on charges for negative externalities, but the latter can be done. Think of the price premiums on **organic foods**–https://www.mint.com/blog/trends/organic-food-07082010/, which are greater than the cost differences in production (which can, in some cases, be lower than for non-organic foods, due to subsidies—another way to reify an externality). By convincing purchasers that there are real benefits to organic foods, suppliers can command a premium price.

Traditional Supply-And-Demand Economics

Many economics textbooks will start with a discussion of supply and demand as the key influences on market price: when demand is high or supply is low, prices go up; they go down when demand is low, or supply is high. The problem with applying this economic structure to software pricing is that supply is infinite: there's no "unit cost," so once the software is made, it can be copied over and over until everybody who wants a copy has one. So how can software be sold *at all* without prices instantly plummeting to zero?

In the face of evidence, some people don't believe it can. That's what **Digital Rights Management** is about: trying to reinsert the scarcity of physical goods into the economics of software (and other digital goods) distribution. But people *do* successfully sell software, music, documents (such as this one), and so on without DRM. Rather than noticing the infinite supply "issue" and trying to limit supply, we need to try to understand the market that *does* exist, *is* sustainable, but that doesn't match long-standing models.

I'll start with a hypothesis: that what's being traded is not the software itself, but *capability* first, and *time* second. Given the desire, but inability, to do something as a problem, *anything* that solves the problem by enabling that thing is valued. This is what economist Herbert Simon described as bounded rationality, or **satisficing**–http://www.economist.com/node/13350892. So, a first solution discovered, whether ideal or not, is still valued. This already explains why the infinite supply "problem" is not real: on discovering that a product can be purchased that meets their needs, a consumer is likely to settle for making the purchase as a satisficing solution–many will not spend extra time on researching a pirated version of the app. (For some people, using a pirated version of an application *does* cost, in terms of anxiety. Any decision, however rational, that runs counter to a person's ethics exerts a mental cost. This is understood by the information security sector as one of the limiting factors of controlling security via policy.)

Having found that the problem can indeed be solved, the customer is then able to spend a little effort on thinking about how to improve that solution. That's where the time-saving part comes in. Now that they know *what* they are capable of, it's possible to improve that capability so that they've got more free time for other things: that's also worth money, as Benjamin Franklin made clear. (This argument applies, in a modified form, to games. Just reverse the two factors. *Given* that I have time available, can you supply the *capability* for me to enjoy its passage?)

In this model, software itself has no value, compatible with the infinite supply problem in traditional economics. But the customer's time and abilities *are* in limited supply, and software can be used as a tool to unlock these. In this sense, paying for software is similar to paying for education: it is not the *teaching* that you want, it is the *having been taught*. We can then say of software that it is not *creating the solution to the problem* that customers value, but *the problem having been solved*. Because of the nature of satisfaction, customers will pay for a solution if the cost and the capability are "good enough."

Looking back to the second paragraph in this chapter, we see that this economic model is just the same philosophy, expressed in economic terms. Our role as people who make software is to *solve problems*–we provide a valuable service to our customers by *solving problems*.

A Management Philosophy of Software

Imagine a world in which programmers are valued similar to middle managers. But first, disabuse yourself of the idea that managers are inherently useless and evil, and let me explain what a manager is.

Managers typically don't get paid for doing work; they typically get paid according to how well their team does work, and how much work their team does. Lots of work done badly isn't very good, but not enough work done well isn't desirable either.

That usually means that they avoid doing work. Given some work to do, their usual action is to find the person on their team most capable of doing the work, and to get them to do the work. They will make that person responsible for doing the work, and (if they're any good) give them the authority to do it.

But they're not paid for telling the person how to do the work, or for the task of delegating responsibility or authority. In fact, if the work isn't done, or isn't done well, it's the *manager* that the rest of the company will hold responsible. They're paid for the work having been done.

Now, imagine a world in which programmers are valued similar to middle managers: a world in which the programmer is the manager and the computers report to the programmer. The programmer is not paid for *writing software* – for explaining to the computer what work needs to be done. The programmer is paid for the computers *having done the work* that was assigned, both in sufficient quantity and to sufficient quality. If the computers don't do the work, it's the *programmer* who will be held responsible.

Again, this is just a restatement of the position taken at the beginning of the chapter. While the restatement in the previous section told us what the people who buy software value, this one tells us what should be considered valuable in someone who makes software. We see that "number of lines of code written," "number of story points completed," "number of features added," and "number of bugs fixed" are not, in themselves, valuable things, but perhaps we can see the extent to which each is a useful *proxy* of our work.

A Social Philosophy of Software

In *Chapter 9, Requirements Engineering*, you saw that software does not stand on its own but is embedded in the social system in which it's used. Much of the rest of this book has discussed a different social system: the system in which software is *developed*. A lot of software is made by more than one person. Even in the rare cases where a single person does all the *production* (the coding, the design, the UI text, the marketing, the sales, and so on), there will likely be some customer input, even if that just takes the form of support emails.

So, how are these two social systems accounted for in the field? The typical image of a programmer is of someone (typically a white male in his 20s), working on his own, staring at a monitor. If the outside world is acknowledged at all, it is through its exclusion: the programmer wears his headphones to avoid distractions as he cuts his code. (At the time of writing, and for my account, the results of *a Google Images search for "programmer"*— https://www.google.co.uk/search?q=programmer&aq=f&um=1&ie=UTF-8&hl=en&tbm=isch&source=og&sa=N&tab=wi&ei=4J2TUbOrOZSV0QWI7YHABQ&biw=2560&bih=1368&sei=452TUcKIFoi40QXmjIDYCQ supported this description of the "typical" image.)

We automatically see all sorts of problems here. The person making the software is a programmer, not any of the other specialists involved. He is male, not female or trans*. He is white, not of any other ethnicity. He is young, not old. He is alone, not working with others. All of these inequalities exist in the *depiction* of software makers. All of which fail to capture the diversity and the complexity of the social systems surrounding software systems. Many of these inequalities exist in the depiction of software makers because they exist in the *reality* of software making.

Social scientists ask two high-level questions of any social system they investigate: How is the society made and repaired? What divisions and inequalities does it support? By examining the "conventional" view of a programmer, we have seen some of the inequalities currently supported by the software industry.

We could potentially find more. Shanley Kane *examined the language used by Silicon Valley start-ups*—http://blog.prettylittlestatemachine.com/blog/2013/02/20/what-your-culture-really-says looking for the underlying biases, for example:

> ### We don't have a vacation policy
>
> What your culture might actually be saying is... We fool ourselves into thinking we have a better work/life balance when really people take even less vacation than they would when they had a vacation policy. Social pressure and addiction to work has replaced policy as a regulator of vacation time.

If true, this implies that those able to work longer hours and take fewer holidays are in a position of relative power within the system. This is turn privileges certain classes of people: those who are younger and do not have children, for example.

So, that's the social system where software is *made*. What about that in which software is *used*? There are inequalities and divisions there, too. Commercial software systems (and even free software systems that run on commercial platforms) are only accessible to those who can afford to buy them.

In the UK, the Office of National Statistics *estimates that over 7 million people have never used the internet.* They identify correlations between ability to access the internet and demographic status, so online services are (for example) less likely to be available to people over 75 and to disabled people (This lack of accessibility is before we even consider whether specific services have "accessibility" features as commonly understood by developers.)

Other inequalities can be found. Many applications have been created to only support the English language, and where they *can* be localized, they don't handle non-Gregorian calendars, right-to-left writing systems, characters with diacritic modifiers, and other "non-English" (or non-American) locale features.

Knowing that these inequalities exist (others do, too) and reporting them is one thing, but probably isn't novel. What are we to do with that awareness?

Which inequalities you feel are *unjust* probably depends on your political views, though the ethics documents described in the previous chapter give us a handy guide. From **the ACM code of ethics**– http://www.acm.org/about/code-of-ethics:

Inequities between different groups of people may result from the use or misuse of information and technology. In a fair society, all individuals would have equal opportunity to participate in, or benefit from, the use of computer resources regardless of race, sex, religion, age, disability, national origin or other such similar factors. However, these ideals do not justify unauthorized use of computer resources nor do they provide an adequate basis for violation of any other ethical imperatives of this code.

That's quite explicit. The behavior the ACM expects from its members is that of no discrimination whatsoever *within the limits of the rest of the ethical code* – as ever, potential ethical conflicts exist. Stealing computer resources from privileged parties for the use of disadvantaged parties (I hereby dub this "Robin Hood scheduling") would be one example of such a conflict.

An important factor to be aware of in discrimination is **othering**. Social psychologists differentiate between **marked and unmarked identities**–http://cak400.wordpress.com/2012/10/01/marked-and-unmarked-identities-and-social-hierarchy/. An "unmarked" identity is what's accepted to be normal, and other identities are differentiated ("marked") by being different from this benchmark. People who talk about immigrants are *marking* some people as immigrants, and by extension implicitly defining natives as normal. People who talk about women are *marking* some people as women, and implicitly defining men as normal.

The important aspect with regard to Othering is the asymmetric nature of this distinction: it is between those who are "normal" and those who are "not like us." It's important to realize that we *do* this, that it's how our minds *work*, to *identify* when we're doing it and to consciously *correct* for it. As *Mike Lee put it*–https://twitter.com/bmf/status/333960606837272577:

We put those qualities into the other that we reject in ourselves. But that blinds us to the reality.

So, next time you think "normal people wouldn't want *that* feature," or "no one with an ounce of common sense would use it *that* way," ask whether you *really* think "people who aren't like me wouldn't want that," then consider whether you're making software for the small number of people who are like you, or for everyone.

A Pedagogic Philosophy of Software

This is the most technical and low-level part of the philosophy chapter, and the one I'm least qualified to talk about. I've done a couple of years of teaching programming at a university but as one of the most obvious features of university teaching is that no one trains you before you start, I'm not sure whether that counts.

It's easy to find assertions that *academic computer science bears no relation to practice*–http://shape-of-code.coding-guidelines.com/2013/05/15/wot-apply-academic-work-in-industry/ and that *computer science is not adequate preparation for a career in software*. Is this a problem? If it is, what is the cause? What alternatives are there?

The divergence between commercial and academic software practices began early in the history of computing. The first version of the ACM curriculum described in *Software as a pursuit* was **Curriculum 68**–http://dl.acm.org/citation.cfm?id=362976. In the introduction to this curriculum, the authors make it clear that the academic computer science course is not appropriate for training professional IT staff:

For example, these recommendations are not directed to the training of computer operators, coders, and other service personnel. Training for such positions, as well as for many programming positions, can probably be supplied best by applied technology programs, vocational institutes, or junior colleges. It is also likely that the majority of applications programmers in such areas as business data processing, scientific research, and engineering analysis will continue to be specialists educated in the related subject matter areas, although such students can undoubtedly profit by taking a number of computer science courses.

So, the curriculum was created with the knowledge that it would *not* apply directly to those who wish to be professional programmers. While vocational courses do exist, it's very common to meet capable self-taught programmers who had no formal introduction to the field – myself included. There's a *lot* of information about how to make software out in the world, which the self-taught must discover somehow: ultimately, much will be learned by trial and error. The **Software Engineering Body of Knowledge**–https://www.computer.org/education/bodies-of-knowledge/software-engineering can be thought of as a guide to what to learn from the published literature on software engineering. When formatted as a book, the guide is longer than this text. Like this book, the guide itself is not at the level of "this is how software is made" but at the level of "these are the things you should bear in mind while making software." So, we have a 200-page guide to 13 "knowledge areas," which comprise lists of things you should know, with *some* references to available literature. The knowledge areas, the topics chosen in each, and the currency and validity of the references are all (as you could probably expect from this field) contentious, so the **SWEBOK (Software Engineering Body of Knowledge)** represents a conservative selection of ideas that have definitely become broadly applied.

How can the self-taught programmer get up to speed on this huge and evolving body of knowledge? Supporters of "software as a profession" would say that they can't; that it's up to professional bodies to teach and maintain the body of knowledge and to ensure that only those who are up to speed may be considered programmers. Supporters of "software as a craft" would also say that they can't: that they need the expert guidance that comes from apprenticeship, then the period of self-searching that comes from being a journeyman.

But, reflecting on *Chapter 10, Learning*, I have to ask: is the SWEBOK anything other than a *curriculum* for learning, whether taught or self-directed? It's presented at quite an abstract level (and in a very dry style), so may work better for instructors to decide what to teach than for beginners trying to find out what to *learn*.

That content – not necessarily the SWEBOK itself, but something akin to it – could easily be adapted into a guide for self-learning. The pattern I find most appropriate for this is the competency matrix: I have evaluated my own knowledge of computer science against **the Programmer Competency Matrix**–http://www.starling-software.com/employment/programmer-competency-matrix.html over the last few years, and in the course of writing this text created **the Programmer Courtesy Matrix**–http://blog.securemacprogramming.com/2013/04/rebooting-the-programmer-competency-matrix/ to summarize the material.

Where the matrix succeeds is that it gives learners a handy way to evaluate their own progress (whether through reflection, or discussion with evaluators or educators) and to understand what's needed to advance in any particular row of the matrix. The columnar layout provides guidance on what's "next" and what can be left to "later."

This ordering is something I struggled with early in my career. I was working at a large company that had progression through technical roles: software engineer, senior software engineer, principal software engineer, and software architect. I was hired at the first level but quickly got promoted to senior software engineer. Because I focused on the next level, I tried to learn about the responsibilities of the principal engineer before consolidating and extending my understanding of the senior role. I therefore didn't make a particularly good senior engineer: a prerequisite for moving onward.

Where the matrix *fails* is at the part the **SWEBOK** does well: giving you references to material at each level, so the learner knows *where* to find the information to progress. That part of a curriculum is much more contextual: a curriculum for self-learning might point to books, articles, conference presentations, or websites for where to learn; a curriculum for directed learning might suggest particular training or university courses, or a problem set to be assessed by an educator. The point is that there's no reason a self-taught programmer can't, with awareness of the field and their own capabilities, provided by a competency matrix, progress as a career programmer – maybe at a different pace to a taught or master-bound programmer, but progressing, nonetheless.

Referring this discussion (and *Chapter 10, Learning*) back to the position statement at the beginning of this chapter, the teaching of software makers should really be considered the teaching of *problem identification and solution* within the context of software systems. From this view, the goals of teaching in the academic and commercial fields are compatible; it's just the choice of problems to solve (and hence the focus on particular areas of the body of knowledge, equivalent to particular rows in the competency matrix) that are different.

For novice programmers, the self-taught, apprenticed, and educated (Beware of reading a false dichotomy in this sentence; self-taught and apprenticed programmers are not "uneducated," they just did not learn how to make software *from an educator*) alike, the course from hobbyist to professional software making – whatever the context in which that software is made, and whatever the specific definition of "professional" we choose – starts with *awareness* of software as a means to solve problems, not as an end in itself. The next step is *awareness* of the gap between their novice competence and the current state of the art. How they choose to close that gap is less important than awareness of the gap's existence.

What Does It Mean to Be "Good" At Making Software?

Statements abound about the productivity of people who make software. Many people claim *that some programmers are 10x more productive than others*—http://www.johndcook.com/blog/2011/01/10/some-programmers-really-are-10x-more-productive/. What does that *mean*?

Presumably, to come up with a quantity, even a relative one like "10x," we have some quantitative measure that can be applied to people who make software in different contexts. What is that quantity? The number of significant lines of code written? If so, should we sack programmers *who write -2000 lines of code in a day*—http://folklore.org/StoryView.py?story=Negative_2000_Lines_Of_Code.txt?

How about the time taken to fix a bug, the measure originally applied (to a small number of programmers) to discover the 10x figure? Maybe the programmers aren't more productive, but *we caught them on a good day*? What about the programmer who spent more time ensuring the bug wasn't present in the first place? Is that person more diligent or wasting time gold-plating?

If you accept the view of software making presented here, then the *amount of software one can write* is, regardless of the way you measure it, irrelevant to the question of how good the maker is. The relevant question is how many problems the software maker removed from (or introduced into) the system in which their customers are working.

One of the most effective demonstrations of this measure of productivity came from a friend who was asked by a potential client to design a mobile app to solve a particular issue the client's business had. Having met with the client and discussed their problems, this person observed that a spreadsheet was a better solution than the mobile app. They thus declined the opportunity to waste the client's money creating a suboptimal solution. That person could get their spreadsheet written, and the software maker could turn their attention to more appropriate uses of their skills.

Unfortunately, the question of whether software's net effect in a system has been to solve or to introduce problems is unanswered, and is perhaps unanswerable, as systems get large. For example, until the 1980s, many offices in Western organizations employed a largely female typing pool, albeit on low wages and in noisy environments. After the introduction of the desktop computer, those typists were replaced by people in traditionally higher-status jobs preparing their own documents with word-processing applications. Those applications and the computers they ran on were supported by a predominantly male IT support workforce.

To the businesses in which those changes occurred, was the IT support department more or less cost-effective than the typing pool? Was typing in a word processor a better use of an executive's time than handwriting a manuscript for a typist? Do desktop computers and office printers cause fewer problems than a few dozen typewriters, or more problems?

At a social level, have the unemployed typists been freed from the tyranny of the typing pool, or have they been excluded from the workforce? Has the computer been good or bad for gender equality? Has software opened up more opportunities than it has removed?

These are complicated questions, and I'm going to finish without answering them. Suffice it to say that, while our new metric for productivity is better philosophically than things like lines of code, it's a lot harder to apply.

Conclusion

I wrote this book to reflect on what I knew about making software and to understand what I didn't know about making software. I published it so that you could take advantage of what I've found over the decade I've been doing this for a living, and to trigger your own reflections on your experiences (with the hope that you would share these with us, just as I have).

I started by looking at the things we do when we're at the coal face: the tools and practices we use to convert ideas into software. Then I looked at how we work with other people: how we document what we've done; how we find out what software needs writing; how we take advantage of opportunities to learn from other people, interpret other people's arguments, and work with them in the context of a team or a business. Finally, I tried to construct a high-level model in which to situate all of that work, by considering the ethics and philosophy of making software, and how to move our knowledge forward by teaching this generation's novices.

Through this process, I found that, while computer science may be able to tell us something about the compilers and languages we use on computers, software products can't be isolated from the *social* systems in which they're made and used. Psychology, sociology, ethnography, and economics: all of the social sciences have wisdom to impart that can help us use our skills as software makers to solve problems for people.

Unfortunately, this work closed on a quandary: while different bodies of software makers have identified the ethical imperative to avoid discrimination, we cannot unequivocally say that our industry has not caused *new* divisions and inequalities in the societies it has affected. Questions of whether to use web or native technologies, or whether functional or object-oriented programming styles are "better" will either be answered, become irrelevant, or both. The question of whether our work removes or strengthens divisions between people will never go away and will be the measure by which history judges what we do.

Index

About

All major keywords used in this book are captured alphabetically in this section. Each one is accompanied by the page number of where they appear.